Chaucer and Dissimilarity

Chaucer and Dissimilarity

Literary Comparisons in Chaucer
and Other Late-Medieval Writing

John J. McGavin

Madison • Teaneck
Fairleigh Dickinson University Presses
London: Associated University Presses

© 2000 by Associated University Presses, Inc.

All rights reserved. Authorization to photocopy items for internal or personal use, or the internal or personal use of specific clients, is granted by the copyright owner, provided that a base fee of $10.00, plus eight cents per page, per copy is paid directly to the Copyright Clearance Center, 222 Rosewood Drive, Danvers, Massachusetts 01923. [0–8386–3814–7/00 $10.00 + 8¢ pp, pc.]

Associated University Presses
440 Forsgate Drive
Cranbury, NJ 08512

Associated University Presses
16 Barter Street
London WC1A 2AH, England

Associated University Presses
P.O. Box 338, Port Credit
Mississauga, Ontario
Canada L5G 4L8

The paper used in this publication meets the requirements of the American National Standard for Permanence of Paper for Printed Library Materials Z39.48-1984.

Library of Congress Cataloging-in-Publication Data

McGavin, John J., 1950–
    Chaucer and dissimilarity : literary comparisons in Chaucer and other late-medieval writing / John J. McGavin.
      p. cm.
    Includes bibliographical references (p.) and index.
    ISBN 0-8386-3814-7 (alk. paper)
    1. Chaucer, Geoffrey, d. 1400—Technique   2. English language—Middle English, 1100–1500—Comparison.   3. Chaucer, Geoffrey, d. 1400. Troilus and Criseyde.   4. Literature, Comparative—English and European.   5. Literature, Comparative—European and English.   6. Chaucer, Geoffrey, d. 1400—Philosophy.   7. Difference (Philosophy) in literature.   8. Philosophy, Medieval, in literature.   9. Persuasion (Rhetoric)   10. Rhetoric, Medieval.   I. Title.
PR1940 .M37 2000
821'.1—dc21
                                                                                             99-047453

PRINTED IN THE UNITED STATES OF AMERICA

This book is dedicated to my family

Contents

Acknowledgments	9
Introduction: Comparison and Literary Language	11
1. Traditions of Comparison and Dissimilarity	31
2. Naming and the *House of Fame*	58
3. Similes	84
4. Patterns of Comparison in *Troilus and Criseyde*	119
5. Persuasive Comparisons in *Troilus and Criseyde*	145
6. The Poem as *Exemplum*	170
Conclusion	200
Notes	207
Bibliography	225
Index	235

Acknowledgments

DURING THE WRITING OF THIS BOOK I HAVE HAD CONSISTENTLY warm support from my colleagues and students in the English Department at Southampton University, and from my friends elsewhere in the faculty, particularly in the History Department, whose cricket team, the Cavaliers, ensured that I kept healthy long enough to complete it. I thank them and all other friends or colleagues who have helped to get the project to this stage. However, I especially wish to thank my immediate colleague, Bella Millett, who has been a good personal and academic friend during the many years of our association; Kate McLuskie, who, as my Head of Department, gave me encouragement, advice, time to work, and her own time to reading the whole manuscript, and Greg Walker and Tim Kirkup, who also read the whole or substantial parts and gave valuable guidance at important stages. Thanks are also due to a colleague in the Wessex Medieval Centre, Phil Cardew, who computerized me at home and away, and to Susan Hartley, Jim Shapiro, Cora Kaplan, Paul Hamilton, David Mills, Ronnie Jack, Joyce and John Swannell, Emily Lyle, and Tim Reuter for their support. I am grateful to my *alma mater*, the University of Edinburgh, where I enjoyed fellowships at the Department of English Literature, and the Institute for Advanced Studies, where I was also fortunate to meet Paul and Betty Olson and, through them, David Anderson; to the University of Southampton for the leave which permitted this, and to the British Academy and the various research committees at Southampton, who gave grant funding towards it. Parts of the book were given early airings at the universities of Southampton, Leicester, Liverpool, Edinburgh, London, Kent, and Aberdeen, and I benefitted from the discussion at all those places. The New Chaucer Society kindly accepted a conference session for which some of this material was prepared. I am also grateful to Houghton Mifflin Company and to the Oxford University Press for permission to quote substantially from Larry D. Benson (General Editor) *The Riverside Chaucer* 3d ed. (Boston: Houghton Mifflin Company, 1987). Lastly, the book is dedicated to my family. In particular, I want to thank my mother, father, and sister, who make my lengthy visits to Edinburgh so pleasurable and productive; my children, Callum and Catriona, who have been encouraging beyond their years, and despite their misgivings about the book's marketable qualities, and my wife, Joan, who manages to combine loving support with a sharp eye for failures of argument or style. Having received so much generous help, it is both a duty and a matter for regret to acknowledge that whatever shortcomings there are in the book are my own fault.

Introduction
Comparison and Literary Language

> ther is diversite required
> Bytwixen thynges like, as I have lered.
> —Geoffrey Chaucer, *Troilus and Criseyde*

IT IS A TRUISM THAT NO TWO THINGS ARE ALIKE IN ALL RESPECTS. Difference is a fundamental of our experience—so fundamental that we are mostly unconscious of it. Language only works by its systematic difference, and does so whether we think of it or not. But when we compare, the underlying difference between things becomes overt, and is no longer a precondition of signifying but is itself significant. When comparison takes place, and difference thus becomes overt, it is no longer difference which concerns us, but particular dissimilarities. That is why comparisons are made: to shift the hearer from an ordinary state in which difference is accepted without examination into a perception of specific dissimilarities and, if the comparison is a positive one rather than contrastive, into a perception of similarities against a background of these dissimilarities.

Attending to such dissimilarities can have a variety of uses, values, and effects, dependent on the context in which they are invoked. When comparing, people are consciously negotiating the terrain of difference, either pointing out specific dissimilarities, or disguising them in favor of similarity, and doing so with a wide range of self-serving strategies, cultural assumptions, tricks, and paradoxes deployed in careful relation to the context in which the comparison is occurring. This book examines the work of a poet who was sensitive to the value of comparison, to the particularities of context, to the persuasive ends and means of comparison, and to the motives behind its use. More than anything he was alert to its deeply problematic character as an ambivalent process which tried to manage the contrary forces of similarity and dissimilarity.

If comparison had its own deity it would be the two-headed Janus, one head looking back to the source from which the comparator was drawn; the other looking ahead to the topic to which the comparator is applied: one looking auspiciously at the similarity which could be fashioned between the two; the other with a more drooping eye at the dissimilarities which undermine it. What particularly defines Janus, however, is the lack of any central head examining the threshold which the two heads mark: the limen itself is unexamined, just as the optimistic assertions of comparison frequently occlude its inherent failings. Chaucer's poems continually urge inspection of the comparative nexus because Chaucer recognized comparison to be fundamental to all language use.

At the heart of his greatest single poem, *Troilus and Criseyde,* written in the middle of his career, Chaucer sets up a discussion about choosing the right words for things. Comparative thinking proves to be central to that choice. Pandarus, who has been busy to bring about an affair between his niece and Troilus, has doubts about how his role could be viewed, and wishes to defend himself. The reader knows how complex has been the process, how dependent on accident and influences outside Pandarus's control, and how far Criseyde herself has been complicit in furthering it. But Pandarus feels that all circumstantiality can be reduced to the single fact that he has become in Troilus's service "swich a meene / As maken wommen unto men to comen" (3.254–55). Pandarus's circumlocution acknowledges, and describes, the thing while sidestepping its name. Though himself an artist in love's persuasion, Pandarus feels the threat of words. Just as Chaucer the Poet's image, "Geffrey," says in the *House of Fame* that he does not seek fame because he does not wish people to have his name "in honde," so love's artist, Pandarus, cannot speak the name which he fears others will subsequently use of him. In the end, the user of words best knows their strength and fears them.

What Pandarus cannot utter, his creator insists on making explicit for him. Despite nearly 150 lines intervening, the matter is later taken up by Troilus. Chaucer pointedly has him use the term which Pandarus cannot speak: "bauderye" (3.397), though Troilus rejects this name as inappropriate for what Pandarus has done. Chaucer thus denies to his amatory "makar" that escape from the world of names and their use which "Geffrey" purports to wish for himself. Chaucer seems to be saying that, in the end, names must be used. They must be used not just because Chaucer is committed to a life of words, but because a mere description of an act or a role is not the same, is not as powerful, is not as morally charged, does not challenge the judgment of the hearer, or imply judgment in the speaker, as much as does the name which is commonly applied to the thing. Pandarus's insinuation is not enough since it obscures that judgment which is ultimately implied in the names we use. Things must and will eventually become names. The writer, Troilus, the reader, and Pandarus must all look hard at the names available for what has been done and decide on their propriety. This Troilus proceeds to do.

The exchange between Troilus and Pandarus develops beyond the mere rejection of the name of "bawd" into an exposé of the means by which names are applied to things and the reliability of the judgments on which such applications are made. Firstly, Troilus rejects the notion that one could judge Pandarus's actions so harshly when they were done "for compaignie" (3.396). When comparing possible names for Pandarus's action, Troilus thus decides on motive as the criterion for choosing one over another. However, his decision is immediately undermined by Chaucer because of the idiomatic vagueness of "for compaignie." The phrase does not adequately reflect Pandarus's motives, which have included a measure of personal sexual frustration together with curiosity, friendship, and concern, not to say the sheer pleasure Pandarus appears to get from verbal persuasion. Intended by Troilus to authenticate his choice of name for what Pandarus does, "for compaignie" is itself a site for possible argument.

Troilus's point is that Pandarus was unprompted by any mercenary consideration. The range of names appropriate to his actions is reduced by this criterion:

> But he that gooth for gold or for ricchesse
> On swich message, calle hym what the list;
> And this that thow doost, calle it gentilesse,
> Compassioun, and felawship, and trist
>
> (3.400–403)

Unfortunately, this response replaces the vague and conventional "for compaignie" with four alternative names for the act, each of which if looked at for more than a second raises questions about its appropriateness and sufficiency. Though the words could easily coexist, each seems at once too large and too restricted an account of the process. Taken together, their plurality counts against them: as elsewhere, Chaucer shows that the problem of naming is not solved by an enthusiastic proliferation of words (even if that is often his own response to a creative problem). Rather, such profusion reveals, and exacerbates, the taxonomic difficulty which it is addressing and failing to control. Attempting to pin the right word on the deed opens up an area for contrast and comparison between the several words chosen, each of which has its own resonances, and some of which resonances are themselves more dissimilar than alike. One thinks here of the amatory associations of "gentilesse," the religious resonance of "compassioun" and the familial duty of the "trist" which Pandarus owes his niece. But the passage also reminds us that naming is a human action. The emphasis of the passage falls as much on the act as it does on the names employed. Words are not naturally attached to their referents but attached by human choice. Though these choices are based on judgment, the judgment is still personal and open to contest.

The credibility of an act of naming, and the truth value which hearers will assign to it, is obviously affected by their estimation of the speaker's authority or insight into the topic. This passage at first seems to undermine the credibility of Troilus's names for what Pandarus has done by showing that love prevents Troilus from really understanding the moral ground on which Pandarus fears the name of bawd might be attached to him. He cannot even see that Pandarus is afraid of more than Troilus's opinion; that it is not Troilus's names that Pandarus fears, but other people's. Troilus is too enslaved to the fruits of the seduction to be capable of judging it correctly: to prove that he does not think the deed shameful or a "jape," he offers to solicit his sister Polixena, Cassandra, or Helen on Pandarus's behalf. Troilus thus ignorantly offers to make himself a bawd while claiming the insight to deny the name of "bauderye" to what Pandarus has done. It looks as if the names "gentilesse," "compassioun," "felawship," and "trist" come from such an inauthentic source that they have no truth value.

And yet, Chaucer is making a subtler point: moral incapacity does not of itself subvert truth. In the *General Prologue* we are told, "ye knowen wel how that a jay / Kan clepen 'Watte' as wel as kan the pope" (642–43). Troilus may be chattering like a jay, but what he says still has some measure of sense, just as the name "Watte" (Walter) can still be spoken correctly, though unknowingly, by a jay. The reader knows that the names Troilus applies are not wholly inappropriate even if they are not the whole story and their speaker falls short in that moral understanding which would authenticate them. The qualities which these names suggest were indeed present in the wooing process. Chaucer has created a fiction which is complex enough to enable us to acknowledge truths independently of any evaluation of their source: what authenticates the language is the reader's experience of the text not the authority of the person who has used it. Responsibility has shifted from a character comparing, contrasting, and assigning names to the reader or hearer doing so. Generations of readers have eagerly embraced that responsibility in developing a range of widely differing accounts of the poems. Within his fictions Chaucer's insight that the validity of language is not always dependent on the character of the user permits him to slide between language which is embedded in character and language which appears free-standing, between truth compromised and uncompromised by its source, between the actions of characters and the heuristic action required in those who read about them. Readers also have to judge where the slide is occurring, and from their differing judgments have developed more or less dramatic theories of the *Canterbury Tales*.[1]

To summarize, showing that blend of fiction and metafiction which is characteristic of Chaucer's best poems, the passage argues that proper use of language depends upon proper distinctions first being made between the things which names are applied to. The responsibility to compare and thus to look for dissimilarities between things before applying names to them is made explicit:

> Departe it so, for wyde-wher is wist
> How that ther is diversite requered
> Bytwixen thynges like, as I have lered.
>
> (3. 404–6)

Though Troilus here emphasises contrasts, they are, of course, part of the larger process of comparison on which language rests. The deployment of words depends upon the user perceiving the dissimilarities which exist between like things. Similarity is recognized; then interrogated; dissimilarities are claimed, then qualified. The similarities and dissimilarities which are revealed determine appropriate names for things, thus fixing in language their perceived likeness or diversity.

Of course, Troilus's discovery of dissimilarities between Pandarus's actions and those of a bawd is wholly determined by his own desires. Human limitations determine which dissimilarities (or similarities) are perceived: the limitations might be personal, as in this case, but elsewhere Chaucer shows them to be variedly cultural. The language which issues from the act of comparison is in turn affected by such limitations. Its truth value, and certainly its acceptability, may be undermined by them. One gives names for a variety of reasons, not all of them morally defensible, and not according to criteria fixed by the real natures of the things to be distinguished, but by negotiating between their natures as one perceives them and one's own desires.

However, the passage also indicates that, even where someone has, from the wrong motives, insisted that things are dissimilar, and has applied those names to them which suit the speaker's prejudices and desires, the names may still themselves be appropriate; they may still have truth value. The Pardoner claims that he can tell an honest tale even if he himself is vicious.[2] To the extent that that is true, the Pardoner is the jay who unwittingly cries "Watte." But one does not need to believe the claim true of the Pardoner in order to recognize that Chaucer believes it possible at the deepest level of language: words can be appropriate for their referents even if the process of comparing and contrasting which underlies them has been affected by unauthoritative and personal motives, and even if the speaker who uses them is not in a position to know why and to what extent they are true. It is this possibility which demands the commitment of the hearer to that same process of comparison and contrast which is present in all use of language: a tacit acknowledgment on Chaucer's part that his own words would not just be read but re-read in the modern critical sense. It is not possible to judge the truth value of words by the authority of their source. Personal experience may indicate that the words used were truer than was recognized by their speaker and truer than they first seemed to the hearer. It is necessary, therefore, to commit oneself to the exploration of similarities and dissimilarities between things so as to judge the rectitude of the words which are applied to them by others. Reading dissimilarity is thus a responsibility which falls both on the speaker and the hearer, covering the whole field of language use.

Without attention to the likeness and diversity of things, it would be impossible for an author to achieve even that ambiguous decorum which is several times invoked in Chaucer's poems. Its first appearance is in his *Boece* where Philosophy says "thow hast lernyd by the sentence of Plato that nedes the wordis moot be cosynes to the thinges of whiche thei speken" (3.Pr.12.205–7). It appears again in the *General Prologue*, where Chaucer uses it as part of a playful and complex justification of his poetic language as an accurate reflection of what was said on the "real" pilgrimage. In this case the words of the supposedly real pilgrims are the "deed" which has to be properly represented. The desire for decorum between what is said and what it reports or refers to is found again at the end of his career in the *Manciple's Tale* where the comparative basis for all linguistic choice, and therefore for decorum, is even more explicitly addressed than it was in the passage from the *Troilus*. The Manciple draws attention to the way in which social prejudices highlight certain dissimilarities between things which are fundamentally alike in moral terms. The names which society applies depend on this comparative process and derive from highly contestable readings of dissimilarity:

> Ther nys no difference, trewely,
> Bitwixe a wyf that is of heigh degree,
> If of hir body dishonest she bee,
> And a povre wenche
>
> (*Manciple's Tale* 212–15)

Despite this similarity, one is called a "lady, as in love" and the other a "wenche" or "lemman." Society prioritizes the women's dissimilarity in wealth and status over the similarity in the moral value of their deed. Similarly, the Manciple sees no essential difference between a "titlelees tiraunt" and an "outlawe or a theef erraunt" except that people dignify one as a "capitayn" over the other because he has greater power to do harm (223–34). One dissimilarity is allowed to weigh more heavily than other similarities when people choose an appropriate name for the person. Seeing diversity in likeness is thus a politically weighted issue, whether the politics are sexual, as in the case of the *Troilus*, or economic as in the Manciple's examples. Here again the grounds for our diverse modern readings of his own works are tacitly acknowledged by Chaucer.

However, although Chaucer's authorial stooge, the Manciple, criticizes failures in the choice of words, and holds out the goal of decorum between names and what they apply to, it is clear that Chaucer himself views the process as deeply problematic.[3] His own fiction serves to reveal this. In the *Troilus* we found that the names "compassioun," "felaweship," and so on, could still be acceptable up to a point even though they derived from a morally inept and self-seeking comparative process in which the speaker had emphasised certain dissimilarities over likeness. In the *General Prologue,* the notion of the word being cousin to the deed is encapsulated in a play upon fiction: the reader knows that there is no "deed" for Chaucer's words to refer to since his poem is not a mimesis of any pilgrimage which actually took place.[4] In the *Manciple's Tale,* the explicit commentary comes from an extremely untrustworthy source, a character who is at once close to Chaucer in his evasiveness, and at the opposite extreme to him because he counsels complete silence as a way of avoiding responsibility for language, a character who, if he utters truth, seems to do so only to quail before its implications.[5] Furthermore, the dictum itself seems to announce argument even as it proposes the kinship of words and "deeds." The problem, yet again, is the name: "cousins" can either be as alike as were Palamon and Arcite in the *Knight's Tale* or as distant as the merchant of St Denys and the monk who claimed "cosynage" of him as a preliminary to cuckolding him in the *Shipman's Tale*. Words are not the natural brothers or sisters of the things they are applied to; they are in a relationship which itself requires further scrutiny, further definition.[6]

Chaucer evidently views the process of choosing words as ambiguous in its goal, unpredictable in its rectitude, subordinate to fictional play, and based ultimately on contestable decisions about the similarities and dissimilarities between things. These comparative decisions will themselves be the product of personal desires, group prejudices, social fears, and historical accident. However, some may actually be accurate decisions, and may therefore issue in a just choice of words.

The language which derives from them may therefore have significant truth value.

When Chaucer playfully, and not infrequently, begs forgiveness if he has written amiss, citing that he had good intentions however poor the result, his wit is not simply a matter of authorial false modesty. Certainly his whole oeuvre is an argument for thinking hard about the distinctions which issue in language, for taking on the responsibility of the comparative process which underlies the linguistic one. With that in mind it does seem important for his writing to have proceeded from good intentions. But the truth value of what he says need not be dependent on his responsible intentions. Troilus's intentions in bestowing laudatory names on Pandarus's action were hardly good, yet the names were not wholly inappropriate. Chaucer's intentions might not be particularly "good"—his delight in fabliau tales is an obvious example—yet what he says, even in his fabliaux, might still at a deeper level be true. Equally, how would one judge that Chaucer had said amiss? Even if one held, as did Christine de Pisan, for example,[7] that there is a common truth which all should strive to access, one could only claim that one's own readings of similarity and dissimilarity between things were more accurate than Chaucer's, thus permitting one to judge his language as inappropriate and as not having much truth value. Inevitably this could only be a claim. Chaucer's game of literary values depends on his already having espoused a theory of language which denies certainty about the link between intention, moral judgment, and truth. The troubled relationship of words, the supposed "cousins" of deeds, has recently been discussed in the ethical context of intention and deception.[8] Chaucer, however, moves beyond human intentionality and ethics by implying that the truthfulness of language, even if it could be recognized in individual cases, would not necessarily have originated in responsible human intentions. As critics we bear out the truth of that perception by re-reading him in ways which will preserve his value despite our continuously increasing and shifting distance from him.

There is no guarantee that the hearer will be able to fix upon the truth any more (or less) than the speaker. Though the hearer of language may contest the underlying decisions about similarity and dissimilarity on which the speaker's choice of words rests, that is no guarantee that the hearer will make the right decisions about diversity in likeness. Though speakers and hearers may argue continually about the justness of words and the comparative decisions which underlie them, they will not be sure, in this life at any rate, about where the truth lies. This is not a denial of truth but a denial that it can be recognized for what it is. In the dream vision world of the *House of Fame*,

Chaucer's "Geffrey" confidently identifies and distinguishes a "lesyng and a sad soth sawe" (2089), but it is only to acknowledge that these become harder to distinguish when they fly off into the real world.

Chaucer seems to promise only a constant deferral of the moment at which dissimilarities and similarities will be finally established and words accurately applied to them; he offers as characteristic of this world's language a constant negotiation of meaning, a contesting of comparison, endless re-readings of dissimilarity. One asks, therefore, how this differs in practice from the modern tropological view of language in which all communication is acknowledged from the outset to involve misprision, and the capacity of all semiological codes to communicate truly is vitiated by their constant metaphorizing of meaning.[9]

The essential differences are, firstly, that Chaucer is more concerned with whether particular instances of language do convey truth than with whether the medium itself conveys truly. Secondly, although words may be used wrongly in the sense that they can be judged inappropriate for what they refer to, Chaucer believes that their wrongness (and that judgment) is open to testing rather than simply to contest. Thirdly, Chaucer believes not only that people can truly understand each other but that what they read or hear may actually be the truth, even if it cannot be recognized as such. Finally, he shows how the *possibility* that truth is being heard or spoken commits people to the business of communication. However complex, evasive, or playful Chaucer might be, his commitment to a prolific flow of words is inseparable from his belief that they may actually carry truth. Despite his evident concern in the *House of Fame* with the difficulties of language, it is not misunderstanding that the dreamer fears, but wilful misrepresentation and callous judgment of his work: people who misjudge it from malicious intention, hatred, scorn, and so on (94–108). In his final bleak myth on language, the *Manciple's Tale*, he does not show a fear of being misunderstood, but of being correctly understood by people who then reject what he has said because of their own psychological need to do so. In that *Tale* it is because the message which the crow delivers to Apollo is impossible to live with that it is finally rejected as false and the crow is punished by its master. The message itself was both true and correctly understood.[10] Chaucer would not play with the complexities of language so much if he believed firmly that misunderstanding was an inevitable feature of all communication. It is his belief that the medium is capable of conveying both the truth and lies, in an untroped form, that makes comparison in its different forms central to his work. In the framing, understanding, questioning, negotiating, and rejecting of comparisons, in the reading of dissimilarities between things like and the claiming of likenesses between things diverse, lies the responsible activity of those who use language and believe that its meanings can be fairly shared, its failures can be inspected, and its truths sought and even, though without complete confidence, enjoyed. Chaucer urges on us a predominantly similaic rather than metaphorical model of language in use.[11]

One can see how the comparative basis of language diversifies for Chaucer into wider social and cultural issues if one looks again at the idea of a "name." So far, names have been used in this introduction as a model for words generally: applying the right name to something was treated as an instance of the general application of words to things. But names do not just pose problems of synchronic application, that is, which name is appropriate at a particular time. They also carry diachronic reputation. Their past uses, and conventional applications (which themselves comprise past uses), form their meaning, and therefore inform their present use. Applying a word to a thing involves imparting to the thing a reputation based on the previous uses of the word. This can be seen more clearly if one considers that the word "name" in Chaucer does actually mean both an "appellation" and "reputation." One can have a bad "name" in the sense of "reputation," just as one can fear that one's actions will be given a bad name, as Pandarus feared the name "bauderye." Following Boccaccio's and Chaucer's poems, Pandarus's own personal name was to shift from being an appellation to becoming a word with a reputation attached: pander.[12] That word could subsequently be carried over to other cases, other people in other contexts, giving them Pandarus's name and his "name."

Applying a word, and hence imparting a reputation, to a thing, carries an implicit claim that the present thing is comparable to the others to which the word has been previously applied. It transfers their reputation through the word to the present instance. It sets up an implicit comparison between things and therefore between past reputations and present cases. However, such a comparison is not just between a single past use of a word and the present instance in which it may be used. Because words take their meanings from a range of past applications, applying them involves a move from the general to the particular, and carries the risk that the particular will be lost in the process, betrayed by the taxonomy into which it is being made to fit. The complexity of Pandarus's motives for wooing, of the context in which he carries it out, and of the woman who is being wooed, defies any belief that a "name," with its freight of past reputations and uses, could be simply or confidently applied to what he has done. The present case is too particular to permit an easy transfer of a word from other contexts. Using words is thus not just a matter of choice in a particular present context but of importing into that context general meanings, connotations, and usage from the past. Comparison was traditionally regarded as the means by which past knowledge could be applied to present obscurities. It was deployed to illuminate the unknown, or less known, by carrying over information from what was already known. Language involves just such necessary and potentially dangerous transactions.

On most occasions the comparisons implicit in the choice of words for things are not worth a second thought; Chaucer, however, constructs contexts in which the dialectic of similarity and dissimilarity between past use and present instance, established meaning and new context, is neither trivial nor ignorable. He knows that the reader brings existing meanings from extratextual sources to bear upon the particularities of the text: he makes it his business to unsettle such a transfer of meaning. This is particularly true of his most contemporary and socially rooted poem, the *General Prologue* to the *Canterbury Tales*. There names achieve their greatest prominence: the poem is structured round them and they are the focus of the reader's analyses. While all words carry the connotations which make up their reputational "name," the words by which we designate professions are the most significant examples of this combination of name and "name" and a socially resonant nexus of established belief and new experience.

The *General Prologue* is a poem built wholly upon names, in both senses of the word: each portrait is tied to a name—knight, reeve, etc.—but each name also carries a set of connotations and thus, like all words, has a reputation. Chaucer chooses names which he knows will not be neutral for his readers but come with considerable preexisting meaning which will arouse prejudices and expectations.[13] Each portrait is designed to exploit, explore, and qualify the reputational name which each of these figures carries, and which is brought to the text by the reader. The portraits open up the names as a site for comparison and contrast between the meaning which the name will already have for the reader and the particular fictional figure who bears it. The particularities of the portrait coexist with the generalities of the "name" which each character already bears for the reader, but they also create a tension: it is not possible easily to transfer knowledge from what is already known to the pilgrim figure one is trying to understand: at the very least individuating detail which coexists with conventional elements, and the specifics of the poetic matrix in which such figures are discovered, create dissimilarities between what is supposedly "known" about people in these professions and the individual figures in the poem.

The *Tales* which then issue from the characters enlarge the site where reading dissimilarity between reputational name and individual narrator can take place. Some critics wish to read towards consistency between name and *Tale*, others wish to exploit the evident dissimilarities between them. At the same time, understanding each *Tale* is made more difficult because the reader is unsure of its source, not knowing whether it reflects the general reputational name of knight, reeve, etc., or the individual narrator's special characteristics. *The* Knight's Tale or *a* knight's tale? Marxist critics are bound to give weight to the latter.[14] The name, knight, has both a past reputation and a present application, and the reader is caught between them, reading dissimilarities and similarities, fashioning and refashioning comparisons between the past and present, the type and the individual, received meanings and discovered ones, the extraliterary contexts of use and the immediate literary one.

Chaucer evidently believes that thinking comparatively is fundamental for humanity. It underlies all language use, and is a necessary and constant resource when people are trying to understand what is new. The achievement that this book celebrates, however, is his recognition that the ubiquity of comparative thinking is matched only by its failures. Though offering a route to understanding, comparison has distinct deficiencies and dangers. It appears to impart continuity and momentum to thought, transferring past knowledge to new situations, preexisting meaning to new contexts, common or generally held wisdom to particular issues, old names for new things. However, no two things, situations, contexts, or issues can ever be the same in all respects; comparison has dissimilarity built into it from the outset. Any illumination or claim to transferable knowledge has to be judged against the resistance of that dissimilarity.

Furthermore, comparison involves a common hermeneutic circularity which qualifies its claim to illuminate. This is evident if we look briefly at three of the commonest types of comparison cited in late classical and medieval academic manuals. Firstly, if one thinks of visual representations of things (whether these are presented to the eye or, through words, to the mind's eye) one cannot recognize the images for what they are unless one already knows, in a sense, the "original" with which they are comparable, and therefore knows what is to be looked for in the depiction. Secondly, one will simply miss the point of a similaic description unless one already knows the salient features both of the topic and the comparator chosen for it. One will also fail to feel its figurative effect since the language of simile is not itself figurative; rather it is the tension between the features of the things compared which creates the effect.[15] One has to know these and to select the appropriate features in order to feel the figuration. Thirdly, if one looks to past events to provide an illuminating parallel to a present situation, one needs already to have decided on the similarity of the cases being compared, and the key features of the present case which one is trying to understand before one can say that the example from the past offers present guidance. These three cases correspond to the three medieval types of comparison: *imago, similitudo,* and *exemplum,* which will be discussed at greater length in the next chapter.

This circularity affects all comparison, though rhetoricians such as Quintilian sought to rank the different types in terms of their probative force. For example, Quintilian considered an *exemplum* drawn from history to be more probative than one drawn from fiction, and he thought *imago* should be less used in rhetorical argument than *exemplum*.[16] Comparison has value as a persuasion to revisit what one already knows, or to remap the relations of discrete things of which one already has experience. What it cannot provide is completely new knowledge or an unforeseen knock-down argument, because it depends on the existing knowledge and acceptance of the person who is being enlightened—yet interpretation and proof are precisely the functions which it is regularly made to serve, as Chaucer shows when he puts arguments based on comparison into the mouths of his characters. One already has to know the end in order to use comparison as the means to illuminate it. Chaucer recognized the circularity and exposed it.

To summarize, comparison seems to promise greater understanding, even if not actually new knowledge; it is fundamental to the use and reception of language, and particularly productive in rhetorical persuasion. But it remains a site for negotiation and contest, flawed by inherent dissimilarity between the things compared; capable more of persuading than revealing; deployed in line with the desires and limitations of the user, and also dependent on the hearer's desires and limitations of judgment for it to be accepted. The present book shows Chaucer constantly employing, and frequently undermining, comparative thinking, and comparative language at all levels in his text—in similes, in the exchanges of his characters, in his poetic structure, and narrative voice, in the value he proposes for his own fiction, and in the heuristic challenges he poses to his readers.

Many of the special literary characteristics which critics have traditionally noted in his work can be understood as dimensions of this central interest. The book will discuss these, and introduce new ones but, for example, the ambiguous relationship between Chaucer the author and his narrator *personae* is best regarded as his fictional playing with a traditional type of comparison, the *imago*. As we shall see later, the *imago* was regarded in the grammatical tradition (with which Chaucer had early acquaintance) as a particularly close comparison which concentrated on visual appearance between the "image" and the original it depicted. Inevitably it contained some measure of dissimilarity, however slight. Chaucer's overweight, bookish, enigmatic, slightly marginal, preoccupied, naive, or inexperienced, amatory amateurs, who act as his narrators in poems such as the *Book of the Duchess,* the *Parliament of Fowls,* the *House of Fame,* the *Troilus,* and in the introduction to *Sir Thopas,* are teasingly offered as comparable with him. They would have been recognizable to Chaucer's readers as instances of *imago,* poetic versions of the paintings of saints, kings, abstract qualities, and so on. His audience would have felt the implicit claim that the physical depiction was accurate and that dissimilarity was slight, but Chaucer denies to the reader an "original" against which the *imago* can be compared: his evasiveness is thus all the more disruptive of judgment because it coexists with an apparent generosity in supplying images of himself.[17] Reading for similarity and dissimilarity is frustrated just as it is being invited.

Chaucer explores the problematics of *imago* within texts as well as at the threshold of author, narrator and reader. The three portraits of Troilus, Criseyde, and Diomede, which memorably intrude upon the action of Book 5 of *Troilus and Criseyde,* are perfect instances of *imago* and of Chaucer's interest in comparison as a process shared by creating author and responding reader. These portraits concentrate on physical appearance and on those qualities of character which could, and would, be represented in a visual representation. They are verbal equivalents of the single figure portraits one gets in Books of Hours. Chaucer is satisfying the reader's desire to have characters portrayed to the mind's eye. In a way, he is also offering the reader the opportunity to enclose the characters within a conventional framework which will make their rejection by the author at the end of the poem more acceptable. But the positioning of the portraits at the end rather than the start of his work, and their placing after we have seen the originals of these *imagines* in action, rather than as the prelude to their actions, will also shock readers who cannot finally limit the characters thus.

Chaucer has positioned these *imagines* so that they will be a crux for reader response. By not putting them at the start of the poem, he has denied the reader a gentler transition from the depiction of an imagined figure to that figure's acts. If he had adopted such a sequence, he would have prioritized the simplicities and conventions of the *imago* over the complex revisionary account which he wished to give of the originals in action. Instead they are positioned so that the reader is challenged by them rather than assisted by them. Like the names which Troilus gave to Pandarus's acts, they are quite consonant with what we have seen—they are in a sense, true—but they are equally evidently not the whole story. Just as Pandarus's wooing preceded the discussion of what names could be applied to it, so the deeds and words of Troilus, Criseyde, and Diomede come first, and the reader is then asked to compare the *imagines* with the originals of the preceeding narrative. Chaucer orders his poem to create occasions for the reader to compare the thing and the word chosen for it, the original and its depiction. Providing information is clearly not the main force behind his *ordinacio* of the narrative. At issue are the readers' acts of comparing: their estimation of the decorum which exists between thing and word, of the sufficiency of the depicted *imago* to represent its original, and in conclusion, their judgment of how much truth is present in the relationship—a judgment which depends on their reading the dissimilarity inherent in all comparisons.

When Chaucer places these *imagines* after the original he is permitting some readers to adopt them and to close down their reading of the poem, but he is also allowing others to deplore the manner in which the complexities of the characters he has revealed are denied by the simplicities of the *imagines,* and by extension, of other reputational names which have been attached to them by tradition. Readers who feel that these *imagines* are unsatisfactory, and I think it by no means certain that all his original readership would have felt that, are valuing the dissimilarity which he has created between his characters and their conventional representation. Chaucer gives the *imagines* first in the *Canterbury Tales* (in the *General Prologue*), but that is because he intends to complicate the preexisting "name" by the portrait itself. The *imago* will defy the original which the readers carry in their heads. In *Troilus and Criseyde,* however, he wants to let the fictional original which he has constructed defy the *imago* and in doing that defy the constraint of existing meanings which the reader will have inevitably brought to the poem.

The examples in this introduction have shown that Chaucer insists on the force of dissimilarity being felt in the basic operation of language, in characterization, narrative voice, and narrative order. But that force can also complicate the status of fiction as a source of illumination. When "Geffrey" emerges from the temple of glass in the *House of Fame,* it proves impossible for him to locate this repository of past literary art in the real world; instead, he finds himself surrounded by desert with no evidence of human habitation. Any attempt to find value in a story from its applicability to life, its capacity to clarify the problems of life or to tell truths about life—in other words, any attempt to raise a story to the status of *exemplum*—embraces comparison and in doing so risks subversion through dissimilarity.[18] For instance, this applies to the past myths, legends, and histories (such as that of Criseyde) which are weapons in the gender war, providing ready-made models for understanding present women. These stories purport to transfer knowledge from the past to the present, from the general to the particular, and to apply old words and their meanings in new contexts. Such stories figure very largely in Chaucer's work: he discusses their claimed transfer of knowledge; he reveals the self-serving motives behind their use, and comments on it through characters like the Wife of Bath. At all points the reader is challenged to be conscious of such comparative strategies, even to adopt them, and is reminded that he or she is also making choices which determine the final meanings which the poem containing such stories will offer. Chaucer shows how his own poems are subject to the same illuminatory impulse which drives comparative thinking, and to the same dangers as those conventional *exempla* whose educative agenda he undermines within his work. Consequently he offers and then destabilizes his own works as potential *exempla*.[19] They resist being applied to life as illuminating comparators. They are not allowed to escape from the disabling force of dissimilarity which undermines all our comparative enterprises. His own work is thus consistent with what he reveals through it. To claim that in exposing the force of dissimilarity Chaucer became immune to it, and could confidently offer his work for our illumination, would make him no better than Troilus. After all, Troilus claims for Criseyde the status of *nonpareil* at the very point where her common humanity is most deeply felt by Pandarus and the reader. Criseyde appears unique to her lover. He orders Pandarus not to compare her to any earthly creature (4.450–51). But even as he asserts this Criseyde is showing all too recognizable human frailty, and is engaging in the betrayal which will make her "name" function as a damaging comparator for other women in succeeding years. *Pace* Troilus, everything and everyone is a potential comparator; everything carries with it its dissimilarities from the things it might be compared with; everything carries both the promise of useful illumination and the likelihood that that illumination will be flawed.

It is conceivable that a writer could believe in the fundamental importance of comparison to language and still not exploit that in his writing, but Chaucer's work displays a particular consonance between his conception of language, the issues which his fiction addresses, and the rhetorical devices and narratological strategies he employs. The present book is designed to reveal that consonance. It discusses the power of dissimilarity within comparison at all levels of his text—in the minutiae of individual rhetorical devices and in the patterns made by larger groups of images; in covert narratorial tricks but also in the explicit dialogue of characters; in the ambiguous likenesses suggested between author, narrator, characters, and reader and in the problematic claim of poetic fiction to illuminate and instruct.

This book will first look at the ways in which dissimilarity had taxonomic force in academic and religious traditions of comparing—those traditions with which Chaucer would have been most familiar from early education, from his contemporary culture, and from his experience of translating Boethius's *De Consolatione Philosophiae*. With an eye to these cultural models, it will look at Chaucer's vocabulary of comparison and at the scope which he gave to dissimilarity in undermining some forms of comparison and empowering others.

The next chapter acts as a bridge between traditional thinking about comparison and Chaucer's literary exploitation of it in his major fictions. "Naming and the *House of Fame*" will look at the relationship between dissimilarity, categorisation, instruction, language as a means of transferring knowledge diachronically, and the function of writing.

A chapter on "Similes" will show how Chaucer and other writers used the dissimilarity which is latent within similes, and on which figurative effect depends: how some authors concentrated on *minimal* dissimilarities between the topic and the comparator chosen for it, and consequently played off simile against apposition to gain local narrative and descriptive effects. On the other hand some writers employed the simile's potential clash of similarity and dissimilarity to associate different worlds and to distinguish between them. Chaucer, however, eschews both these goals, preferring to create a dialectical play of simile and context—a play which can even extend beyond the boundaries of a single poem.

When comparison is put in context, or rather when the reader chooses a context as the appropriate one for understanding a comparison, the reading of comparison shades off into the interpretation of the poem as a whole. This book seeks to show that Chaucer uses comparisons as nodes to which various interpretative issues are joined. When comparisons form a narrative pattern in the work, they construct a special context for their own interpretation, forcing readers to examine their own part in making the text. These issues and readerly responsibilities are examined in a chapter on "Patterns of Comparison in *Troilus and Criseyde*." They are extended in the next chapter on "Persuasive Comparison" through Chaucer's exposé of comparison as a device of persuasion, of self-deception and seduction. Chaucer demonstrates the use and abuse of comparison through the exchanges of his characters in *Troilus and Criseyde*, but their errors have metapoetic significance and offer a model for the process of reading poetic fiction.

The final chapter studies areas in which Chaucer prevents the reader from feeling that his fictions are "known," that they are comparable with the reader's experience, or that their dissimilarities from such experience can be managed. He prevents his poems from being categorized by various means: by generic shifts; by sudden changes of direction; by situating them uneasily between fictional particularities and conventional models; by locating his narrative voices somewhere between an individuated character and a social model in the mind of the reader, and in the case of the Wife of Bath, in whom the problems of comparative thinking reach their literary apogee, by constructing a literary illusion which sometimes seems to offer a realized character and sometimes only a collection of voices. When the poems escape the established taxonomy of literary function they are prevented from contributing to the matrix of generalized ideas by which the reader can be educated. When their source cannot be clearly established the "fame" of what they say cannot be confidently judged. Their exemplary function is thus undermined. This constitutes the highest level at which Chaucer analyses comparative thinking within the literary process, but the present book contends that comparison is an important critical issue because of its omnipresence in the poems, from his poetic figures to the status of poetry itself. Reading dissimilarity is an activity which Chaucer insists upon at all levels of his mature work.

Chaucer and Dissimilarity

1
Traditions of Comparison and Dissimilarity

As the *Introduction* indicates, I have not restricted the present study to a single type of comparison, such as the visual image, simile, or argumentative example.¹ The dense texture of Chaucer's literary works suggests that such a restriction would be too limiting. But his own accent in exploiting comparison indicates the means by which such a heterogeneous and ubiquitous process as comparison can be controlled. The defining feature of comparison for this chapter, as in the book generally, is *dissimilarity:* the dissimilarity which exists between everything and everything else, and which is therefore latent in any comparison between things. It is that dissimilarity which comparisons try to bridge that authors either limit or enlarge according to the goals of their discourse, enforcing their comparative claims or subverting them; restricting or opening up the distance between the topic and the comparator by which the topic is supposedly illuminated. Comparative claims can be supported or subverted by measuring the dissimilarity latent within the comparison. As the distance between the topic and the comparator is restricted or opened up so is the comparison's power to illuminate increased or reduced.

It is unnecessary to cite a particular source either for Chaucer's interest in comparison or for his insight that all comparisons contained a negative charge of dissimilarity. Chaucer must have been exposed to the business of comparison, with its argumentative pretensions and disabilities, through many cultural conduits—from the *exempla* of a simple sermon to the claim of any proverb to clarify the present case by implicit comparison with past experiences, or from the *figurae* defined in his basic grammatical education through the omnipresent portraiture of the saints to the profound similes of Dante. He may also have been influenced in his rhetorical understanding by French literary models, as James J. Murphy suggests, though one can still find him preferring a Latin to a French source when translating Boethius's terms of comparison.² No one area or work could be considered the single "source" of his interest in the comparative mode of thinking and its literary forms, just as we shall see that his use of comparative terminology was not dependent on that of any one author. Similarly, any serious attention to comparison inevitably brings with it the recognition that comparative claims can be contested. It is not possible to develop comparative modes of thought without also giving potential value to dissimilarity.

This chapter looks at two components of the medieval understanding of comparison which Chaucer was exposed to in a formal manner, rather than simply *en passant:* firstly, the academic tradition, represented variously in rhetorical and grammatical writings and, secondly, the religious tradition, particularly as it is exemplified in Boethius's *Consolation of Philosophy*, which Chaucer translated as the *Boece*. Taken together they illuminate for the modern reader the types and goals of comparison which Chaucer would have recognized, though he would not necessarily have understood them in specifically academic or theological ways, and certainly did not have academic or theological goals in using them. More importantly in view of what Chaucer subsequently did with comparison, these traditions already bore witness to the paradox of comparison: each had already bifurcated in ways which gave varying scope and value to dissimilarity, and each fed contrasting (and sometimes confusing) accounts of it to later writers. In Chaucer's literary works, however, dissimilarity was to constitute a creative self-interrogation which depended on its silent copresence with positive comparison.

The academic traditions and the *Consolation* differ markedly in the degree to which their direct influence on Chaucer can be claimed. There is no doubt about the importance of the *Consolation*, and we will see the ways in which Chaucer worked with Boethius's practice, and diverged from it. The *Consolation* was no simple source for Chaucer's use of comparative figures, but it may well have shifted comparison as a mode of thinking into the prominent place which it held in his middle and later fictional work. On the other hand, the academic traditions have often been considered more dubious sources for Chaucer's thought, and this is virtually inevitable given the overtly different ends of academic and fictional writing, and the fact that scholars have to work back from the fictions to nonfictional lines of possible influence.

Chaucer was not university educated, and it has been argued that there is little evidence that he studied rhetoricians.[3] However, it is clear that he was in charge of some basic vocabulary from the tradition of the *figurae*, just as he was able to refer to, and borrow from, such an important rhetorical writer as Geoffrey of Vinsauf.[4] It is just not the case that he "does not name . . . any of the one hundred or more *figurae*," as Murphy claims,[5] unless by that one means that he does not name them explicitly *qua figurae*. On the contrary, Chaucer is very aware of certain terms for the figures of comparison, and in some contexts clarifies them according to the immediate requirements of his text, and the expected capacities of his audience.

Chaucer's exposure to grammatical writing is more easily claimed. He would almost certainly have studied Donatus's *Ars Grammatica* as part of his elementary education and if, as is likely, he read Book 3 of that work, the part known as the "Barbarismus," he would have been directly in touch with one of the main medieval traditions for understanding figures, amongst them, of course, the figures of comparison. He would therefore have been faced with an account of these figures which differed significantly from the rhetorical tradition. The understanding of comparison which Chaucer shows, and which he reveals in his terminology, supports the strong argument which Murphy put forward for influence from the grammatical rather than the rhetorical tradition.[6] But to study the disagreement of the traditions before Chaucer is not just to be introduced to an academic tradition of which he almost certainly had experience. It is to understand better the conceptual shape which comparison had in the grammatical tradition, and hence for Chaucer, through looking at the features which were most contested between it and the tradition of rhetoric. Scholars have not fully appreciated that one of the significant distinctions between the rhetorical and grammatical traditions of the figures was that the latter insisted on the taxonomic force of dissimilarity in a way that the former did not. Chaucer was thus more influenced by the tradition which had given dissimilarity greater prominence in the configuring of comparison.

While making this claim for the significance of the grammatical tradition in Chaucer's concept of comparison, I am not wanting to claim that, because of that tradition, Chaucer would have envisaged comparison as a predominantly learned activity. Certainly he treated it with respect in learned contexts such as his translation of Boethius, but Chaucer would also have shared the common usage and conceptions of an educated cultural élite, whose employment of the terms of comparison would carry traces of their etymological and critical development in a mixture of senses but would by no means be restricted by academic tradition. What academics might regard as subtle distinctions were happily accommodated and merged in common usage. Use of the terms by a generally educated person like Chaucer need not imply any particular interest in the academic discourse at the time he used them. Nevertheless, it is possible to define Chaucer's conception of comparison in relation to these traditions, however literary his treatment of it and, in significant respects, these traditions can serve to open up the complexity of this mode of thinking for the modern reader.

Comparison was from the time of Aristotle divided into three types:

(1) *eikōn* which appeared in Latin as *imago*, (2) *parabolē* appearing variously in texts under its Greek name, or translated as *similitudo, comparatio, collatio,* etc., and (3) *paradeigma* translated as *exemplum*. It is useful to have a general working distinction between these as theoreticians defined them with varying degrees of idiosyncrasy.[7]

The first type of comparison, which this book will refer to as *imago*, concentrated on giving a vivid description of the appearance of something. It was comparative in the sense that the image was comparable to that which it represented, or depicted. However, the semantic range of the word extended from meanings which stressed its deictic function to those which implied a very close likeness between the image and its original. The *Oxford Latin Dictionary* shows the range of classical usage, which includes the notions of imitation, pictorial likeness, manifestation, and visible appearance and—with greater emphasis on close similarity—a death mask, duplicate, copy, or the reflection which one gets in a mirror.[8] It was this range of meaning which led to a bifurcation in the academic tradition.

The second type of comparison, here called *similitudo*,[9] was more varied than *imago* in its subject matter: it was not restricted to the depiction of appearance. It was also closer to our modern understanding of simile, and would include what we call simile, because it made a point of drawing a comparison from dissimilar things.

In its classical definition, the third type, *exemplum*, occurred when the case of another person or persons (perhaps their deeds, words, or both) was cited to compare with the topic under review. There were two ways in which example functioned comparatively. Firstly, if an example is understood simply in relation to the argument of which it is part, comparative thinking is involved: the hearer has to be convinced that there is a strong enough likeness between the particular example and the argument which it is adduced to support. All rational induction thus involves establishing a persuasive string of similarities. Certainly example was often acknowledged as a contribution to proof—more so than other forms of comparison.[10] But the comparison which *exemplum* generated was not simply the formal one between the example and its argumentative matrix, but between the example and the real problem or situation which the writer was addressing. For rhetoricians or theologians, who were dealing in applied arguments with legal or moral persuasion as their ultimate goal, *exemplum* was comparative in a different sense, and this is the sense in which Chaucer primarily understood it: the example functioned as the comparator to elucidate, illuminate, or clarify a particular case or topic which it was supposed to be like.

As was usually the case in academic traditions, different writers had different emphases in their definition of *exemplum*.¹¹ Usually, however, the final end of *exemplum* was noted: that it was designed to exhort someone to action or deter them from it, and we shall find that that is a principal feature of its use in Chaucer's works. Fritz Kemmler has noted that the functions of the *exemplum*, though they varied locally according to context, were more defined than its content.¹² Some writers had a very broad conception of what narrative genres might function as *exempla*, and Chaucer's use of the term suggests that he envisaged a wide range of material from proverbs through historical allusions to whole poems as potential *exempla*. Evidently, content or function or both might lie behind an author's use of the term *exemplum*. This was true for as authoritative a writer as Boethius, and certainly for a fiction writer like Chaucer. While the classical definition was frequently relevant, and Chaucer uses many *exempla* which fit it exactly, a writer might well term an *exemplum* any supposedly true event or state of affairs, whether historical, contemporary, or proverbial, which was employed to illuminate a particular case, and through that illumination persuade the hearer to behave in a particular way. The case which was to be illuminated by comparison might be explicit as when, for example, Pandarus offers Troilus *exempla* which should help Troilus decide what to do in a particular situation. But equally an *exemplum* might be offered as a comparator for a state of affairs which was only implicit—as when a poem is presented to illuminate the lives and experience of the reader/hearer. Then it is supposedly relevant in a comparative way, offering itself as a "known" by which confusing experience in real life can be clarified and ordered.

We will see later how Chaucer's understanding of *imago, similitudo,* and *exemplum* relate to these broad definitions and to the narrower academic traditions which tried to refine upon them. In the following pages I have set out the main lines of the rhetorical and grammatical accounts of comparison with particular attention to the taxonomic value which each gave to dissimilarity. Consequently, my focus is on the first two kinds of comparison, *imago* and *similitudo*. Although instances of all three types of comparison, including *exemplum*, will inevitably contain dissimilarities between the topic and comparator (and Chaucer was quick to exploit this feature of the *exemplum*), it was between the first two forms of comparison that the nature and extent of latent dissimilarity had classificatory force. It was here that rhetorical and grammatical traditions varied most in their understanding of comparison, and individuals were most likely to show their own emphasis in definition. Though Chaucer may have felt only that he was using the common vocabulary of comparison and the customary distinctions between different types of comparison, that vocabulary had not always been uncontested; the distinctions had not always been clear; and Chaucer's own usage was actually much closer to the grammatical than the rhetorical conception of comparative figures.

Throughout the classical and medieval tradition there was a tendency to describe the second type of comparison as joining dissimilar things, and a tendency not to make this point explicit of the first kind, *imago*. However, writers varied markedly when explaining this distinction. Because *imago* covered similarity of appearance, it could also imply similarity of genus between the things compared: where there was a close resemblance in externals, it was not unlikely that the things compared were in fact of a similar "kind," e.g., a statue and a person; a face and its reflection in a mirror. For some writers this became an essential aspect of the academic definition of the figure *imago*. Consequently, it had for them a much higher proportion of similarity to dissimilarity in it than *similitudo* had because the similarity of topic and comparator extended to their ontological natures. Thus we find *imago* glossed by Martianus Capella: "imago, id est veri simile" [*imago*, that is, true likeness].[13] Here any comparison which *imago* might make rests upon an implicit identity of genus. However, other writers on *imago* did not require this degree or kind of similarity as long as the emphasis fell upon the appearance of the topic. We can see this difference emerging within the traditions of rhetoric and grammar.

In Book 3 of his *Rhetoric*, Aristotle cites as an instance of *imago* the comparison of someone called Idrieus to a terrier dog.[14] Early rhetoricians like M. Cornelius Fronto also embrace such dissimilarity in *imago*. For Fronto *imago* is more distinctive for its relation to painting: finding an appropriate comparison for a subject is like painting its picture.[15] Dissimilarity between comparator and topic is significant only in so far as a correct impression has to be given, whether respectful or critical. This power to elevate or degrade was particularly valued by some rhetoricians, who recognized that *imago* was inadequate for forming irrefutable arguments, but could add colorful support to probable ones. While searching for an apt *imago* for himself and for Marcus Aurelius's father, Fronto is quite prepared to consider non-human comparators (he chooses an island as an appropriate *imago* for the latter). In describing himself he does actually end up with a comparator of the same genus (the poet Orpheus), but does not insist that the constituents of *imago* always share genus.[16] The later rhetorical tradition was equally open on the generic aspect of the figure.

The pseudo-Ciceronian *Rhetorica ad Herennium,* which was to become the *rhetorica nova* of the Middle Ages, also emphasizes appearance as the definitive subject of *imago:* "Imago est formae cum forma cum quadam similitudine conlatio."[17] This is best translated "*Imago* is a comparison of appearance with appearance under some similarity."[18] The following is the *Rhetorica*'s example of *imago* used to praise: "Inibat in proelium corpore tauri validissimi, impetu leonis acerrimi" [He entered the combat in body like the strongest bull, in impetuosity like the fiercest lion].[19] The example given of *imago* used to blame is considerably longer: it compares a man moving through the Forum to a crested serpent, with fangs and poisonous look. There is no doubt that depicting appearance is the key to the figure, and the rhetorician thus distinguishes *imago* from *similitudo*.

Similitudo is simply described by the *Rhetorica:* "oratio traducens ad rem quampiam aliquid ex re dispari simile" [*Similitudo* is a way of speaking which carries over to one thing an element of likeness from a different thing].[20] The *Rhetorica* evidently does not use the extent of dissimilarity between the topic and the comparator, far less a difference in genus between them, to be the criterion for distinguishing *imago* and *similitudo*. In neither type of comparison is there any constraint on the genus of the things associated. For *similitudo*, correctness in the point of comparison is more important than the dissimilarities between the things compared, which can be extreme: "Non enim res tota totae rei necesse est similis sit, sed id ipsum quod conferetur similitudinem habeat oportet" [The resemblance between the two things need not apply throughout, but must hold on the precise point of comparison].[21] Indeed the orator is encouraged to think about all aspects of the material and imaginary world in order to gain facility in comparison.

On the other hand, *imago*, though restricted to a comparison of appearances, is not thereby bound to link things of the same genus, as was evident in the examples which linked man with bull, lion, and serpent. Such a restriction would curtail the power of the orator to praise or blame through a careful association of dissimilar things. As far as the *Rhetorica* is concerned, there is not even a coincidental association of like with like such as in the example of Orpheus adopted by Fronto as an *imago* for himself. Dissimilarity within the comparison is not a taxonomic issue for the writer of the *Rhetorica;* subject matter is.

The rhetorical tradition's emphasis on visual similarity without similarity in the area of genus is shown clearly in the minor fourth-century Latin rhetorician Julius Rufinianus in his *De Figuris Sententiarum et Elocutionis*.[22] He says that *imago* occurs "cum perfectae formae similes conferuntur" [when complete outward appearances are brought together because of their similarity].[23] The priority of imaginative portrayal over generic similarity is evident for he exemplifies *imago* by Cicero's comparison of the Roman populace to the sea: naturally tranquil, but customarily agitated by the force of the winds.

This understanding of *imago* is transmitted through the rhetorical writers of the Middle Ages. Geoffrey of Vinsauf distinguishes between the types of comparison in the following way. He says of the second type, *similitudo*, "ex re / Dissimili similem traho" [I draw a similarity from dissimilar things]. But of *imago* he says, "collatio facta / Formae cum simili forma sub imagine recta" [I make a comparison between similar appearances under the influence of a true likeness].[24] To Geoffrey, *imago* seems to imply strong similarity between the things compared, while a simile is fashioned out of dissimilarity. But it is also clear from his example of *imago* that the true likeness it carries need not have a generic basis:

> Abstulit illum
> Ille pugil noster, mira virtute leonis,
> Astu serpentis et simplicitate columbae

[He, our champion, rescued him with the wondrous valor of the lion, the guile of the serpent, and the innocence of the dove].[25] Geoffrey is transmitting the doctrine of the *Rhetorica ad Herennium* to his contemporaries, and accurately reflects its emphasis on appearance without shared genus in the definition of *imago*.[26]

The rhetorical account of comparison appears to have had a rival in the grammatical tradition from Donatus's *Ars Grammatica* (also known as the *Ars Maior*).[27] Although, as James J. Murphy says, Donatus and the *Rhetorica ad Herennium* "in large measure shaped the doctrine of *figurae* in the middle ages,"[28] they differ substantially in their treatment of comparisons, not only in the respect that the grammatical tradition sees them as tropes, and the rhetorical does not, but specifically in the criteria employed for their classification. It is the extent and nature of the latent dissimilarity in the comparison which is crucial. The *Rhetorica ad Herennium*'s claim that both *imago* and *similitudo* could involve generic dissimilarity was unacceptable to the grammarians, who saw this as the very feature which distinguished the figures from each other.

The difference between the grammatical and rhetorical traditions in their criterion for separating *imago* from the *similitudo* type of comparison reflects the different goals of their discourse. The grammarian values exactitude in definition of kinds, as shown in the distinctions drawn between parts of speech, and the rhetorician stresses the effectiveness of communication and the function which particular types of speech have in context. They accordingly emphasize different aspects of the natural connection between similarity of appearance and shared genus/species (a connection borne witness to by the Latin word "species," which contains both "visual appearance" and "subdivision, species" among its meanings). The grammarian emphasizes the generic because it is the scientific foundation upon which shared appearance depends; the rhetorician emphasizes visual appearance because the descriptive effect is more immediately important to the discourse than the ontological status of the things he compares, though that may have an implicit value as the basis on which the subject being described is praised or blamed through association with a higher or lower creature.

The difference between the two traditions is well seen if we compare their examples of *imago*. The rhetorician Julius Rufinianus, whom we earlier found classifying as *imago* the comparison of the citizens of Rome to the sea, also cites as *imago* the following quotation from Virgil: "talis Amyclaei domitus Pollucis habenis / Cyllarus" [Such was Cyllarus, tamed by the reins of Amyclaean Pollux].[29] Virgil is describing the physical characteristics and appearance of the ideal war horse and compares it to famous horses of the past, of which Pollux's Cyllarus is one. The grammarian Diomedes, writing firmly in the Donatan grammatical tradition, quotes this latter example as an instance of *imago* but he rejects the comparison of the citizens to the sea as *imago*. Revealingly, he adds this note to the Virgilian example of *imago* which he finds acceptable: "hic enim equus equo comparatur" [for here a horse is compared to a horse].[30]

Imago for the grammarian does not show dissimilarity in the area of genus or, indeed, species. Donatus makes this clear through both his definitions and his examples. He writes "icon est personarum inter se vel eorum quae personis accidunt conparatio."[31] That is, for Donatus *imago* is a comparison of persons themselves or of those things which appertain to persons. Donatus does not mention visual appearance, but he does wish to constrain the generic area within which things can be linked in *imago*. His example makes clear that description of appearance is the expected result. The example he gives of *imago* was to become seminal for the tradition and was still being quoted at the end of the seventeenth century by Vossius: "os humerosque deo similis" [his face and shoulders were like a god's].[32] The description is of Aeneas suddenly revealed to Dido in a beauty of divine quality (and source, since it has been imparted to him by his mother, the Goddess Venus). The semi-divine Aeneas and a god are sufficiently similar in genus to permit this striking depiction of appearance to be an instance of *imago*.

By contrast, the second type of comparison, *similitudo* "est rerum *genere dissimilium* conparatio" [is a comparison of things different in kind].[33] The example given (also from Virgil's *Aeneid*) compares the cries of the priest Laocoon as he is killed by sea serpents to those of a sacrificial bull wounded by a badly aimed axe. Here, although the exact point of comparison is the frantic sound of priest and bull, it is the clear difference of genus in the comparison which is most prominent to Donatus: the linking of man and animal, of priest and his customary sacrificial victim. Such a yoking of significantly different topic and comparison constitutes *similitudo*.[34]

The encyclopaedist Isidore of Seville is even more explicit:[35]

> imago—cum figuram rei *ex simili genere* conamur exprimere, ut 'Omnia Mercurio similis, vocemque coloremque et crines flavos et membra decora iuventa.'

[*Imago* is when I try to depict the appearance of something from something of a similar kind, as 'Like Mercury in all respects: in voice and complexion; in his golden hair, and his pleasing youthful limbs.'] The degree of similarity implicit in the phrase *ex simili genere* becomes more evident when we follow up Isidore's example in Virgil's *Aeneid*, 4.558–59, for the person being described *is* indeed Mercury whose shape appears to Aeneas in a dream. The topic and the comparator are the same. Here the demand for similarity of genus is at its most extreme: the image and its original have merged into a kind of identity, separated only because the image is visionary. From the range of meanings testified in classical Latin, the grammarian clearly insists on very close likeness as the defining characteristic of *imago*, while the rhetorican looks to its deictic function.

By contrast, citing Lucan's comparison of Caesar to a lion in *Pharsalia* 1.205–7, Isidore defines *similitudo* as "conparatio ex dissimilibus rebus . . . ubi leoni Caesarem conparavit, *non ex suo, sed ex alio genere* similitudinem faciens" [a comparison from dissimilar things . . . in which he compared Caesar to a lion, making a comparison not from his own, but from a different, genus]. At this point the wheel has turned full circle: the very type of comparison adduced by the *Rhetorica ad Herennium* and other rhetorical works as an instance of *imago* because of its emphasis on appearance, is now being classified by a grammarian under the second type of comparison on the grounds of its containing generic dissimilarity.

Using the terminology and definitions of Donatus, Bede exemplifies *imago* by the biblical text "Vidimus gloriam eius, gloriam quasi unigeniti a patre" [We have seen his glory, a glory as of the only-begotten of the Father].[36] Here, Bede chooses the mysterious separateness in unity of the Persons in the Trinity to show the relation between the things linked in an *imago*. He thus presents the grammatical stress on genus at its most extreme and perfectly replicates in Christian terms the identity of genus evinced by Donatus's pagan example "os humerosque deo similis." By contrast, *similitudo* is exemplified by

Christ's parable in which the most extreme dissimilarity of topic and comparator is exploited: "Simile est regnum caelorum grano synapis" [The Kingdom of Heaven is like a mustard seed].[37] This intentional use of extreme dissimilarity for didactic purposes is recurrent in Christian tradition, and reaches its fictional apogee in Chaucer's contemporary, the *Pearl*-Poet.

While the evidence so far adduced does indicate that the rhetorical and grammatical traditions divide in their treatment of dissimilarity in comparison, it would be misleading to imply that the sources are always clear or the traditions consistent. Consistency is not always evident even in texts which became highly influential. This is well seen in the case of Victorinus, who wrote a fourth-century commentary on Cicero's *De Inventione*. Victorinus's *Explanationum in Rhetoricam M. Tullii Ciceronis* was much used in the Middle Ages.[38] Mixing a taxonomy which reflects rhetorical tradition and examples from Donatus he proceeds, unusually, to conflate his definitions of *imago* and *similitudo* and their Donatan examples, under the single head of *imago*.[39]

After the early thirteenth century, the two chief grammatical texts in the schools and universities were the *Graecismus* of Eberhard of Béthune and Alexander of Ville-Dieu's *Doctrinale*. They reveal the constant fraying of the edges of definition which characterizes writing on the *figurae*, even though knowledge of these devices was considered a matter of elementary education. James J. Murphy writes, "whatever the motivation for the notice taken of *figurae* by authors of non-grammatical works, it is apparent that most medieval writers assume their study to be an *elementary* subject. It is regarded as something that every educated medieval person would have absorbed at an early stage of his training."[40] Eberhard does not include *imago* in its traditional setting with *similitudo* and *exemplum* as tropes, but substitutes *allegoria*, presumably because he does not consider that *imago* is a device which truly "tropes," turning language from its proper use.[41] In another part of the book he associates *imago* firmly with the appearance of things, but is not concerned with it as a figure.[42]

Alexander of Ville-Dieu, on the other hand, includes *imago* in its traditional association with similitude and example, and maintains the grammarians' distinction between it and *similitudo* (which, like other grammarians in the Donatan tradition, he refers to under its Greek name *parabolē*). But at lines 2564–67 he also reveals that the terms are not so distinct in usage:

> in simili genere qui comparat, efficit icon
> haec solet ex usu quandoque parabola dici.
> sed dici poterit de iure parabola, si quis
> inter dissimiles res comparat

[Whoever makes a comparison within a similar genus is making an 'icon'; in practice, from time to time, this is said to be 'parabola.' But it can be truly called 'parabola' if someone makes a comparison between dissimilar things].[43] Here Alexander acknowledges a tendency to promote the term for the second type of comparison to the status of superordinate, that is to make *similitudo (parabola)* stand as the general term for comparison, but he himself wishes still to maintain the practical criterion of generic dissimilarity to distinguish between the first and second types of comparison.

Both Eberhard and Alexander show the potential in academic discussion for *imago* to disappear as a type of comparative figure, either into the portrayal of appearance, with no special comparative or figurative force, or into a general category of figurative comparison. The potential was always there for, as has been shown, *imago* was both comparative and depictive in function. Consequently, it was traditionally grouped with types of comparison but also had descriptive affinities with other kinds of portraiture, such as *effictio*, which often followed it in lists of *figurae*,[44] and *characterismus*.[45] When Chaucer was writing, however, *imago* had not lost its status as a comparative figure, and he uses both the term itself and the device in ways which reflect the grammarians' sense of it as involving the depiction of appearance together with a close generic likeness between the image and its original.

Most of this book is given over to an account of how Chaucer responded in his literary practice to the configuration of comparison which he inherited. The grammatical tradition shows us that Chaucer would have had a concept of comparison which was refined both by the degree of dissimilarity between the terms compared and by the different functions of the figures. It was a rich and complex conceptual area with immense potential to be exploited in practice. Functionally, at one end of the spectrum there lay the depictive or manifesting power of the *imago*, particularly valuable for the poet aiming at emotional force or imaginative vividness; at the other the persuasive, supposedly educating, force of the *exemplum*. In the middle was the immense, functionally unrestricted, world of likenesses explored through *similitudo*. Analytically also, the three figures offered a range of possibilities: *imago* asserted itself as a close likeness to that which it imaged; *similitudo* positively exploited dissimilarities between the terms compared; *exemplum* proposed a similarity but was, in a sense, tied to that proposal—it was a similarity offered, but open to rejection. While the other two forms by their assertive rejection or embracing of dissimilarity were suited to the complex, tortuous, ironic, and subversive techniques of the poet, *exemplum* had the additional attraction of dramatic potential: it was a form of comparison which could serve as the focus of contest between characters, and between the author of the poem and its readers or hearers. In his fiction Chaucer proceeded to exploit all areas of comparison. But his own poetic and philosophical agenda led him to extend into them an interest in the potential of comparative dissimilarity—into *exemplum* where it had been implicitly constrained by the need to persuade by analogy, and even into the area of *imago* where his basic education had suggested it was limited or absent. Against the background of the academic traditions outlined above, this radical commitment to the tension in all comparison, whatever subcategories it might form, shows up more clearly; but the rhetoricians and grammarians studied here show that dissimilarity had proved a taxonomic challenge long before Chaucer took it up.

Dissimilarity was not just an issue in academic writing on rhetoric and grammar. It also had a long history in theology and, since we are to look more closely at Chaucer's work with Boethius, a brief introduction to this aspect of the comparative tradition is required. Chaucer was cultural heir to the Christian religion's deeply comparativist outlook and, consequently, to the hopes, anxieties, and negotiations which attend any attempt to say that something is like something else. We have already seen, in the Christian examples which Bede gave for the figures of *imago* and *similitudo,* the extremes of theological and didactic comparativism: the mysterious mutual reflection between the persons in the Trinity on the one hand and, on the other, the extravagant dissimilarity employed by Christ in his likening the Kingdom of Heaven to a grain of mustard. But the issues of comparison were also deeply embedded in the Christian's theological self-construction.

Christian theology was constantly engaged in acknowledging, comprehending, measuring, and trying to traverse the dissimilarity between the Creator and a creation which still bore signs of its divine origin, even although it had added the Fall to the fundamentally unbridgeable gap between it and the perfection of God. As comparison uses that which is known in order to elucidate that which is less well known or unknown, so Christian theology used the creation as the comparator to work towards an understanding of the topic, its Creator. Saint Paul had sanctioned the attempt when he said that Christians can understand invisible things through the things that are made (Rom. 1:20), that is, that the divine could be traced and partially comprehended by examining the characteristics of the creation. But Saint Paul had also stated that earthly understanding could not be complete; humanity only saw the truth "per speculum in aenigmate" [as in a mirror, obscurely].[46] For example, St Augustine devoted Books 9 through 14 of his *De Trinitate* to showing how the Trinity was adumbrated in the associated human powers of mind, knowledge, and love; and memory, understanding, and will. But in Book 15 he showed how these comparators were still inadequate since they were not unified, immutable, or eternal as were the persons of the Trinity.[47]

Humanity was understood as the *imago* which manifested, though imperfectly, its original, God. As in all comparisons, there was a latent tension which came from the coexistence of dissimilarity with similarity. In the Vulgate, God says, "Faciamus Hominem ad imaginem et similitudinem nostram" (Gen. 1:26) using words which implied for Jerome and medieval Christians both close physical similarity and a likeness which had basic dissimilarity etched into it. How much dissimilarity that nature included; whether it could be reduced; the influences which might lead it to increase; the promise of its final removal which was given when Christ closed the terms of the comparison by taking on human flesh—all these issues were predicated upon the comparability of humanity with the divine, of the creation with the Creator.

It would be inappropriate here to follow up the immense theological tradition of comparativism. But, since this book will argue that Chaucer powerfully exploited dissimilarity in comparison in his literary work, it is as well to recall that one of the main traditions of scriptural interpretation had long embraced the creativity of dissimilarity. Within this area of Chaucer's cultural ambience it was wholly traditional to place a high value on dissimilarity. In particular, dissimilarity was regarded not as destructive of comparison but as essential if comparison was to convey any degree of truth. With such a culturally formative emphasis behind him, it should come as no surprise that Chaucer also embraced dissimilarity, though his attitude to it was more overtly ambivalent than that of the theologians, his use of it was more forensic than optimistic, and, working at a lower level of discourse, and with earthly communication rather than the scriptures, he was not able to depend upon the absolute truths on which theologians relied when exploiting dissimilarity for their purposes. A brief look at this theological tradition also offers a valuable perspective on Boethius's more modest, but no less comparativist, *Consolation,* with which Chaucer had direct working experience.

The tradition of biblical interpretation established by the early sixth-century Neoplatonist known as the Pseudo-Dionysius had wide currency in the Middle Ages.[48] This tradition allowed for an extravagant use of dissimilarity in framing earthly images to speak about the divine. In two extant works, *The Celestial Hierarchy* and *Mystical Theology,* Pseudo-Dionysius was concerned with how to interpret those biblical images which referred to God and other heavenly beings. He defended images against the accusation that they were indecorous or spiritually dangerous when they appeared to drag God down into incongruous materiality by referring to Him as a sun, star, fire, ointment, corner stone, or even as an animal.[49]

He did not distinguish as contemporary rhetoricians and grammarians would have done between simile, metaphor, imagistic name, or poetic symbol. He did, however, regard the relationship between the images of earthly things and God as a comparative one, and he described them with deliberate word play as "dissimilar similarities."[50]

Pseudo-Dionysius defends the imagery in a variety of ways. Firstly, by employing material and perceptible things to describe immaterial, spiritual intelligences, scripture is using the means of instruction natural and necessary for material humanity. In other words, comparison must draw upon what we know. But he also envisages the comparison as a means of *preventing* understanding by those who are not suitable recipients of sacred knowledge.[51] The function of comparison is here turned on its head: the comparator becomes not a means of leading people to understanding, but an obstacle, a protective veil, a digression.

To those who might feel that there is too much dissimilarity between God and the imagery of material things employed to speak about him, Pseudo-Dionysius replies that any comparator would be inadequate "for the Deity is far beyond every manifestation of being and of life."[52] Consequently, while it is better to speak of God in terms of what he is not, rather than what he is, if one does aim to find comparators for heavenly beings, they should include a high degree of dissimilarity, and it is their very inappropriateness for God or the angels that will impel the Christian (of adequate intelligence, that is) to pass beyond them, realizing that they are figurative rather than taking them literally.[53]

In this tradition, the danger of using comparisons with a high degree of dissimilarity to illuminate a divine topic was reduced because it was assumed that Christians did really know *something* about the topic. Belief about God's nature could act as a restraint and a control on any outrageous comparison. To employ such a radical comparative method would have been impossible had it not been assumed that Christians were able to select from the possible characteristics of the comparators those which were appropriate, and to reject or, better still, include as contrastive, those features which were evidently and grossly inappropriate.

Pseudo-Dionysius is thus involved in paradoxes which are latent in all comparison but are accentuated by its theological use. He wants to say that the comparator can stimulate the Christian towards understanding the topic, but he depends on the Christian's already knowing the topic sufficiently well to recognize that the comparator must be understood figuratively, not literally. As was pointed out in the Introduction this is a hermeneutic circularity which all comparison suffers from. This circularity makes the educative force of comparison more problematic than is suggested by the optimistic traditional formulation that comparison leads us to understand the less well known, or unknown, by similarity with what we know. Chaucer's treatment of comparison, both through his narrator *personae* and his characters, shows that he understood this circularity and consequently regarded comparison as a matter of debate and negotiation.

However, there are other paradoxes more particular to the theological use of comparison. Pseudo-Dionysius wants to say that comparisons promote understanding, but also that it is acceptable when they do not, because then they protect rather than clarify. He wants to say that God is beyond comparison, but also that comparisons are useful to us in learning about him. He wants to say that the gap between topic and comparator is unbridgeable but, when it comes down to it, he is committed to reducing the gap if he can, and to implying that there is a real ground which the topic and the comparator share in a positive sense, not just by contrast: "Matter . . . owes its subsistence to absolute beauty and keeps, throughout its earthly ranks, some echo of intelligible beauty."[54] The imagistic obfuscation of the word "echo" in this passage cannot disguise the fact that Pseudo-Dionysius, as he is bound by scripture to do, needs positive comparability at the base of his dissimilar similarities, because the alternative would be to cut the Christian off from God, and to imply that God's creation bears no marks of its origin.

The theological embracing of dissimilarity thus depends upon assuming a number of things. Firstly, it depends on a certain bedrock of "knowledge" or belief about the topic of the comparison. Furthermore, it is not committed to educating every Christian in the mysteries through comparison, and so can countenance comparison which, by its very dissimilarity, will frustrate the less intelligent. Thirdly, because it can depend upon the faith of the believer it is untroubled by the circularity built into the comparative process—affirmation rather than proof is sufficient. And fourthly, it can claim a real similarity between the heavenly topic and earthly comparators to authorise their comparative linkage. However dissimilar they may otherwise be, there is a solid ground to the comparison, provided by the divine goodness of which the comparators partake. Given these safeguards, dissimilarity can be promoted theologically as a decorous and truthful acknowledgment of God's supernal distance from us.

As his *persona*, Geffrey, makes clear to the Eagle in the *House of Fame*, Chaucer did not wish to fly so high.[55] Though he may well have ultimately believed in spiritual absolutes circumscribing the force of dissimilarity,[56] his own writing concentrated on a world of human discourse and anxiety in which dissimilarity was indeed productive of doubt and confusion, though this same dissimilarity could also be used positively to illuminate the difficulty of human understanding, the prejudicial manner in which we employ comparisons, and to subvert easy conclusions.

Chaucer must have had at the very least a general sense of the creative value of dissimilarity as it was embraced by theologians trying to mediate between earthly and heavenly things. However, his immediate and proved access was to the more restrained tradition of Boethius's *Consolation,* in which dissimilarity was modestly acknowledged or directed to the needs of consolation, while similarities between the realm of the transcendent and the earthly were employed for illumination and to give a consolatory assurance of divine values.[57] Boethius combined didacticism with consolation in ways which led him to exploit dissimilarity at times but also to limit it at others.

Through his translation of the *Consolation* Chaucer would have had direct experience of the notion that the universe was part of a comparison *ab initio* because it was the realized imitation of the divine thought which created it. Dignified by this relationship, comparison could have a correspondingly lofty didactic goal. This is borne out in passages such as the following, in which Philosophy is explaining to Boethius the nature of eternity: "Eternite, thanne, is parfit possessioun and al togidre of lif interminable; *and that schewethe more cleerly by the comparysoun or collacioun of temporel thinges.*" (5.Pr.6.13–17; my emphasis)

At the same time dissimilarities between the two realms had to be acknowledged if for no other reason than to show the appropriate humility of the fallen creature towards the perfect Creator. Throughout the work, dissimilarity in comparison is signaled to avoid spiritual impropriety, but from a basic assumption that positive comparison is fair and valuable. The delicacy of this task is shown when Philosophy qualifies her parallel between God's and humans' sight, a parallel based on the similarity between eternity and the continuity of created things:

> Certes, thanne, *yif men myghte maken any digne comparysoun or collacioun of the presence devyne and of the presence of mankynde,* ryght so as ye seen some thinges in this temporel present, ryght so seeth God alle thinges by his eterne present. (5.Pr.6.130–35; my emphasis)

However, Boethius is also prepared to assert that there are areas where comparison simply should not be made, although this runs counter to his prevailing comparativist method. While arguing for the worthlessness of earthly renown, Philosophy will admit only comparison between different amounts of measurable, temporal fame. Comparison between such fame and the attainment of eternal glory is inadmissible "for of thinges that han ende may ben maked comparysoun, but of thynges that ben withouten ende to thynges that han ende may be makid no comparysoun." (2.Pr.7.106–10). This strict separation is prompted by the text's consolatory function as much as by spiritual respect. In the immediate context of the argument, where Boethius must be shifted away from regret for his political downfall, the dissimilarity between earthly and heavenly glory has to be presented not just as too great to measure, not just as a qualified comparison, but as a comparison fatuous from the outset.

The consolatory function of Boethius's text enjoins strict constraints on where dissimilarity can be acknowledged if the similarity of things earthly and divine is at issue. There is no consolation in being left room to fear that our connection with the divine is only tenuous, or that the gap is too great to be bridged by the imagination strengthened by faith. However, a comparison which acknowledges a well-defined dissimilarity between earthly and heavenly things can be a source both of education and of gladness when it teaches us not to desire that which is of lower worth, or mourn it when it is lost. Thus Philosophy compares, and contrasts, the shining beauty of earthly jewels with heavenly light. The persuasion depends both on laying open the positive comparison between the beauty of the jewels and of heaven and defining the dissimilarity between them. It is important to the educative power of the comparison that the beauty of the earthly jewels be genuinely appreciated, for this is also helping us towards understanding divine beauty, even if these jewels are to be set aside as ultimately worthless compared to it. Their beauty comes through even in Chaucer's wordy translational style:

> Alle the thinges that the ryver Tagus yyveth yow with his goldene gravelis, or elles alle the thinges that the ryver Hermus yeveth with his rede brinke, or that Indus yyveth, that is next the hote partie of the world, that medleth the grene stones with the white . . . Al that liketh yow here, and exciteth and moeveth youre thoughtes, the erthe hath norysschid it in his lowe caves. But the schynyng by whiche the hevene is governed and whennes that it hath his strengthe, that eschueth the derke overthrowynge of the soule. (3.Me.10.11–25)

In the *Consolation* comparison provides a spiritual dialogue on the relative values of topic and comparator through which the user can be both educated and consoled.

Chaucer also found throughout Boethius's work the buoyant view that different aspects of the created universe were *mutually* informing

1: TRADITIONS OF COMPARISON AND DISSIMILARITY 49

because their Creator had established analogies between them, and that thus we could gain knowledge from comparatively adducing what was already known to clarify new topics. Frequently, Boethius uses comparison not towards its higher end of linking the earthly and heavenly but to illuminate one aspect of our earthly condition by another. Thus, he uses the ever-changing sea and seasons to explain the nature of Fortune, concluding: "Yif the forme of this world is so zeeld stable, and yif it torneth by so manye entrechaungynges, wiltow thanne trusten in the tumblenge fortunes of men?" (2.Me.3.16–20)

While the *Consolation* employed comparisons for traditional didactic purposes, the dramatic context of Philosophy's dialogue with Boethius gave them a special color. Chaucer would have seen them used to impart spiritual assurance; for structuring an argument powerful enough to convince a fearful and desolate Boethius; for persuasion; and for the degradation, praise and illumination of the topic. He also found a literary attraction towards using comparison in ways extraneous to the strict demands of argument. At one point Philosophy narrates a comparison at length, as in the mythical *exemplum* of Orpheus and Eurydice which ends Book 3, at another she clusters comparisons for intensifying effect, as well as for proof, as in the recitation of classical *exempla* which ends Book 4. Often this exuberance of comparison shows up in the *metra*, which may be made up of one or more poetic comparators, extended to the point where the beauty of the image is as prominent as its function, and one feels a delight in the sheer contemplation of the comparator.

> And ryht by ensaumple as the sonne is hydd whan the sterres ben clustered *(that is to seyn, whan sterres ben covered with cloudes)* by a swyft wynd that hyghte Chorus, and that the firmament stant dirked with wete plowngy cloudes; and that the sterres nat apeeren upon hevene, so that the nyght semeth sprad upon erthe: yif thanne the wynde that hyghte Boreyas, isent out of the kaves of the cuntre of Trace, betith this nyght . . . and discovereth the closed day, thanne schyneth Phebus ischaken with sodeyn light and smyteth with his beemes in merveylynge eien . . . Ryght so, and noon other wise, the cloudes of sorwe dissolved. (1.Me.3:4–Pr.3.2)

Here we see scholarly detail and imaginative and tonal modulation combined in a way readers of Chaucer's fictional works will recognize.[58] These instances of fulsome comparativism adumbrate Chaucer's own delight in detailed or reduplicated example as a generator of narrative. They constitute narrative and rhetorical pleasures which coexist with the main argumentative thrust of Boethius's consolatory project, but function as an aesthetic trope upon it.

Chaucer also probably borrowed actual similes from Boethius, such as the thunderbolt and the tower used in the *House of Fame* (534–40); the ass and harp image with which Pandarus rouses Troilus (1.Pr.4.2–3; *Troilus and Criseyde* 1.731–35); the comparison with a drunk man unable to find his house which Arcite employs in the *Knight's Tale* to show the human condition (3.Pr.2.86–88; *Knight's Tale* 1261–65); or, from a much later period of composition, the Manciple's image of the bird which prefers freedom to good treatment in a cage (3.Me.2.21–33; *Manciple's Tale* 163–74).

Translating Boethius meant not just that Chaucer was exposed to his generally comparativist outlook and his local deployment of its devices in argument and consolation. It meant working closely with his terminology of comparison, choosing between words like *exemplum, collatio, imago, simulare* (vb.), and so on, and glossing them when the simple English equivalent seemed inadequate. Recent research indicates that he left the *Boece* in an unpolished state.[59] Nonetheless, in its rougher form the *Boece* shows Chaucer responding to the promptings of his main text and his parallel and commentary sources in the area of comparison, and deciding how to represent its terms in English.[60]

When translating Boece, Chaucer clearly aims to maintain visibility and consistency in the terminology of comparison; to clarify it through using doublets if necessary; and to remain close to his source.[61] As one might expect, his terminology for comparison throughout his oeuvre, not just in the *Boece*, is derived from Latin rather than Greek (though his elementary education in Donatus would have introduced comparative figures under their Greek names).[62] From the vocabulary traditionally used for the first kind he typically uses the word "image"; for the second type he employs "similitude" (rarely), "collation" (in translation), "comparison," "likeness"; and for that of the third kind he typically uses "example." His vocabulary thus reflects the variety of terms traditionally used for the second type, and the narrower range of terms customarily employed for the first and third types.

"Example" is Chaucer's most frequent term of comparison, and this reflects a fictional emphasis on persuasion as it is attempted both by characters and narrators. For him, as for Boethius, an "example" is defined as much by persuasive function as by content. One finds that comparisons which look, in terms of content, like instances of *similitudo* since they draw upon widely dissimilar things, are nonetheless termed "examples" because they are part of a persuasive argument.[63] For example, the Wife of Bath uses the word "ensample" for a comparison which associates quite dissimilar things and, indeed, she provokes the hearer to find the hidden ground of the comparison—a gesture more suggestive of the dissimilarities in *similitudo*. She is talking of men and women in the same bed: "For peril is bothe fyr and tow t'assemble; / Ye knowe what this ensample may resemble" (*Wife of Bath's Prologue* 89–90). Here it is the persuasive function of the comparison, its intention to deter, that justifies the use of the word "ensample."

Chaucer concentrated most heavily on comparison in the ten-year period, approximately from 1378–87, before he wrote the majority of the *Canterbury Tales*. Significantly, it was this period in which he wrote his translation of Boethius's *Consolation of Philosophy*. It cannot be coincidental that the period which saw the *Boece* also saw the theoretical analysis of the linguistic base of comparison in the *House of Fame;* two attempts to frame a collection of tales by establishing an exemplary agenda for them—the *Legend of Good Women* and the tragedies which became the *Monk's Tale;* and, in the *Knight's Tale,* which seems to have originated at this time as "Palamon and Arcite," a thematizing of comparison in the extremely dissimilar fates which very similar people can receive. This was also the time when Chaucer chose to revise an existing *exemplum* for his longest single narrative, *Troilus and Criseyde.* In doing so, he drew attention to his own poem as a potential *exemplum*. He also gave immense scope to similaic comparison to operate as a structural device, linking and defining the voices in the poem, and forming thematic patterns; and he developed a depth of realism through having characters use comparison as a persuasive device. If the *Tales* of Part 7 of the *Canterbury Tales* were also written at this time, we must add to the above list the intensely playful invitation that we draw morality from the fable of the *Nun's Priest's Tale* (3438–43), thus claiming its similarity to our own lives. In that comic mélange of all that Chaucer took seriously elsewhere a world of exemplary meanings is opened up, but teasingly without the selective thematic focus upon which a successful *exemplum* depends almost as much as it depends upon exact comparability.

However, by analyzing, undermining, and dramatizing comparison these poems move far from Boethius's confident adoption of this mode of thinking. What Chaucer did not find in Boethius was what he particularly developed himself: exploitation of the dissimilarity latent in all comparisons. As we have seen, Boethius employed this only within limits; he stressed the positive ground of his comparisons and did not invite close investigation of their justice. Chaucer, on the other hand, was fascinated by the tension which dissimilarity could create in positive comparisons such as instructional *exempla* or supposedly close likenesses such as *imagines*. Much of what he was to write in the ten years surrounding, and succeeding, his translation of the *Consolation* was empowered by a dual sense of comparison's worth and disability.

Chaucer uses the word "comparison" as the superordinate term for the comparative process. Significantly, when employing it outside his translation of Boethius, he tends to give it a formulaic slant which shows comparison as contested. Claims that comparison cannot, or should not, be made recur: "thanne is ther no comparison"; "mak no comparysoun"; "comparisoun may noon ymaked bee," and so on. This is an important sentiment for an author who wishes to show that, while comparison is the natural recourse for someone trying to understand a problem, dissimilarities can disable the comparisons of which they are part; and that persuasions by comparison or claims for incomparability may be self-serving and deceitful.

Though the *Consolation* had shown him the subtlety of comparison used in a resonant dramatic context, Chaucer framed the comparisons which he took from Boethius with fictional contexts of greater complexity than was appropriate for the philosophical argument of the vision in the *Consolation*. Thus the fulsome, example-packed, arguments of Pandarus work in context as a comic rewriting of the intensely argumentative style of Philosophy, with whom he is implicitly linked when he challenges Troilus's attention in the words Philosophy uses to challenge Boethius: "artow lik an asse to the harpe?"

Arcite's view that we are unable to find true felicity, as a drunk man cannot find his house, is not left part of a single line of argument, as in Boethius, but has the wider complicating context of a fictive opposite in Palamon's opinion that the fault lies more in the gods than in ourselves and we are victims of divine indifference (*Knight's Tale* 1303–14). These conflicting views are then bound into the subtler ironies of a plot which shows Palamon elevated despite his personal failure, and Arcite cast down by divine machinations.

The caged bird example, as used by the Manciple, has its tone altered by the narrator so that the bird's desire for the "agreables schadewes of the wodes" acknowledged by Philosophy (3.Me.2.29) becomes an inexplicable, and ungrateful preference for "a forest that is rude and coold" (*Manciple's Tale* 170). Philosophy uses the example to propound a doctrine of nature: "Alle thynges seken ayen to hir propre cours, and alle thynges rejoysen hem of hir retornynge ayen to hir nature" (3.Me.2.39–42). Chaucer, however, divests it of this value and of the optimistic spiritual end which this instinct serves, and instead catches it up into an increasingly gendered, derogatory, and evasive pattern of *exempla* which not only displays the duplicity of the Manciple but also reflects metapoetically on the author.

Since Chaucer repeatedly problematizes comparative thinking where Boethius had not, the poems of the years from 1378–87 cannot be in any obvious way the *result* of Chaucer's translation of the *Conso-*

lation, but they owe much to the prominence, functional variety, and subtlety which comparison has in the *Consolation*, and they help to constitute the "Boethian" strand in his writing.

The poems which Chaucer wrote before this time certainly contain comparisons, but with much less of a charge. There is the same tendency to list classical *exempla* in the *Book of the Duchess* that we find in the *House of Fame*. Indeed we find in the earlier dream vision some of the same comparators (though not making the same point) as appear later in the *Legend of Good Women*. The assertion that Blanche was as true or as gracious as Lucrece, Penelope, and Hester is an affirmation of the *exempla* of female goodness which reappear in various forms during the poems of the Boethian period and beyond, though in the early work such affirmation is part of a more indiscriminate tendency towards making the poet's learning overt.

When scholarly bravura shows itself in the dreamer's and the Man in Black's shared penchant for listing *exempla* (*Book of the Duchess* 725–39 and 1054–87), we are seeing an early version of a stylistic univocality which Chaucer was to employ to powerful effect through the similes of the *House of Fame*, and *Troilus and Criseyde*, and in the mixed voices of the *Canterbury Tales*. In the *Book of the Duchess* it is less sophisticated, however, and lacks the implications which it will have later.

Other similarities with later work are also evident: Geffrey's claim in the *House of Fame* that his dream surpasses notable previous examples is rehearsed in the *Book of the Duchess* where previous interpreters are found inadequate. The *Parliament of Fowls* introduces Chaucer's delightful trick of blurring similes into their context by literalizing them. The dreamer says:

> Withinne the temple, of sykes hoote as fyr
> I herde a swogh that gan aboute renne,
> Whiche sikes were engendered with desyr,
> That maden every auter for to brenne
> Of newe flaume
>
> (*Parliament of Fowls* 246–50)

Here figuration blends into physics and both into iconography, for the sighs, hot as fire, become the flames on Love's altars. This play of the literal and figurative is marked in *Troilus and Criseyde* and in some of the *Tales*.

The most striking adumbration of the poet's later interest can be found in the *Book of the Duchess*. There a triple comparison is permitted between the lovers, Ceys and Alcione, whom Chaucer reads about; the dream couple, the Man in Black and the Lady White; and the real couple, John of Gaunt and Blanche of Castille. The comparison which is formed between Ceys and Alcione on the one hand and the Man in Black and his lady on the other expresses Chaucer's interest in the relationship of book and experience, but does so wholly within the fiction.[64] In *Troilus and Criseyde* and later works, he will challenge the reader to find exemplary value in fiction despite its troubled and uncertain relationship with life. When Chaucer implicitly compares Alcione's sad loss of Ceys with John of Gaunt's bereavement, and enforces this at the end of the poem by waking up to find the Ovidian book, he is extending this relationship between book and experience beyond fiction into real life—the real but single life of his patron. And he is also restricting it to the instructional function of *exemplum*. In later poems he generalizes it to the reader and presents it as the problematic condition of all communications. Also, unusually for *exempla* in Chaucer's poetry, this story appears designed to deter rather than to exhort, persuading John of Gaunt to understand grief as something which should not be terminal.[65] It is also only an implicit example with no meaning proposed for it. Generally the value of such an example depends on its exemplary function being clear, however tendentious or unacceptable its meaning might prove to be. This comparison, as with many others in Chaucer, does include a degree of dissimilarity between comparator and topic for, unlike John of Gaunt's situation, the story is about a woman's bereavement. However, all these features—a fiction separated from life by being a book itself, with a bookish source;[66] connected with life through indirection and dream, and with a focus limited to the patron—all derive from the tact and constraint which the poem's occasional purpose requires. While the contribution of example is important, its form and significance are limited by the ambience in which consolation is offered by a young poet to one of the greatest lords of the realm. If the poem is a foreshadowing of later subversive work with *exemplum* it is very shadowy indeed and, in my view, its features can all be explained by the "occasional" context for its production. What is missing here, as in the other poems before the Boethian period, is the sense that comparison itself is on the poetic agenda, or that basic dissimilarity between the example and the situation which it is to illuminate threatens failure in the attempt.

The incomplete *Anelida and Arcite* also evidences the substantial shift in the prominence of comparison from the early poems to the ones which fall in the period after 1378. Features which will recur in the greater works are present: the subject matter is a wronged woman from the past; the reader is given direct access to her feelings through her complaint, and she is compared to other great women, Penelope and Lucrece. In addition, her tale is presented as an *exemplum:* the poet says, "Ensample of this, ye thrifty wymmen alle, / Take her of Anelida and Arcite" (197–98). However, there is a significant difference between the apparent aims of this poem and those which come after. The poem is offered as an act of recovery in which the poet retrieves the "known" and safeguards it against Time's depredations; it is not a "known" which will then be problematized:

> For hit ful depe is sonken in my mynde,
> With pitous hert in Englyssh to endyte
> This olde storie, in Latyn which I fynde,
> Of quene Anelida and fals Arcite,
> That elde, which that al can frete and bite,
> As hit hath freten mony a noble storie,
> Hath nygh devoured out of oure memorie.
> (*Anelida and Arcite* 8–14)

Anelida and Arcite is showy about its metrical experimentation, and it is an important exercise in the dramatizing of a woman's emotions within a thematic context of male betrayal, and with an exemplary slant, but the *exemplum* here is not compromised as the *exemplum* of the betrayer Aeneas in the *House of Fame* will be; it is not put in the difficult context of a sustained revisionary narrative or a variably complicit narrator, as in the *Troilus*. It has many of the elements of comparison to be found in the later poems but not the analytical drive.

Clearly Chaucer's engagement with comparison and its latent dissimilarity in the poems after 1378 developed an already established practical interest in comparison, shown in theme, simile, and example. Boethius did not drive him towards exploiting dissimilarity, but there can be no doubt that the prominence and character of that engagement changed around the time Chaucer worked on his translation. One should not deny to Boethius's comparativist method the influence over Chaucer which has been claimed for other aspects of his thought.

Some years ago A. C. Spearing showed in an important article how Chaucer undermines the exemplary function in the *Friar's*, *Pardoner's*, *Nun's Priest's*, and *Manciple's Tales*.[67] However, Spearing was also anxious to limit the implications of his perception so that it would not be anachronistically generalized to the *Canterbury Tales* as a whole or, one suspects, adopted as Chaucer's prevailing philosophy by critics anxious to modernize him. Spearing warned that his analysis might show

a growing scepticism on Chaucer's part about the link his age expected between narrative and moral wisdom; but the *Canterbury Tales* is too rich and various a collection to serve as an exemplum or fable illustrating the "truths" of late-twentieth-century thought about literature.[68]

In contrast to Spearing's historical prudence, the present book argues that the roots of Chaucer's scepticism were strong and consistent with tradition even if they did not need to be the product of tradition. They can be found in the formal structure of comparison itself, a mode of thinking designed to illuminate but inevitably undermined by dissimilarities between the topic and its elucidatory comparators. Longstanding traditions in rhetoric, grammar, and theology had encountered, managed, exploited, or sought to constrain this dissimilarity. Comparativism was a mode of thinking to which Chaucer was exposed by a variety of influences, not least his direct experience of its figures encountered in elementary academic training; the general value given to dissimilarity in similarity by Christian theology and, in particular, his practical work with Boethius's *Consolation*. These influences helped to carry over to him a consciousness of the significance of dissimilarity within comparison. If anything, I would argue that, rather than marking a "growing scepticism," the *Canterbury Tales* shows an intermittent revisiting of an earlier interest in dissimilarity, which achieved its most powerful expression in *Troilus and Criseyde*. The narrative method of the *Canterbury Tales* exploits the insights of Chaucer's middle period work. Sometimes they do so with a more intense effect through the shorter length of the poem, but the *Tales* develop what was already there.

However, I would also argue that Chaucer's interest in dissimilarity was not limited to *exemplum*—the most attractive type of comparison for us because of our modern fascination for the unreliability of authoritative moral pronouncements. Dissimilarity in comparison informed Chaucer's work at different levels and for different reasons. Certainly it showed up in the undermining of the *exemplum*, but the *exemplum* showed up partly because, as a literary form, it was a productive generator of stories, and satisfied a deeper need in Chaucer for narrative multiplicity and reduplication. In addition, dissimilarity was stylistically productive through its use in *similitudo*, showing up in forensic, ironic, and ornamenting similes. These similes could then be fashioned into narrative structures and sequences which made different points, and had different implications, from the individual similes. And dissimilarity even informed Chaucer's treatment of *imago*, particularly through his portraits of the pilgrims in the *General Prologue*. There it served to further his fascination with the unfixable origins of language.

We need to look at comparison not with a focus on the binary values of a single type or figure, but rather with a more holistic attention to the interconnectedness of different features of style and thought. A device which may carry philosophical criticism of authority or received truth may also convey the poet's positive aesthetic pleasure in an alternative world of words, just as a comparison may serve to elucidate a topic but in doing so may introduce a comparator which escapes subordination to the topic and carries its own independent appeal. The ecosystem of the text insists that modes of thought and their individual figures have long lifelines, interconnected, and stretching through quite different areas of the literary project. That is why one could never hope to posit an actual source for Chaucer's distinctive treatment of dissimilarity in comparison, though one can still look closely at the cultural influences which bore upon it.

2
Naming and the *House of Fame*

Traditionally the principal function of all comparisons was that they should illuminate something less well known by adducing something better known.[1] Certainly, comparison cannot work without some presumption (however mistaken that presumption might be) that there is a "known" which is being called on to assist. Even if neither term in a comparison is fully understood, they are compared in respect of features which are better known. Comparison therefore always involves a transfer of ideas from the past, real or notional, to the present; the application of things known to things still to be known.

In the *House of Fame* Chaucer gives a critique of the linguistic medium which conveys to people what they claim to know.[2] That medium either transmits communications from the past through books or provides news which will become the prior basis of further thought. By undermining the trust one might place in the words received from texts, from cultural traditions, and from other people, Chaucer thereby also questions comparison as a means of illumination because, if what one "knows" is imperfectly, or incorrectly, known, it cannot be relied upon as a comparator to assist understanding what one does not know.

Chaucer roughly divides what is known into two categories: those communications which come from books, and are thus historically past, and those which are received from the turmoil of communication in the present, but which become notionally past when known. The first are discovered already situated in the House of Fame, built into the architecture in many cases, and the second are seen flying in and out of the House of Rumor, but bound inevitably by natural laws, which the eagle explains to the dreamer, to pass through Fame's House before she lets them go again into the world, where they will join the mass of information which constitutes the world of the known. The reason everything has to pass through Fame's House is that no communication is ever received without a reputation of some kind attached to it—Chaucer's word for this is "name":

> Thus out at holes gunne wringe
> Every tydynge streght to Fame,
> And she gan yeven ech hys name,
> After hir disposicioun
>
> (2110–13)

The implication of this process is that knowledge is essentially a word by which people dignify the reputation or "name" which each communication has received. Chaucer suggests that all one reads, or hears about from others, comes with a reputation attached, either as a truth or a falsehood, or as something new, or something insignificant or, perhaps, if truth were really told, as something merely rumored. But whatever the reputation, it has been assigned by a deity called Fame and it is important to understand what kind of deity she is, what her "disposicioun" might be, for all of these communications, with their "names" attached, comprise what is supposedly known about the world in its historical and recent state; they are therefore the bases of the comparisons which people make to help them acquire new understanding.

While the tidings which we have just seen flying to Fame's House are orally transmitted and current ones, and thus represent well what Chaucer believes happens to all communication, they are not the only ones in which a writer will be interested. Chaucer is concerned with the tidings which come from the texts of other writers and speak to him in his study. Furthermore, he tends to realize abstract problems by grounding them in the condition of individual people—we are told that when tidings appear in the House of Fame, they appear embodied as the person who uttered them, an idea which adumbrates the dramatized narrative of the *Canterbury Tales*. Taken together, these preferences lead him to look to past writers for their accounts of significant people from the past. Consequently he discusses reputations in the sense in which we commonly understand the word: as applied to the condition of fame or notoriety which people have received as a result of their actions—in other words, these people's significance for us. This kind of fame has a direct bearing on comparison, as the following instance shows.

In a lengthy interruption of her own *Tale*, the Wife of Bath tells the story of King Midas and how his wife revealed the secret that he had the ears of an ass. When the wife is begged not to divulge the secret, she swears that she would never cause her husband "han so foul a name" (963). Just as with the tidings which fly from Rumor to Fame's House for their "names" this kind of reputation fixes a person's significance through time and society, and as a consequence, prescribes the use which others will make of him or her. In this case the revelation of the ears will ensure that Midas is used as a figure of contempt and may become a point of comparison in admonition or insult. There is no need to press the point but it helps to recognize that the concept behind his wife's promise to safeguard Midas's reputation is still represented in today's admonitory idioms: "there's a name for people like you" or "he's got a name (reputation) for it." Such meaning can be good or bad and can be lost as well as gained. In the *House of Fame* Dido complains of both:

> For thorgh yow [Aeneas] is my name lorn,
> And alle myn actes red and songe
> Over al thys lond, on every tonge.
>
> (346–48)

In the *Troilus* Pandarus commends Criseyde for her "good name" (1.880), but by Book 5 the actions which have lost her this name and gained her another lead the author sympathetically to withhold criticism, for her name is "publysshed" widely, and that should be enough punishment for her fault.

The significance of such names for the present study of comparison is that someone who has a "name" may then become an *exemplum*. Such a named person forms part of what people claim to know and therefore of what is used comparatively to achieve further understanding. Dido functions as an *exemplum* of a woman foolish in love: "Loo, how a woman doth amys / To love hym that unknown ys!" (*House of Fame* 269–70). She even begins to use herself in that way: "Now see I wel, and telle kan, / We wrechched wymmen konne noon art" (334–35). Similarly, Chaucer's Criseyde expects to become the *exemplum* of a faithless woman which Chaucer is trying to qualify. In the Prologue to the *Legend of Good Women* the God of Love has evidently read Chaucer's *Troilus and Criseyde* and accuses him of peddling this very *exemplum:* "And of Creseyde thou hast seyd as the lyste, / That maketh men to wommen lasse triste" (F: 332–33). Chaucer is accused of publishing her name in a way which permits other men to use her as a damning comparator for other women. It would appear that the literary revisionism of the poem, its attempt to qualify *exemplum* through a deeper understanding of detail, circumstances, motivations, and so on, is irrelevant if the poem reiterates the facts of the betrayal. The God of Love is evidently no more a sensitive reader of Chaucer than Harry Bailley is when he hears *Sir Thopas* and *Melibee* or the people whom Chaucer warns about misinterpreting his dream in the *House of Fame*. Reputation and comparison, "name" and "example," are closely connected, for the one permits the other. The significance of a person is first controlled through their acquiring a "name," and they can then form part of an argument as an *exemplum*. Midas's wife, who was so reluctant to give her husband a contemptible name but could not stop herself from revealing his condition, implicitly gets a name herself from the Wife of Bath, for she is being used as an *exemplum* of how women cannot keep their mouths shut—an insulting comparator to which one can have recourse if seeking to know what kind of creature a woman is; or if one wants to prove this to others (as the Wife is doing here); or to bolster and reaffirm existing prejudices.

The fear of gaining a bad reputation comes in part from recognizing that, when such meaning is acquired, other people will not take the trouble to investigate the justice of the "name," or may *need* for their own selfish purposes not to do so. In the *Manciple's Tale* Phoebus punishes the crow not for revealing his wife's adultery but for, in Phoebus's view, making a false accusation. He deceives himself and wrongly injures the crow because he cannot live with the reputation of cuckold, a reputation brought ominously close to the name itself in the crow's cry of "Cokkow!" One of the first things Phoebus does while convincing himself that he is not a cuckold is to give names to his wife which will preserve her "name": "O deere wyf! O gemme of lustiheed!" (274), and a name to the crow, which will blacken his: "Traitour" (271). If "names" constitute what is known, and can therefore shape our understanding of what is still unknown, the significance of comparative *exempla* is very great, and the responsibility of those who employ them is commensurate. Dido laments that her "actes" will be "red and songe / Over al thys lond, on every tonge" (*House of Fame* 347–48). She knows that she will become public property, her name handled by all and published abroad through various media. Perhaps, if a person's name is good, this general use will constitute a pleasure to them: fame, in its modern positive sense. But if not, it becomes a cruel punishment, almost a dispersal of the person for the uses of others.

Although Dido regrets that her deeds will become the knowledge that others acquire from books, she does not herself dispute the value of acquiring knowledge in this way. However, Chaucer elsewhere does call it into question. At the start of the *Legend of Good Women* he pointedly says that we should honor old books where "we han noon other preve" (F:28). Despite the rebuke which he receives from the God of Love, Chaucer's intensive study of how Criseyde came to fall in and out of love is intended to constitute a sort of fictional proof; the naturalism in her portrayal creates an alternative world of experience which, though fictional itself, can be read against the old books which have given her a less sympathetic "name." His study of Dido and

Aeneas in Book I of the *House of Fame,* and his account of Fame herself are similarly designed to problematize the fabric of received "names," although he does so here as part of a larger concern with language, and in a more abstract way than in most of his other poems. Chaucer frequently fictionalizes himself as being blamed for representing women badly and tries to exculpate himself through blaming men also or by writing fresh works in praise of women. This apparently playful motif appears much less trivial when we put it against the background of comparative thinking, its *exempla,* and the consequences which publishing them has for our understanding of the world.[3]

In fact, Chaucer is very ambivalent in his attitude to *exempla,* and employs them as much as he undermines their authority. We see this ambivalence in his Book I retelling of the story of Dido and Aeneas. Just as his two authoritative sources, Virgil and Ovid, differ in their accounts, the one presenting a more favorable picture of Aeneas, and the other providing the grounds for a sympathetic presentation of Dido, so Chaucer leaves a quite divided sense of the significance of the story. He starts with the untruth of which Aeneas was guilty when he abandoned Dido, first introducing it as an example of a general trend in the world:

> For this shal every woman fynde,
> That som man, of his pure kynde,
> Wol shewen outward the fayreste,
> Tyl he have caught that what him leste;
> And thanne wol he causes fynde
> And swere how that she ys unkynde,
> Or fals, or privy, or double was.
> Al this sey I be Eneas
>
> (279–86)

Having urged his readers to use Aeneas as a comparator to help them understand the ways of the world, he then gives force to his admonition through the plaintive direct speech of Dido, together with his own sympathetic responses. This is then built up into a pattern of reinforcing *exempla* which cites seven other instances of such betrayal of women by men, and which uses the word "fals" on six occasions. However, when he returns to his first example, it is to report the fact that the *Aeneid* finds grounds for excusing Aeneas "fullyche of al his grete trespas" in the divine commandment he had from Mercury to abandon Dido and settle Italy. In the end, it is difficult either to ignore the weight of example and feeling which Chaucer has built up or the fact that the last part of this comparative section undermines the force of the very example which initiated it. Given the severe critique which Chaucer is going to mount later in the poem against the trustworthiness of reputation, the quiet way he moves from reporting this excuse for Aeneas into a list of all the other things which happened to him on his voyage sounds highly disingenuous.

What Chaucer has not done here is to set one authority overtly against another; indeed he invites the reader to see no difference in value between them: "Rede Virgile in Eneydos / Or the Epistle of Ovyde."[4] His main concern is to make the reader experience the fragile foundation of exemplary comparison, but without implying that it is simply a problem of relative textual authority and could be solved by abandoning one of the sources. It is typical of Chaucer to juxtapose details, sections, styles, opinions, and voices of conflicting force.[5] The possible responses to this juxtaposition are very much like those which are prompted by a comparison. One can press for resolution of the dissimilarity latent in the comparison, perhaps by prioritizing the similarity or by incorporating the dissimilarity into a homogenized reading, or one can use those dissimilarities, latent in every comparison, to open up the comparative claim to question without necessarily showing it to be absurd or rejecting it because it is not, and never could be, exactly true. To imply either that the excuse made for Aeneas is irrelevant to the exemplary case, or that it wholly undermines it, is to claim an ability to detect the truth in the effects of Fame's work. All Chaucer claims in this poem is a capacity to see what Fame does, not the insight to work back from her effects to the truth in a given instance. One can feel the strength of the exemplificatory case against men's untruth while also recognizing its susceptibility to analysis, and while still confused by the details of its central case study of Aeneas.

This ambivalence of response is given formal, and implicitly historical, justification when Chaucer demonstrates Fame in action, assigning different "names" to different groups of people. The episode (1526–1867) is designed to show in a very systematic way the different disjunctions there may be between what Fame's petitioners ask for and what they get. Chaucer is overtly concentrating upon the grounds of human tragedy or happiness, though his interest in the theoretical possibilities of his topic lead him here to stress the ironies of Fame's disposition rather than to show the responses of her victims, which he is quick to foreground in other places, as in the misery with which Dido and Criseyde contemplate an exemplary notoriety which they would not desire. But he is also exploring the extent to which the names people receive truly accord with their actions. It was this question which lay behind his introducing Virgil's excuse for Aeneas. Today's petitioners to Fame are potentially tomorrow's *exempla* and therefore behind the personalized drama of Fame and her victims' desires lies the general issue of founding our understanding of the world upon the "name" which past events have received.

Fame's disposition of different reputations to different groups of people is sometimes just. When a crowd of traitours ask for good renown, she replies,

> Nay, wis . . . hyt were a vice.
> Al be ther in me no justice,
> Me lyste not to doo hyt now,
> Ne this nyl I not graunte yow.
>
> (1819–22)

The process by which reputation is acquired is amoral, but its results sometimes are morally proper. Such people will prove good *exempla* even if only accidentally so. Valuable also will be those "shrewes" who ask for, and receive without comment, a fame which is "In alle thing ryght as hit ys" (1837). Furthermore, Chaucer shows that the disparity between fame and deserving, and therefore between one's supposed knowledge of the past and the truth of the past, may be merely a matter of degree rather than of kind. When a group of worthy petitioners to Fame arrives, she agrees to broadcast their good works but also says that they shall have better praise than they deserve (1667–69). Anyone who uses them as *exempla* will not be wholly mistaken but will probably be wrong in the importance which is attached to this overrenowned group. These groups give some hope that comparisons with the past will be well-founded. People may still be self-serving or inadequate in using *exempla*, but Chaucer prefers to demonstrate this aspect of comparison dramatically through the interaction of characters such as Troilus, Criseyde, and Pandarus, and in a context more directly reflective of the real world, rather than in a dream with its unsituated characters, theoretical emphasis, and problematic relationship to reality. But, as comparators, these groups do constitute a reliable "known."

However, among the truths and near-truths are lost truths, misrepresentations, and untruths. The first group which approaches Fame seeks a full reward for their good deeds (1557–58). They are told that they will be completely ignored—neither good nor ill will be spoken of them. This does amount to a misrepresentation of the past through these people even if it does not take the form of positively lying about them. Anyone who wishes to use the past as a comparator to understand the present will thus be denied valuable material simply because of the operation of Fame down the years. There are gaps in what is known and missing *exempla*.

Equally, some people will receive attention when they have not merited any: they will be regarded as highly as if they had done something good, and others will receive notoriety though they did nothing particularly bad. Quite apart from the incongruence between these groups' wishes and Fame's rewards, Chaucer is revealing a further misrepresentation by Fame of the past reality from which we draw comparison. The map of the past which Fame provides to us includes features which should not be there as much as it ignores some which should. He also shows how other aspects of the past will be wholly travestied and betrayed by the action of Fame, good people receiving "a shrewed fame, / And wikkyd loos, and worse name" (1619–20). The writer who wishes to use *exempla* and innocently employs this group will be passing on downright lies under the guise of illumination.

This is the disposition of Fame which every communication receives when it is about to leave Fame's House. It is an unreliable basis for any understanding of the present. But Chaucer adds to this the fact that individual messages, in whatever form, may be unreliable even before they receive their reputation from Fame. He shows how truth and lies can mingle and fly off to Fame as one item (2108–9). It is quite possible that this tiding will not receive a reputation which accurately reflects even this deceitful composition.

However, it is in this area of Chaucer's account of language that I disagree with recent studies of the poem. There has been too great a readiness to view the *House of Fame* as offering a medieval equivalent of the modern, essentially deconstructive, view that all language is tropological, twisting meaning so that communication is, in Harold Bloom's phrase, a map of misreading.[6] Robert W. Hanning writes,

> philosophy, since it deals with the record of the past and its exempla, and passes that record on, can also not avoid the true-false mixture inherent in all verbal communication, cannot escape from its own world of words.[7]

While it is true that Chaucer shows the mixture of truth and falsehood, he does not show it as "inherent in all verbal communication." Boitani has a similar emphasis to Hanning. He also implies that truth and falsehood are always equally mingled.[8]

The view that Chaucer showed falsehood to be general throughout language may have come about because of the twentieth-century topos that language can never accurately communicate an extralinguistic reality. This position, though usually referred to Saussure, derives from Nietzsche's claim that all epistemology is metaphorical and that language is consequently rhetorical rather than referential:

> When we talk about trees, colours, snow and flowers, we believe we know something about the things themselves, and yet we only possess metaphors

of the things, and these metaphors do not in the least correspond to the original essentials.[9]

Even for critics who did not agree with him, the 1980s were very much colored by the question Paul de Man raised as to "whether the entire semantic, semiological, and performative field of language can be said to be covered by tropological models."[10] In this context, it is understandable that Chaucer's presentation of language in the *House of Fame* should have taken on a more absolutist character than it actually possesses. Boitani writes, "Reality as told is different from reality as it existed before it was told,"[11] and Hanning sees

> a nexus between *fama*, poetry, and philosophical discourse as three versions of the linguistic after-life of deeds, all subject to an uncontrollable process of transmission and accretion in which truth and falsehood intermingle so as to be indistinguishable.[12]

There is much to agree with in both these claims, and they certainly catch the sensation one has of Chaucer's justified unease with language, but they also rather overstate the case and misrepresent the source of that unease. If their position were true, one might expect to see Chaucer turning away from an anxious involvement with language towards the view that it is predictably untrustworthy. Not many of his works would have escaped retraction with such a philosophy.

The essential problem which Chaucer poses is not that Fame is arbitrary or unjust and always misrepresents tidings, or that lies and truth invariably get mingled, or that good things get ignored, and so on. Admittedly, the walls of Fame's House are made of beryl which magnifies everything, as is natural (though not inevitable) in the operation of Fame (1289–92). Boitani comments, "Once more, reality, its truth dissolved, is distorted into mere appearance."[13] But although Chaucer proposes this "kynde" for Fame in his iconographical program for her, Fame's actual workings prove to be less predictably falsifying. Robert R. Edwards correctly notes that the episode "shows Fame's naming of reputations as capricious not malicious."[14] Similarly, the lies do not always mingle with truth as they emerge from the House of Rumor. The real problem for judging language is posed by the fact that all this only happens "somtyme" (2088). The dreamer only sees lies and truth mingle sometimes; sometimes Fame gets it right, "ryght as hit is" (1664), however capricious or indifferent she might be. This means that sometimes the oral and written communications which come to us are correct; they do accurately represent the past; they provide well-founded *exempla* for use in comparison; they convey other people's meanings without distortion. However, we just don't know when this is the case. We are thus locked into the existing scheme of knowledge, doomed to further reading and listening but without any guarantee that the more we know, the better we know. To understand the world, one is forced to use comparisons which might be truly illuminating, but can never be wholly trusted and to which there is no alternative.

The human condition is not unlike that of the two knights, Palamon and Arcite, in their prison cell. When Palamon groans, Arcite advizes him: "taak al in pacience / Oure prisoun, for it may noon oother be" (*Knight's Tale* 1084–85). Perhaps if their prison had had no window, they might have got used to being cut off, but through the thick iron grill Palamon, and then Arcite, sees Emily, and Love becomes the force which compels them to be miserably part of the outside world. In the same way, if Fame could be relied upon to be always wrong, people could cope with the condition of language. It would be predictably misleading, but if one *may* be glimpsing truth, one cannot avoid feeling commitment to the medium, and one turns to it again and again, perhaps more in hope than expectation of truth, but nevertheless unable to "taak al in pacience / Oure prisoun." Chaucer's perception about language is actually productive of more anxiety than the stoic, perhaps masochistically buoyant, embracing of mingled truth and falsehood which informed earlier studies. One might compare this with Mary Carruthers's conclusion, based on her study of memory in the medieval literary tradition, that "themes of deconstruction and psychoanalytic criticism are not socially subversive when we detect them in medieval Literature; they are the tradition itself."[15]

Unreliable *exempla* challenge one's ability to order. Comparisons are a means of mentally controlling the rush of experience and explaining it by significances which are already established and organized. Like taxonomic systems, while promising understanding, comparisons defuse the challenge of the new by incorporating it in the known. They establish categories: for example, the eight cases of male betrayal cited in Book 1 are clearly thought to belong to the same class. In the same way a taxonomic system, which is ipso facto a system of comparison, asserts that a phenomenon belongs to a particular class on the basis of similarities between its salient features and those of other members of that class. The classificatory system itself has already been arrived at on the basis of similarities and dissimilarities which were perceived earlier. Taxonomy establishes a "name," that is, a significance based on a thing's perceived character, and then usually proceeds to assign a classificatory name to it. Comparison also draws upon known "names" to control new experience, to categorize it, and hopefully to permit understanding of it. However, the perceptions, the assumptions, the traditions of belief, which lie behind the establishing of a taxonomy or the applying of a comparison, are themselves shaped by previous knowledge, and Chaucer has shown the unreliability of this knowledge through exposing the operation of Fame.

Taxonomies, like comparisons, are open to debate, therefore, as decisions about assigning individuals to classes, the unknown to the known. Should Aeneas remain in the class of betrayer after he has been excused by Virgil? Can he be confidently adduced as a comparator for male betrayal, or will the comparison always be subverted by the detail that he was divinely instructed? Taxonomy and comparison are related processes which show a similar desire for understanding through the control of new meaning by past meaning. Chaucer shows them both to be seriously qualified by the condition of language.

His attitude to taxonomy is as ambivalent as his treatment of the *exempla* in Book 1. The *House of Fame* actually opens with a section on the taxonomy of dreams. The dreamer declares his bafflement. He cannot understand what causes dreams, why some prove to be true and others not:

> Why that is an avision
> And why this a revelacion,
> Why this a drem, why that a sweven,
> And noght to every man lyche even;
> Why this a fantome, why these oracles
>
> (7–11)

However, it is impossible to say whether Chaucer is exasperated by the baffling multiplicity of experience which taxonomy tries to control or with the taxonomy which, in trying to control it, seems almost to mimic that multiplicity. The "grete clerkes" may disagree on dreams, but Chaucer has decided not to tax his mind with the different types of meaning which they have (16–18). However, in this example of *occupatio,* there is as great a commitment to outlining the different types of dream as there is to bravely declaring them unnecessary. The effect is to remind the reader that there are canons of interpretation which the reader can ignore but which exist nonetheless. Similarly, he asserts the wonderful uniqueness of his dream in Book 2 against the traditional comparators of Isaiah, Scipio, Nebuchadnezzar, Pharaoh, Turnus, and Elcanor, but his claim is grandiose enough to carry a wry self-mocking undertone which actually affirms the importance of the comparators cited and of the comparative process which he is employing merely to enhance his own experience. It seems that he would like his dream to be classed with these even as he claims its superiority to them.

A taxonomy organizes the multitude of its phenomena by names, and exemplary comparison does the same for the multitude of new experiences, applying to them "names," and actual named people from the past, to be their illuminators. The *House of Fame* constantly expresses this multiplicity of experience through the device of listed names. Whether the predominant tone is serious as in the exemplification of male betrayal in Book I or comic as in "Geffrey's" claim that his dream is more wonderful than its predecessors, the same impulse to represent plurality is found. It is not enough for the dreamer to threaten those who might interpret his dream badly; he has to list the kinds of motive they might have: presumption, hatred, scorn, envy, spite, trickery, and villainy (94–96). It is not enough for the eagle to promise Geffrey more tidings about love than there are strings on an instrument or grains of corn in a barn; Chaucer has to recreate the plurality through citing upwards of twenty different kinds of love tiding (675–98). It is not sufficient for Geffrey to record that he heard rumors about every conceivable experience that this world can provide; we have to have forty of them listed, and "dyvers accident" in case all has not been covered (1961–76). This is a phenomenon not restricted to the *House of Fame:* Lee Patterson has described the Canon's Yeoman's language as "multiplying itself—proliferating uncontrollably—yet never finally grasping the essence it seeks."[16] While taxonomy is designed to control multiplicity, the poem shows it almost as *evidence* of multiplicity. One leaves such listing as much with a sense of the unmanageable particularity of things as of their capacity to form clear categories. This is an important tension to recognize, for the issue of whether comparisons are useful aids to understanding the world is in part an argument about particularity: whether one thing can ever be wholly illuminated by another; whether the plurality of experience is also an irredeemable discreteness of experience. Achieving understanding through comparison may be like achieving order through taxonomy: at best, a pyrrhic victory of hope over the facts; at worst, a wilful, self-serving assertion of general rules which ignore individuating detail. Patterson sees "the impossible dream of accurate naming" as present in several of the *Canterbury Tales*,[17] but, like the scepticism about *exempla* found in the *Tales* by Spearing, the problem is given an earlier powerful airing in this mid-career work.

This need to realize the plurality of experience through rhetorical list actually comes from the same impulse which leads Chaucer to realize problems in fiction at all, and which leads him to realize them more intensely through the dramatized form of the *Canterbury Tales*. It is a need to make rather than to tell, to recreate rather than to report, and it thus empowers his fiction-making, even while the fiction suggests that the plurality of experience will always escape attempts to control it.[18]

This paradox is represented metafictively in the attempt of Theseus to control the tournament in the *Knight's Tale*. He sets up a highly artistic amphitheater with rules to control the unpredictable violence of a general melee. He manages the genre and the rhetoric of battle, and there is no doubt that he achieves much by this (though not, of course, his principal object of resolving the rivalry of the lovers), but the reader never finds out if he was wholly successful in his desire to prevent loss of life: we are told that no one has died when the combatants return from the fight, but Chaucer chooses to mention the fact that one of them in particular was seriously wounded, pierced through the breastbone by a spear. The detail is left hanging, as was the recorded excuse made for Aeneas.

Just as one can never know whether the "name" which a communication receives is a just one, and therefore whether a comparative *exemplum* has been justly applied to the particular case, or whether in a given tiding truth and falsehood have joined, so the writer can never quite manage nature through art. Battle may be turned to tournament; the multiplicity of experience can be rhetoricized into a list, and made to serve the larger argument of the poem; one may seek to control the present by the past through *exempla* drawn from what is already known, but the control is never sufficient nor reliable. And, to carry the metafictive significance of the episode further, Theseus has actually increased the total violence of things by his transmutation of a personal battle into a tournament just as Chaucer seems driven to recreate the baffling multiplicity of experience, with the added power of rhetoric, rather than just to record it.

Chaucer's paradoxical commitment to what he regards with suspicion is typical of the *House of Fame*. The dreamer happily stands apart from Fame, only observing since he does not wish it for himself, but the writer grasps at Fame's disposition with an almost logical force, giving us no fewer than nine ways in which one's name can relate to one's desires and deserts. The poem is made out of a set of contrary impulses which show at all levels of the work's content and style, and may even help to explain why an apparently unfinished poem feels finished. The most significant of these for the present study is the tension felt between expansion and constraint.

At the end of the poem, the forward movement of the narrative, which has been intimated by the introduction of a new character, is frustrated by a sudden, unpredictable breaking-off. But this is only the last, albeit artistically the largest, in a long series of such contrary movements, and it is because of this that the reader is subliminally prepared for the experience. So much can be claimed without implying that Chaucer intended such a truncated ending. If one looks at the poem's central abstraction, Fame, one finds that she similarly contains the

2: NAMING AND THE *HOUSE OF FAME* 71

principle of expansion and contraction. At one moment she seems less than a cubit long; the next she stretches to the heavens (1368–76). The direction which this change takes as the dreamer watches clearly tells something about fame's capacity to grow however inauspicious its origins, just as the walls of Fame's House are of beryl, which makes things seem larger than they are; but this is not the only direction in which such change occurs. The dreamer, though transported into the heavens to the point where the earth "No more semed than a prikke" (907) voluntarily limits his travels, stopping short of visiting the stars (991–99).[19] The soaring flight of the eagle has its contrary comic pull in the weight of the dreamer, who is "noyous for to carye." Even the geography of the poem seems to change extension. The dreamer is set down within a spear's throw of the House of Fame, yet in true dreamlike fashion his proximity turns into a labored and lengthy approach in which he tells us that he is climbing up at line 1118 and then again at 1165. The expanding ripples of water which the eagle says represent the movement of sound have their centripetal contrary in the gathering together of all speech in Fame's House. A significant figure in this dynamic is Eolus, who commands the winds, torturing them by the pressure of fierce constraint until they roar like captive bears (1586–90), and then selectively releasing them at storm force (1598–1601).[20] The fictional impulse for the dreamer's experiences with the eagle is just such a release of constraint, whereby a man who locks himself away until he looks dazed is taken beyond the study door into a whirl of experience, though he spends much of that locked in the eagle's talons. The ambivalence in this world of contrasting forces is well-represented in the architecture of the House of Rumor which, though its cage-like shape promises constraint, yet, because of that very construction, allows passage to the news which flies in and out of it. Conversely, even a tiding which has been swelled by retelling, like a fire growing from a single spark to destroy a city (2075–83), is next seen much diminished as it tries to creep out of a crevice in the House (2086). Other tidings block each other, though the window is available for them to escape. Imprisonment and freedom; control and escape; reclusiveness and cosmic travel; centripetal and centrifugal movement; expansion and contraction; narrative promise and cessation—the action and imagery of the poem offer more examples of this tense dynamic of opposites than it is necessary to recount here. If we add this pattern to the prevailing narrative tempo which, as in so many of Chaucer's and his contemporaries' works, is shaped by passages of fluid forward movement interspersed with substantial sections of rhetorical or expositional stasis, it becomes easy to see why the ending should feel less incongruous to this poem than it might to another.

Even the layout of the *House of Fame* reveals such contrary impulses, for the poem is ambiguous about its own overt structure and this, together with the kind of narrative dynamic which we have already described, has led to attempts to give it greater order than it probably has. All internal divisions, such as are usually found in modern editions, are indeed editorial. It was Caxton who introduced the Book division, which is not found in the manuscript versions. If we look at the division at line 508 between the sections now set out as Books 1 and 2 we can see the consequence of this practice. The striking structural division which is introduced when we separate the poem into Books 1 and 2 comes on top of a natural division which Chaucer formed by interposing remarks between the approach of the eagle and its descent (508–28). That is why the editors have chosen to make the formal division there.[21] However, the effect of this is to disguise the narrative character of the lines by a formal order which purports to serve a larger purpose—the structuring of the poem as a whole. Taken without such major division these lines show the poem's characteristic contrary movement of forward impulse and retardation: the approaching eagle is held up by the narrator's admonition to his audience (509–11); his assertion of his dream's uniqueness with its delaying employment of *comparatio* (512–17) and his equally rhetorical and static invocation of Venus and Thought (518–28), and then finally by a renewed description of the eagle with an elaborate comparison to a thunderbolt which, while asserting the swiftness of the descent, actually leaves it pent up for a few more lines (529–37). The eagle then descends with that much more force. When a book division is imposed on this, the emphasis is shifted away from the dynamic of the narrative movement into a more thematic concern with the division of subject matter, in which we find ourselves seeing the material of Book 2 as an answer to the dreamer's worries about where he is, worries which are strangely ignored by the eagle but now seem to have climaxed Book 1. What started as editorial good faith and sensitivity ends up as an organizing, even classicizing, of the poem's dynamic into a dialectic.[22] It is much the same as arguing that the incompleteness of the poem is metapoetically intended—it shifts a stylistic paradox under scholarly, critical control. Yet the poem also suggests at one point that Chaucer had a sense of it falling into books, for the poet prays to Apollo to guide "this lytel laste bok" (1093). There is no indication of whether there were divisions other than this one, or indeed whether the "book" he refers to was more than a book in the mind, but nonetheless the author shows, at one point anyway, the same attraction towards order that the editors have, albeit an attraction which the manuscript tradition suggests he never realized fully in the poem. The poem hints at the ordering of its dynamic flow, but not much more than that. We should not be surprised to find such inconsistency in the degree to which the poem is overtly structured, for the central ambivalence of the poem lies in its attitude to the order and control of meaning. All these contrary impulses to constraint and freedom extend Chaucer's problem with the means by which the new, unknown experience is controlled, turned towards the known, and imprisoned by the processes of comparison and taxonomy—processes which are never fully sufficient to the task or reliable in their results.

Chaucer is ready to set limits on the arena in which he will struggle with such imperfect means of dealing with experience. As James Simpson and others have pointed out, he is unwilling to extend his struggle into the higher realms visited by Dante. The mythical *exempla* of Icarus and Phaethon, which were to become such potent Renaissance emblems of anxiety about control are only hinted at here. Though they anticipate their later exemplary use they do not anticipate the function they were later to serve, for Chaucer does not need to be told "casus ab alto gravior" [a fall from height is more serious] as do Marlowe's over-reaching heroes, for example.

Chaucer includes Icarus simply as one of the comparators by which he can measure the height of his own ascent with the eagle (920–24), but the detail he gives—that Icarus's folly led to his death—together with the comparative function which the reference serves, affects the way one reads both this myth and the account of Phaethon shortly after.

The apparent motive for telling the tale of Phaethon is only that it should be a kind of ornamental trope upon the Galaxy, rather like the alternative names which are cited for it:

> Se yonder, loo, the Galaxie,
> Which men clepeth the Milky Wey
> For hit ys whit (and somme, parfey,
> Kallen hyt Watlynge Strete),
> That ones was ybrent with hete,
> Whan the sonnes sone the rede,
> That highte Pheton, wolde lede
> Algate hys fader carte, and gye.
>
> (936–43)

The play upon the white color of the Milky Way and the red color of the sun, and the development of the story as a mere appendage to the act of naming the Galaxy serve to obscure its exemplary potential, but working against this is the reader's memory of the comparative function given to the story of Icarus and both myths' implicit concern with aspiration which outstrips capacity. By the end of the Phaethon episode what seemed like digressive narrative has emerged as full-fledged *exemplum:*

> Loo, ys it not a gret myschaunce
> To lete a fool han governaunce
> Of thing that he can not demeyne?
>
> (957–59)

Appropriately in a dream, with its ambiguous significance for waking life, the poem does not specify a topic for which the story of Phaethon might function as a suitable, illuminating comparator, but its self-reflexive relevance can be seen in Chaucer's subsequent refusal to investigate the stars with the eagle, and to be satisfied with a lower literary orbit than great predecessors such as Dante. Here the *exempla* bespeak the poet's determination to limit himself to what he can control; they do not, as in the Renaissance, reveal existing poetic worries about an aspiration which outstrips ability.

As we have seen, Chaucer does have concerns about the manageability of things even within the realm of experience which he delimits for himself; it is clear that he believes experience to be too heterogeneous and language too unreliable, but at the same time as he exposes these problems he is wholly committed to the business of controlling them through the literary medium. That experiencing, understanding, communicating, and being informed by others pose real difficulties in life authorize this apparently paradoxical literary enterprise. What he could not accept is the further paradox of claiming to illuminate, by use of what he already knows, areas which are not part of his immediate world. Only at a distance, through translating Boethius, does he get involved in that comparative project, with its arguing up from the evidence of the fallen world to truths about the perfect world and, as we saw in an earlier chapter, even Boethius acknowledged its possible impropriety. When Geffrey decides not to fly as high as Dante, Chaucer the writer of fiction, as opposed to the translator, is also refusing to take the similaic path of insight, which had led Dante to draw on the world of the Arno when describing the nature of Hell and Heaven. Chaucer's refusal to mount up beyond what he sees as the realm of experience is also a definition of the limit of his similes.

Perhaps the strongest evidence for claiming a nexus in the *House of Fame* between comparison and the problematic managing of experience by literary means is the poem's remarkable set of similes for the sound of language in its various forms. One might expect such a central topic to attract rhetorical decoration or intensification, but the development which the similes receive, and the patterns which they occasionally form, suggest a serious literary program of instruction. These similes are more than decoration of a central theme: they are an affirmation of the ordering and explicatory power of the writer. They are comparisons which Chaucer draws from the world of the known to illuminate a topic, language, which is as yet imperfectly known by his readers, by Geffrey and, at a deeper level, by their author. Yet, while the use of simile constantly asserts rhetorical control of the subject, the comparators chosen increasingly argue that language is an uncontrollable force.

When the eagle is confidently explaining to Geffrey through comparisons how sound made by speech is simply the breaking of air, he employs two similes which reflect the human control of musical sound:

> For whan a pipe is blowen sharpe
> The air ys twyst with violence
> And rent—loo, thys ys my sentence.
> Eke whan men harpe-strynges smyte,
> Whether hyt be moche or lyte,
> Loo, with the strok the ayr tobreketh;
> And ryght so breketh it when men speketh.
>
> (774–80)

The poem later overtly associates language with violence, but the suggestion is here also in the twisting of air and the beating of the harp strings, whether lightly or heavily. Common to both images at this point in the poem is the notion of individual human control over the sound, its stopping and starting, and the musical, presumably harmonious, end to which the sound is directed. However, the poem moves towards less optimistic images for speech than the musician at work: the idea that speech is singular, controlled, and issues in harmony changes to a vision of mass speech, which has its own momentum, and results in human destruction. The latent violence, which seems merely to intensify these early musical images for didactic effect, becomes the central ground of the later comparisons. Human agency changes to threatening, nonhuman forces: when Geffrey hears the sound issuing from Fame's House, the image of the musician striking a string changes to one of Jove beating the air with thunder (1039–41) and the sea beating on hollow rocks during tempests when ships are sunk (1034–36). Chaucer intermittently through his oeuvre shows two related, and deep-seated fears: the *force majeur* of the unpredictable mass, and of the supervening authority. Both inform his similes for language here. But equally striking is his reminder that the similes are part of a tutorial discussion between him and the eagle:

'Herestow not the grete swogh?'
'Yis, parde,' quod y, 'wel ynogh.'
'And what soun is it lyk?' quod hee.
'Peter, lyk betynge of the see'

(1031–34)

These similes are not just passing rhetorical controls on the fearsome nature of language; the scene actually dramatizes the capacity of the individual to exert such control. It foregrounds intellectual and poetic management, even if Geffrey is still sweating for fear at the end of it. Appropriately, when Geffrey passes from the House of Fame with its architecture of past writers, and describes the House of Rumor, where book learning is less evident, his similes emerge as an immediate rather than a studied response. The dramatizing of control is gone, and one is left simply with the poet's rhetorical grasp on his experiences. Here the paradox is at its barest, for similaic device and content are directly opposed. The sound of Rumor is like "the rowtynge of the ston / That from th'engyn ys leten gon" (1933–34). The pause for reflection, for analysis, and for illumination which this simile, like all others, momentarily imports into the flow of language is quite at odds with what it says about the nature of ordinary communication: that it is unstoppable and destructive; it breaks down the structures which people erect to define and safeguard their lives, just as the stone from a catapult breaks down a city wall or, as we are told in a later simile, just as a spark turns into a conflagration which can destroy a city from within (2078–80).[23] But the pattern of comparators which Chaucer employs for this topic is involved in a deeper paradox than that of rhetorical control over uncontrollable language.

In a poem which concentrates so much on reputational names, and the unreliability of what is conveyed in such names, Chaucer pointedly does not name any of those whom he meets in the course of the dream. The person he encounters in Fame's House is simply someone who had been standing right behind him (1869), and the poem only breaks off once Chaucer has established that the new character is a man whom he is unable to name (2156). Given that the former seems more a device to maintain the dramatic discourse through which the dreamer and his desires can be characterized, it is not surprising that he should not be named. The latter is presumably unnamed because it is more important that he represent an authoritative figure than that authoritativeness should be defined and delimited by his identity. In each case, it is lack of information which ensures anonymity. However, in the case of the eagle who carries Geffrey through the experiences of Books 2 and 3, and who instructs him in the nature of sound, the opposite holds good: he is too polysemous and his connotations are too diverse to permit identification. He has intertextual affinity with the eagle in Dante's *Purgatorio* 9.19, but he is a servant of Jupiter not God, and Chaucer is not being carried to Purgatory; as a purveyor of wisdom he might be seen as a down-market version of the eagle of St. John; however, he speaks to Chaucer in the voice of someone known to him, and known in a particular relationship, the unhappiness of which is suggested without any identification being made.[24] Different kinds of "name," textual and nontextual, are thus hinted at for the eagle, and between them, they serve to keep him semiotically neutral: a provider of instruction without a defined source of authority for it other than the conventionally fictional notion that he is a servant of Jupiter. Technically, as the servant of Jupiter, he exists beyond the unreliable medium of language which he reveals. But this is only one of his "names" and, when the others are taken into account, he fails to achieve a clear "name" which would raise his speech above the status of communications which have passed through Fame's House; he cannot provide us with a point of reference which would permit us to judge correctly of what we hear, thus increasing the entropic dynamism in the poem—just as the man who seems to have great authority is never allowed to justify his promise because the poem breaks off.

Although one does not realize it at the time, Chaucer's description of the descent of the eagle is the only "name" which he receives, and it is one which ties him deeper into the linguistic medium rather than raising him above it:

> But never was ther dynt of thonder,
> Ne that thyng that men calle fouder,
> That smot somtyme a tour to powder
> And in his swifte comynge brende,
> That so swithe gan descende
> As this foul
>
> (534–39)

The thunderbolt which destroys a tower, and the burning both prepare the way for the similes which the sound of communication will receive later in the poem. Clearly other literary sources lie behind this description. Dante provides the tense delay between the sight of the eagle and its descent, and his eagle is also associated with fire since it carries Dante up into the purgatorial flames. The image of the thunderbolt hitting the tower ultimately comes from Boethius's *Consolation of Philosophy* 1.Me.4, and has a close verbal parallel in Machaut's *Jugement du Roi de Nevarre*. But these intertextual relations do not provide the striking significance of the description. I cannot see any special point in comparing the descent of the eagle upon Geffrey with the Boethian source, where we are told that a virtuous man is unmoved by anything, including the thunderbolt which hits a tower. It is the pattern of simile *within* the poem rather than the comparative allusions made to other works which seems more remarkable, for while Chaucer is apparently describing the power of the eagle, he is actually anticipating his later descriptions of language (which, as we have seen, include a thunderbolt). The eagle is fearsome, sudden, unstoppable, and seems to threaten destruction when he comes—like the stone from the catapult, or the fire, or the raging sea, or the bullet from the gun, which describes the speed with which the sound of Fame's evil trumpet (1642–44) passes round the world.

Of course, this is quite at odds with the way the eagle conducts himself towards Geffrey: the unpleasant features of language which are first imagistically introduced when he arrives are very unlike his confident, schoolmasterly discourse with its frequent use of helpful *exempla*. While the poem elsewhere indicates the questionable efficacy of *exempla,* the eagle makes a special point of their usefulness, distinguishing them from more difficult methods of instruction:

> Have y not preved thus symply,
> Withoute any subtilite
> Of speche, or gret prolixite
> Of termes of philosophie,
> Of figures of poetrie,
> Or colours of rethorike?
>
> (854–59)

But despite this harmonious atmosphere of pedagogical directness, Chaucer has tied the eagle imagistically into language because he wants to emphasize that the eagle's communication does not exist outside the world of damaging, unreliable language which his coming permits Geffrey to experience. The eagle may be the servant of Jupiter, and the means by which Chaucer is brought to see the problems that affect communication, but on a deeper similaic level he is made to participate in them. Perhaps it was Dante and Boethius that Chaucer had in mind when he described the arrival of the eagle but, as the poem progressed, the authority of the eagle was increasingly compromised by the developing pattern of comparisons for language. All that people receive to help them understand the world comes through language; there are no guides external to the world of experience which Chaucer has chosen to concentrate on. Thus, comparisons, taxonomies, teachers, and past and present writers are all complicit in the problems of the medium which they employ. It is significant that the great prolixity of philosophical terms, poetic figures, and rhetorical colors which the eagle eschews is highly prominent in the poem. Even if the educational discourse on the movement of sound is presented as reliable straight-talking, Chaucer ensures that its source, the eagle, and its context, the poem, will remind us of language's more intimidatory and tortuous aspects.

The *House of Fame* is not altogether a coherent work. David Wallace has memorably described it as "that nervous breakdown in short couplets."[25] As we have seen, it is shot through with paradoxes, and forces which take it in contrary directions. Sometimes, this dynamic is overtly represented in the imagery or ideas of the poem; sometimes it is implicit in the writing. Before I characterize this quality further, it might be helpful to summarize the poem's more obvious relevance for the topic of comparison.

The *House of Fame* sees the following problem: adducing the known to help in understanding what is not yet known is a project bound to fail. It will fail because the claimed knowledge has been undermined by an arbitrary principle built into the linguistic medium by which that knowledge is transmitted. Processes, like taxonomy and exemplary comparison, by which one attempts to order new experiences and to control particular cases on the basis of what one "knows," are thus the most likely to be vitiated by the unreliability of the linguistic medium; their claim to give illumination is particularly fragile.

The source of failure lies not in a disconnection between language and truth but in its arbitrary and unpredictable connection: all comparisons are not bound to be false; some may be true, since the arbitrary principle produces both results. Unfortunately, people do not know which kind of comparison they face or are making. If, as Chaucer does, we choose to restrict ourselves to the world of experience, we are bound to live with its central challenge: the possibility of true understanding coexists with the possibility of being deceived. The difficulty of finding out which is which is the only certainty.

Chaucer's poem shows all the paradoxes of such a commitment: rhetoric which controls what is recognized to be uncontrollable; taxonomy which, in ordering multiplicity actually replicates it; exemplary comparison which does and yet does not prove its case; a voice which supposedly surmounts the unreliability of Fame's communication but is imagistically tied to it; and, more than anything, a poet who makes illuminating fictions from a position of doubt about our capacity to be illuminated by what we hear. In choosing the dream genre for his poem, Chaucer embraces a representation of all that is difficult in applying communicated past experience to present cases. He is unable to give it a classification in the order of dreams, but he plays with the reader by pretending to give information which would enable the reader to do so: he gives its exact date; the fact that it was not a daydream; that he was in his usual bed; that he fell asleep quickly (111–15). Appropriately, this apparent helpfulness is routed into a jokey simile which pretends that the problem is accessible through the reader's extratextual knowledge: Chaucer says that he fell asleep as quickly as someone who had gone two miles on pilgrimage to Saint Leonard (114–17). The problem posed by such a claim is paradoxically compounded for the modern reader by the *inaccessibility* of the image.[26] Chaucer is challenging the reader to classify the dream and hence define its usefulness; to apply Chaucer's unfathomable experience to the reader's own life. In the last analysis the dream is itself a comparator which is as little known as the experiences which one might wish to illuminate by it, and in doing this he is introducing the true condition of understanding.

Chaucer responds in various ways and with varying degrees of overt fictionality, to the problem he has perceived. Through his fictional persona, Geffrey, he envelopes his opening bafflement about taxonomy with a folksy shrug: "God turne us every drem to goode!" (1 and 58), and he diverts the interpretational challenge of his dream into a comically exaggerated curse on anyone who misjudges it. He represents the difficulty of connecting the world of past written exemplars with the present through Geffrey's sense of disorientation in the Temple of Glass. He does not know where in the world this past material is and that, in a sense, will always remain true for Chaucer and for everyone. In the desert, which stretches to the limit of Geffrey's perception, he shows imagistically, and with a sense of fear, that people cannot of themselves make the connection between the world of the Temple and the real world. Our perceptions do not enable us to bridge the gap between the comparator and the topic, the example and the present case, the past communication and the present experience which we want it to clarify. This recognition brings fear, and the eagle guide proves to be more of a comforting companion than a means of arriving at safe connnections between the known and the new.

However, the poem itself constitutes another way of responding to the problem: it does offer a flawed kind of linguistic success despite the inadequacies which disable all communication; it offers *sententia* despite recognizing that we cannot rely on what we hear as being true. More specifically, it shows comparison to be an empowering force for, while it is unreliable as a mode of knowledge, it is intimately connected with Chaucer's narrative drive. Just as taxonomy may have been revealed as heuristically facile but its mass of names can still prove rhetorically creative, so exemplary names, however untrustworthy as wisdom, are potential stories.

The most striking response which Chaucer makes to the problems he perceives is to thrust himself deeper into narrative, even into narrative within narrative. So we find him taking time to narrate the story of how Theseus betrayed Dianira (405–26), though this retelling adds nothing either to the weight of his eight examples or to the larger question of how reliable such examples are. In many respects these are the most trivial and, literally, eccentric lines in the poem, but they are also very revealing, for they show that *exemplum* does not simply furnish Chaucer with abstract challenges, but possesses a narrative impulse of its own. These two aspects meet in *Troilus and Criseyde,* where Chaucer meets the challenge of renarrating traditionally "named" exemplary characters. But that poem is unusual for the extreme length of its revisionary narrative.

More typical is the multiplication of examples in the *Legend of Good Women,* where Chaucer was engaged in promoting or revising the "names" acquired by twenty-five famous women, or the seventeen "ensamples trewe and olde" (out of the hundred available) which form the fragmented narrative of the *Monk's Tale,* or the twenty instances of virtuous suicide recalled by Dorigen in the *Franklin's Tale*.[27] Example seems to promise Chaucer narrative form and dialectical challenge but also the attraction of recursive storytelling. There may be an untraversable space between what people claim to know and what they would illuminate by it, between the past example and the present instance, but this insight impels Chaucer to fill the desert with a proliferation of narrative, never writing one story where several dozen can be promised, never employing one example where a further halfdozen can fill the space. Such recursiveness is, in a sense, mere supplementarity; an obsessive generation of words which has its attractions, but also its failings. One cannot know the circumstances which led to the *House of Fame* existing in an incomplete form, but what remains was going nowhere; it had come too close to a condition of reiterative supplementarity both in its individual sections and in its central argument, where it had proved its point about the unreliability of language several times over.[28] Without wishing to claim that it was abandoned with deliberate metapoetic intent, one cannot help noticing a further similarity with the multiple narratives of the *Legend of Good Women* and the *Monk's Tale:* the former, like the *House of Fame,* is incomplete under circumstances unknown to us; the latter is also incomplete, but its incompleteness is overtly dramatized—cut short by a character within the poem as if Chaucer was signaling that he had surmounted, and was punishing, a pleasurable feature of his own poetics.[29] From the point of view of fiction-making, reiterative narrative is a joyful force of propulsion and creativity; it is *amplificatio* at the highest level. But for problem solving, it is as much use as pouring water on a desert which stretches to the horizon and has sand grains "As smal as man may se yet lye / In the desert of Lybye."

The contrary forces present in the poem are thus expressive of deep creative paradoxes in Chaucer's writing. In him there was a constant tension between divergent and convergent thinking; between the desire to achieve understanding by the analysis of the dissimilarity between things and an equally attractive accommodation of different things to each other; between, on the one hand, the joys of literary supplementarity which revels in plurality and heterogeneity, and on the other, the mental control which is exerted in perceiving similarity, linking, and grouping things. I said earlier that the numerous names which Chaucer lists were evidence of attempted taxonomic control but also suggested a plurality which escaped true control. Reiterative narration is paradoxically both a force for forward movement and narratorial stasis. It offers more stories, but possibly just more of the same. That was certainly the Knight's view when he stopped the Monk: "That ye han seyd is right ynough, ywis, / And muchel moore" (*The Prologue of the Nun's Priest's Tale* 2768–69).

There is a corresponding paradox in the "voicing" of the stories. Chaucer adopts the mixed voice in which both narrator and characters speak, and this gives a quasi-dramatic quality to his poems, but he also tends to blur those voices. The similes which tie the eagle in with what he is expounding constitute an early version of what Chaucer does when he conflates voices from different aesthetic levels into each other, for example, making a character in *Troilus and Criseyde* share the same simile as the narrator,[30] or having the crow speak like the Manciple and the Manciple speak like Chaucer,[31] or apparently making a Canterbury pilgrim into an "extra" within another *Canterbury Tale*.[32] There is thus a drive for similitude in the writing which asserts the single plane of language against the hierarchical structures we would employ to give different value to different communications, the author's over the narrator's, or the narrator's over a character's, an eagle guide's speech as against his subject. Dramatic perspective is thus inconsistent, and sometimes altogether absent.

All these contrary pulls express a central tension between similarity and dissimilarity. The many different words for Fame's tidings express immense heterogeneity in language but massed together rhetorically seem to lose individuality; the many examples of male betrayal build up intensively but to prove a single point; the many legends of good women address the single penitential agenda set by Alceste; the different voices in Chaucer's poems tempt some critics to dramatic readings of the *Tales* but by losing their differentiating qualities return others to a purely stylistic or thematic reading. In the same way an *exemplum* claims a likeness between known and unknown which will result in illumination, but it may also carry disabling dissimilarities. It offers itself as the result of a process of comparison, but it may be just the start of a new one.

The *House of Fame* gives us an account of the problems which the linguistic medium poses for the writer, and it also constitutes an expression of them. Embedded in both account and expression is evidence that Chaucer feels contrary impulses towards dissimilarity and similarity. It is impossible to know whether this ambivalence empowers his writing more than his perception that language is a medium which only unpredictably conveys truth. We only have his words, and he expresses these contrary impulses through the practical problems which language throws up, such as the seductive unreliability of comparative *exempla*. The *House of Fame* constitutes an intense critique of the process of transference by which knowledge was supposed to beget knowledge through the comparison of things. But it also shows the rich creativity of such a failing enterprise.

3
Similes

IN THIS CHAPTER I WILL BE CONCENTRATING ON THE CLASS OF comparisons for which dissimilarity was a defining feature in all traditions, *similitudo,* and will look at how dissimilarity at the level of figuration was exploited for different ends by Chaucer and other writers of the period. Although we will see how striking dissimilarity can be exploited figuratively, and how the structure of comparison can be used as a formal representation of otherness, the chapter begins at the less flamboyant end of similaic figuration with the subtler effects which arise when figuration is barely perceptible; when dissimilarity is held in strict check by similarity, and, consequently, the figurative and literal are allowed to blend and play off against each other. In such cases one feels that the modern term "simile" is barely appropriate and that the author is really playing with the difference between such minimal dissimilarity as is allowed in *imago,* and the more overt and substantial dissimilarity at the heart of *similitudo.* This first section will move from poetic contexts where dissimilarity is figuratively constrained for rhetorical pleasures to others in which this constraint has a powerful dramatic, moral, or imaginative charge.

The central section, on Chaucer's use of similes, stresses the importance of context to the reading of simile, in particular to judging the extent or effect of dissimilarity. For example, some clichés recover their vitality remarkably in favorable contexts. Furthermore, the visibility and force of a simile depends on whether other similes have appeared in the text; whether they are sporadic or clustered; how conventional they are; what topics they have been attached to; whether they have formed a pattern; what voice utters them; whether the comparator has some kind of supplementary relationship to the immediate context independent of its function in the comparison; what the prevailing tone of the work is (for example, satiric or parodic), and so on. This means that decisions have to be made about what constitutes the relevant context for a given figure. Reading dissimilarity in simile thus engages larger issues of meaning. Unlike ordinary conversation, in which the speakers will probably use similes with a shared and narrow sense of the context relevant to understanding them, in a literary work relevant context itself is a matter of debate, a reflection of the overall reading within which the simile is allowed significance by the reader.[1] The context which the reader judges to be relevant may not be the same as the writer's or another reader's. Thus rhetorical figures are not so much ornaments to their local context as nodes for a wider interpretation. Reading a simile can involve the same interpretative activities as we associate with reading whole texts. This is evident in Chaucer's longest narrative, *Troilus and Criseyde*, where he dramatizes the interpretative challenge of comparison through the struggles of his characters, and maneuvers the reader by offering patterns of linked *similitudines*. But such issues are adumbrated in the central section of the present chapter within a broader range of poetry.

The last section will address the special function which simile can perform in mediating between different realms of existence. As we saw in chapter 1, the religious tradition in general, but particularly that from the Pseudo-Dionysius, felt that comparisons which involved dissimilar similarities were the most appropriate for expressing to the human imagination that which was beyond the human. Such comparisons paraded their lack of decorum in a way which protected the ineffable topic, but also goaded the human intellect to aspire to understanding it. In addition to such didactic advantages, they also formally reflected the connection and disconnection of the supernal and earthly realms. Goodness ran from one to the other, and so there was a ground to support comparison, but the gap between the spiritual and the material was vast (properly speaking unbridgeable), and so nothing really was adequate to express a positive similarity between the two realms. Dissimilarity had to inflect any link between the two.

Chaucer restricts himself to the earthly world, and he does not use similes in this way. But other writers, both popular and courtly, do not restrict themselves thus, and can be found using the intrinsic tension in similaic comparison to represent the different worlds which they are drawing together, and to help carry the imagination from one to the other. In the last section, therefore, I will be looking not simply at the operation of similes but at simile itself as a structure for representation and mediation between the other and the world of the known. Chaucer can be defined against the other writers of his age in part by his largely ignoring the two extremes of comparative dissimilarity: the bare figuration to be discussed next, and the extreme structural use of dissimilarity to be discussed in the last section of the chapter.

Dissimilarity and Figuration

Anyone who has read widely in the romances (and the present book reflects the reading of several dozen even if they are not actually mentioned) will be familiar with the tendency to employ description of an irritatingly pleonastic type, such as when someone, whom the reader knows to be a knight, is described as fighting bravely "like a knight." Such statements appear comparative, and employ the same phraseology as comparisons, down to the use of the words "like" and, more usually, "as." They certainly share the functions which one associates with similes: description, intensification, praise, blame, etc. But they also look very much like statements of apposition, for their description of the topic includes a minimum of dissimilarity: the comparator is simply the topic viewed from a slightly different angle.

To understand why these constructions should recur so often in medieval narrative, and yet sound so superfluous, even fatuous, to the modern ear it is necessary to retune our sense of what is figurative in a way which will allow for a different transition between literalness and figurativeness. Fashions change and even if the same subtlety of effect can be enjoyed by readers from different periods, the means by which it is brought about will differ, and may be so alien to later taste that the effect itself is lost. This is what has happened to statements of the kind in question. And it must be admitted that even though their original raison d'être can be recovered and explained, it is still virtually impossible for the modern reader to *enjoy* them in the aesthetic sense.

Statements which say that a knight "stert up ase a man" or fought like a knight are best seen as a special use of language which blends apposition and comparison. The result is a verbal *imago* or portrait, belonging to that class of comparison which produced depiction of appearance from a base in generic similarity. They represent the topic as very closely similar to its source which, in this case, is the ideal knight against which this particular knight can be truly and closely measured. These statements exist at the point where type and instance, original and copy, topic and comparator, genus and individual are least distinguished. They do not incorporate that degree of dissimilarity between topic and comparator that creates a figurative effect. On the other hand, they are not simple quantitative comparisons which, it is generally agreed, are not figurative in effect.[2] There is a notional, perhaps only theoretical separation between the topic and comparator, or in this case between the *imago* and the original which it represents, but there is dissimilarity which is not just of a quantitative kind.

It must be acknowledged that some poems are of such general banality or literality that such remarks do indeed seem to be simple cases of an author pretending to say something when nothing is being said. *Generydes* is such a work.³ In its many thousand lines it so far eschews any figurativeness that the whole begins to look like a genre of its own, a literary *grisaille*. For example, faced with the opportunity to describe the arming of Generydes, the author avoids all figurative pointing, and brings the scene to triumphant conclusion with the remark "A knyght hym semyd for to be right stought" (3311). Later what looks as if it is going to be a simile comparing someone to a pilgrim, "a pilgrim as he were" (3667), turns out after seven lines to be a literal description of someone who *is* a pilgrim. The author does use one simile in the poem. He describes black warriors as being "As blak as cole" (1942). But although the comparison is so tired one almost misses it, the author still remembers it over one hundred lines later, and clearly feels that now is not the time to confuse the audience by change. He reiterates that they were "As blak as coole, as I befoore haue told" (2076). In such a poem nonsimilaic "as" and "like" statements remain embedded in literality, and any notional difference there might be between the topic and the comparator is unproductive of effect.

In another poem and another local context, however, a quasi-figurative effect can be created. In *Athelston* the King is warned in the following terms: "thou shalt ligge in an old dike, / As it were an heretike" (480–81).⁴ Here the dramatic context of the threat and the evident desire to picture the King's condition to the imagination of King and audience help to make this feel more figurative. But, if it is figuration, it is of the *imago* kind that involves minimal real dissimilarity between topic and comparator for, in the situation being described to the King, he will indeed be an excommunicate. So he will be lying in a ditch as a heretic in a more appositional than similaic sense.

There are places where such statements are brought into close proximity with comparisons of a clearly similaic nature which also employ the word "as," and the writer seems to play with the apparent association between them. Here verbal *imagines* and *similitudines*, each with their very different freight of likeness or dissimilarity, are played off against each other. A very basic example of this is to be found in *Guy of Warwick* where the same combatants are described thus, "Als lyouns þai fouȝten þo" (3600), and two lines later is the appositional version, "Þai wered hem as douhti men."⁵ The description of the battle is conventional: it attracts a cluster of similes (the first cluster of the poem) and their topics and comparators are all highly clichéd. But part of the conventionality of the section is, in fact, this association of the two different "as" phrases, an association no more unique to the poem than its tendency to cluster similes.

A more developed example of this association can be found in the following lines from the description of a storm at sea. The author of the *The Destruction of Troy*,[6] from which the passage comes, particularly favors this rhetorical game:

> With a leuenyng light *as* a low fyre,
> Blaset all the brode see *as* it bren wold.
> The flode with a felle cours flowet on hepis,
> Rose vppon rockes *as* any ranke hylles.
> So wode were the waghes & þe wilde ythes,
> All was like to be lost, þat no lond hade.
> The ship ay shot furth o þe shire waghes,
> *As* qwo clymbe at a clyffe, or a clent hille—
> Eft dump in the depe *as* all drowne wolde.
>
> (1988–96)

I have my doubts about whether the second "as" italicized is comparative, though it subliminally introduces the image of a fire; I am sure that the last one is not even imagistic in the minimal sense, but the others are.

The most striking feature of similaic comparison as used in such passages from popular romance is that its figuration is often subordinated to the rhetoric of phrasal patterning in a way which suggests that our modern concentration on the figurative, with its striking dissimilarity, is inappropriate. One finds whole sections of verse which are structured by repeated use of the word "as" serving quite different types of statement. This happens often enough to suggest that it became a literary convention—not one, it should be said, that Chaucer employs to any degree, even though he frequently uses repetitive rhetorical devices such as lists and anaphora. When Chaucer blurs the literal with the figurative it is in the area of meaning, not of mere rhetorical phrasing.

It appears that writers of these romances started with the notion that a topic to be intensified should be extended by a statement introduced by "as." This word could lead to a whole range of developments, some renaming the topic in the appositional way which I have described as *imago*, some making purely quantitative comparison with no figurative effect, some genuinely figurative, some even incidental but beginning with "as." The result was a tendency towards a string of "as" phrases at moments the author considered particularly striking. This strategy for intensifying appears mechanical and obsessive to the modern reader, but it is not impossible that the mixing of different kinds of "as" phrase was originally recognized and appreciated by writer and reader, and constituted a rhetorical pleasure of modulation over and above the intensificatory purpose which the statements served. Figuration could have a subtle effect deriving from its place in a rhetorical matrix rather than from the specific claim that it made. A writer could thus create effective mixtures of appositional naming of the topic, in which there was minimal dissimilarity, and similitudinous naming, in which dissimilar things were brought together with figurative effect. This was, in turn, part of a larger interest in playing off literal statements against figurative ones. This occurs in the following description, from the *Laud Troy Book*:[7]

> As he were a hors, he neyes & ondes.
> His eyen were lyke to brennande brondes;
> He fferd, as he scholde men haue brent
> With spark of fire that fro him glent;
> His vice was red as any fir.
>
> (7729–33)

There is a subtle modulation between types of statement here. The adverbial description of how "he" behaved—as if he would have burned men up—is literal. But it merges on each side with similes which compare his eyes to firebrands and his countenance to a fire. The reader or hearer knows that the opening of the description, "As he wer a hors," is carefully poised between *imago* and *similitudo*, for the whole passage is describing a centaur, which both is, and is not, a horse. The doubleness of comparison, the way in which it links topic and comparator, or *imago* and original, is a perfect medium for communicating the ambivalent condition of the centaur, and the author supports this oscillation between literality and figurativeness with other lines which also vary as to fact or figure.

If one needs proof that some writers knew perfectly well that they were making different kinds of statement, although they would not have defined the difference in our terms, it is provided by their employing for strategic purposes the ambiguity in the phraseology common to apposition and figuration, as in the following example from *Guy of Warwick*:

> Gij seye Herhaud yfeld,
> Tohewen his hauberk & his scheld
> (& of his hors feld he was,
> As ded man lay on þe gras;
> He seye þe blod þat cam him fro).
>
> (1441–45)

Guy thinks that Herhaud is dead, and so does the reader because the surrounding detail encourages one to interpret the phrase "As ded man" in an appositional way: being dead, he lay on the grass. The statement seems like an *imago* of Herhaud, depicting him as a dead man because he is one. In fact, it should be interpreted more similaically: he lay like a corpse. Some 220 lines later the wounds have proved curable and he has recovered. An appositional naming has turned out to be figuratively comparative naming. *Imago* has turned into *similitudo*. Comparable with this is the statement in *The Earl of Toulouse* that the Earl and Sir Trylabas "kyssyd togedur as gode frende" (415).[8] While one of them thinks that they are good friends; the other knows that they are kissing only *as if* they were friends. What such authors lack in finesse they compensate for with basic narrative cunning.[9]

The above examples show how comparisons with very different degrees of latent dissimilarity are mixed for rhetorical purposes, and made ambiguous for strategic narrative ones. But they must also be seen as part of a larger interest in defining nature and status through names. In militaristic verse romances authors promote a sense of strict codes of conduct and social propriety. This is built upon a belief in real and fixed natures. Accordingly they show considerable respect for the names, such as knight, prince, man, churl, which encapsulate their society, stratified as it is by rank and duty, and which thus assist the clear delineation of achievement within the terms of that society. So it is that a nonfigurative statement saying that Sir Dégaré "stert vp ase a man" (379) has equal value with a figurative statement which adduces a nominal comparator of greater dissimilarity to its topic.[10]

It would be a mistake to regard such appositional descriptions, like the one of Sir Dégaré, as just periphrastic adverbials, another way of saying that he leapt up "in a manly way," for the whole point is the giving of the name, the defining of status in a title. That is why such statements regularly appear in nominal form; frequently could not be reduced to an adverbial statement anyway, and have rhetorical affinities which lie beyond adverbial description. If *exemplum* derives from existing reputation and contributes to the transmission of reputation, *imago*, in the form discussed here, is a depiction of a person which implicitly compares him or her closely against an original reputational "name."

In religious drama such namings carry a considerable didactic charge: they reveal the spiritual condition of the person who gives the name; and they challenge the audience to judge the degree of dissimilarity involved in the comparison. Within the spiritual contest dramatized and extended into the hearts of the audience they act both to focus theme and control response. What is uttered by a character as an *imago*, or a *similitudo* in which little dissimilarity is intended, may be taken up by the discerning spectator in quite a different way. Or, indeed, a comparison intended as an insulting *similitudo* by a character can be perceived as an *imago* in a deeper sense by the spectator.

3: SIMILES

The *York* cycle of plays, for example, gives considerable scope to such statements in its Passion sequence:[11] there Christ is described as a king, thief, knave, lad, fool, king of fools, sacrificial beast, magpie, jay, and so on, in "as" or "like" phrases which vary in similaic or appositional force. Sometimes the comparisons are straightforwardly insulting and the audience rejects the close similarity claimed between Christ and his comparator:

> *I Miles.* We, harke, he jangelis like a jay
> *II Miles.* Methynke he patris like a py
>
> (35.265–66)

The structure of the play itself undermines and reverses these insults: Christ only speaks twice in the play, whereas the soldiers have barely stopped talking since it began.

At other times, however, deeper significance links the claimed simile and the apposition which truly underlies it, as when the first soldier says at the *Crucifixion:* "And sen he claymeth kyngdome with croune, / Even as a kyng here hange shall hee" (35.79–80), or as when Christ before his Passion is described thus "he is boune as beeste in bande / That is demed for to dye" (34.341–42), a simile which recalls Christ's status as sacrificial lamb. Both of these statements purport to be *similitudines* but both are *imagines,* if properly understood: Christ is not *like* a king, but is one; is not *like* a bound beast awaiting death, but in a mystical sense is such a beast.

In a context like the *Crucifixion* these spiritual alternatives are clear, even if the emotional involvement of the spectators is complicated by the entertainment they get from the soldiers. With less stark alternatives, particularly colored by comedy, the status of the comparison becomes more ambiguous, less a choice of opposite readings. In the scene of Peter's betrayal of Christ, *York* brings out the power of simile to create emotional conflict. Peter is described by the Jews round the fire by three comparisons within a dozen lines or so: "He lokis lurkand like a nape" (29.105), and

> *Mulier.*   he lokis like a brokke
> Were he in a bande for to bayte
> Or ellis like an nowele in a stok
> Full preualy his pray for to wayte
>
> (115–18)

The Christian might well wish to reject such comparisons for the founder of the Church as purely vituperative *similitudines.* But there are several forces working against this. Peter is, in a sense, alienated from the scene and from the audience by being decribed at a distance by people who could talk to him but talk about him instead. This whole passage, though within drama, is actually narrative, and it draws upon the technique frequently found in popular romances of using a cluster of similes, particularly when a romance beast or some other monster, is introduced. Peter is thus objectified by narrative, debased by the literary topos employed for him, and also, in the time-honored fashion of simile, is dragged down by the individual comparators to the level of the beast. The comparators themselves present him as something to be laughed at, but also speak of his ugliness, his aggressive fear, and his predatoriness. It is a remarkable passage for it forces the audience to subscribe to the judgment of the Jews. Peter as a sinner, a fearful betrayer, an injurer of his master, is rightly described in their terms. These are not casual *similitudines* of insult, but are actually *imagines* and occur in an episode not of direct dramatic intercourse, but of deictic representation. The audience observes Peter, and sees him through the comic and critical *imagines* supplied, at the same time as it must feel sympathy for him, morally identify with him, and respect him as the saint holding the power, through his church, to bind and loose the sinner.

It seems that rhetorical taste, the analytic demands of a genre like drama, and audience interest in the fixed values of status all go towards encouraging a play between the figurative and nonfigurative, between some statements which encapsulate a high degree of dissimilarity and others which do not, in other words, between *imago* and *similitudo*. Sometimes the effect is crude or minimal; at others it appears more striking and creative. The above examples are all taken from works of a popular or civic character, but a high literary version of this play on dissimilarity can be found working almost at the level of pure imagination rather than rhetoric or morality.

The author of *Sir Gawain and the Green Knight,* perhaps surprisingly in a work so imaginatively rich, does not use many similes.[12] If anything, he offers a poem more effectively brought out of Arthurian myth towards reality through the two forces of conversation and material things, clothes, architecture, dismembered animals, and so on. That "realizing" impulse can be seen in the way he treats the following simile. He gives new life to one of the most clichéd comparators of the period by literalizing it: he removes its latent dissimilarity and blends it into its context. But he also sustains another simile in its full figurativeness at the same time. The combination is powerful. Having flinched once, Gawain is steadfastly awaiting what he believes will be the Green Knight's final blow, but which will prove only a feint. The poet describes him thus,

> Gawayn grayþely hit bydez and glent with no membre
> Bot stode stylle as þe ston oþer a stubbe auþer
> Þat raþeled is in roché grounde with rotez a hundreth.
>
> (2292–94)

As the image of the tree is extended from a simple comparator by placing it in its locale, the poet's mind slides from the simile of the stone away from the figurative into the literal, harsh landscape of the valley where Gawain is standing. In this place of stones—of cave, crag, and "ruʒe knokled knarrez with knorned stonez" (2166)—the similaic stone finds its literal setting. The simile stone becomes part of the "roché grounde" in which the trunk of the tree, to which Gawain is also compared, is fastened by its hundred roots. The *similitudo* of the stone thus loses even the minimal dissimilarity of *imago* and is blurred into factuality. However, the *similitudo* of the tree, the "stubbe . . . þat raþeled is," remains as a figurative descant upon the literalness of the first comparator.

This is not rhetorical play. If anything it is an imaginative shift of symbolic significance for, while still describing Gawain figuratively for the purposes of enhancing his bravery, the passage declares that he has to become one with the harsh, testing world of the Green Knight before he can return to the court. As the conventional simile sinks into the literal, so Gawain becomes a rock in the rocky landscape. But the accompanying image of the tree in its full similaic claim actually preserves Gawain as a knight who is only *like* a tree. These two similes with their contrasting elision and acknowledgment of dissimilarity function like the similes which mediate between the world of earthly perception and the world of supernal values which humans need access to. The effect is here created on the cusp of the literal and figurative.

Chaucer also blurs the literal and figurative at this higher level. He thereby naturalizes what is conventional, and makes what is generic and highly conventional contribute to an impression of realism. He frequently harmonizes his comparisons with the context in which they are placed so that what is *similitudo,* with all its figurative dissimilarity, also does service on the literal level of the work, helping to "realize" the fiction. I would wish to add this technique to others which have been identified as constituting the "realizing" and "particularizing" dimension of literature at this time.[13]

In the *Parliament of Fowls* sighs "hoote as fyr" (246) are transformed into the real flammable cause of altar flames. In the *Knight's Tale,* the highly conventional description of Emily places her in a garden and compares her to the stock romantic comparators for women, the rose and lily flower. But although all is done within the constraint of convention, the elements within the description support each other in a way which gives the impression of reality. The flowers which are similitudes for Emily are also, one feels, growing literally in the garden where she is seen. Dissimilarity in the overtly functioning comparison is thus elided in the imaginative subtext. In the *Reeve's Tale* the students come back in a horse-like manner from chasing their horse through the fens: "Wery and weet, as beest is in the reyn" (4107); John lies in the Miller's bedroom like a sack of chaff (4206). In the *Canon Yeoman's Tale* the alchemical canon's forehead sweats like a still, imagistically anticipating later literal revelations. The most remarkable slide from simile into literal context occurs in the *Squire's Tale* where a similaic comparison of Canacee to the young sun "That in the Ram is foure degrees up ronne" (386) turns into giving the time of day: "Noon hyer was he whan she redy was" (387).

In all of these cases there is an imaginative decorum between the simile and its context which is attractive in its own right. But the effect is greater than ornamentation, and a deeper power of imagination in the author is implied by it. It reveals a writer whose imagination is poised between the reality of the scene he envisions and the poetic figures and conventions which he has at his disposal to express it. And not just "poised": he blurs and merges the two, using the power of dissimilarity, and its removal, to mediate between the language of poetry and the reality in the imagination. *Similitudo* stands at the heart of this aesthetic mediation.[14] In such a world, where the figurative plays with the literal and artifice is intermittently obscured, the potential for a poem to offer exemplary truths by implicit comparison to the real nonfictional world is increased and its attractions are made more seductive.

In an earlier example from *Guy of Warwick* the reader was encouraged to think of a statement as an *imago* whereas it later turned out to have been a *similitudo*. The dissimilarity between the topic and the comparator was found to be much greater than expected—a simple enough narrative trick. In the cases just studied, Chaucer elides the dissimilarity in *similitudo* with the result that the scene is made more effectively real. In the following example an enhanced version of this effect is created. Chaucer uses a set of flamboyant similes, with marked and comic dissimilarities between topic and comparator, in such a way as to leave the impression of *imago*, a depiction with minimal dissimilarity between the image seen and the original it represents. These extravagant poetic comparators paradoxically blend with their topic rather than serving it.

The rhetorical *amplificatio* which Alison famously gets in the *Miller's Tale* (3233–70) recalls by its packed comparative style, though not by its chosen comparators, the model of *descriptio* outlined by Geoffrey of Vinsauf for beautiful women.[15] This ironic glance at a higher rhetorical form is playful rather than subversive of the romance genre or the immediate topic, Alison. Using fifteen explicit similaic comparators and three other covert comparisons in forty-three lines, the passage manifestly goes beyond generic point. The most evident feature of the portrait is actually the author's own literary complicity with the sexual object he creates.

As an example of high style for a low subject it is a comic, if rather trivial, success. As a description of Alison it is almost totally irrelevant to the plot of the tale in which it appears, for she could perform all (or perhaps both) the normal fabliau functions, and satisfy the plot demands of the story with a good deal less description. However, as part of a tale which dramatizes one character's ability to paint vivid and persuasive pictures for another, as Nicholas does for the carpenter, and which expatiates upon the power of imagination to overcome sense, it is central: "Men may dyen of ymaginacioun, / So depe may impressioun be take" (*Miller's Tale*, 3612–13). Chaucer offers an *imago* of Alison as her own world, its animals, trees, fruits, drinks, money, and other objects. They are used as comparators to illuminate her as the topic but, in the end, as the similes build upon each other and mass together, topic and comparators are more symbiotically sensed by the reader, so that the portrait becomes a comparison of closely related kinds. Alison seems to constitute her world and to be constituted by it. Its components cease to be dissimilar comparators within a *similitudo,* and become more the original of which she is the *imago*. She certainly seems larger than anyone whose haunches could be grabbed, and that is Chaucer's point: she lives largely to the imagination, and that imaginary picture is made real. The resulting effect is much more serious than those paintings in which the artist constructs a face out of the different fruits and flowers of a still life. That is visual trickery of a fantastic kind, whereas this is an affirmation of the realizing power of the imagination made by the management of dissimilarity in a mass of similes.

Similaic comparators supposedly import knowledge of things from outside the specific textual location of their use to inform our understanding of the topic within the text, but Chaucer here avoids a clear distinction of poetic and nonpoetic world. This amalgamation of fictive character and the real objects which are adduced from the world of the "known" derives from a deep associative mechanism in Chaucer. It produced those similes whose comparators were in harmony with their context, and blended with it literally. It also gives us the portrait of the Monk who loves "venerie" and is then described with a mass of animal references, some of them similaic: several to horses, a plucked hen, a fish, an oyster, greyhounds, birds in flight, and a roast swan.

When the comparators which are used in similes thus merge with their topics, Chaucer creates an imagistic equivalent of narratorial univocality. Elsewhere in his poems voices blend or mimic each other across the aesthetic boundaries of author, narrator, and character, creating a plane of speech which is almost self-authorizing in its independence of source. In *Troilus and Criseyde* even similes can become the medium for this sharing of voice. In such places the framework of voice which keeps in place our power to distinguish levels of reality is collapsed. In the description of Alison, however, image rather than voice creates this poetic reality which is neither figure nor fact but glances at each.

As we will see later, Chaucer often seeks out the dissimilarities which prise an *exemplum* away from that to which it is adduced, and he thereby reveals the failure of the comparative route to truth. But the *similitudines* just studied indicate his contrary attraction towards blurring the figurative with the nonfigurative or less figurative, the similaic comparator with the topic which it illuminates. Whereas the *exemplum* has its dissimilarities exposed for analytical purposes, the *similitudo* has its dissimilarities reduced for imaginative ones. Alison's *imago* and the other *similitudines* which flow in and out of their literalizing contexts assert the joy of the fictive process, of making and associating things of different genus, of joining here, separating there, rather than questioning comparison's claim to illuminate the unknown by the known. The power of comparison to assist the poetic process is elevated over its pretensions to transfer meaning.

Similes and Dissimilarity in Context

Chaucer's originality does not often show itself in unusual figurative comparisons. The same similes appear in different places. Things shine like gold; people are jolly or loquacious as magpies and jays; they can be as meek as maids; pale as ashes; grunt, fight, or even just look, like wild boars; be still, hard or blind as stone; they are busy or murmur or swarm like bees, and so on. A rudimentary variety is maintained in that the same comparator can have several qualities attached to it and, conversely, a single quality may have more than one potential comparator, or the same comparator can be expressed in different ways. Thus eyes can be grey as glass or goose, and Hypermnestra is described as quaking "as doth the lef of aspe grene" at one point and "As doth the braunche that Zepherus shaketh" shortly after (*Legend of Good Women* 2648, 2681). The idea may not be unusual but an attempt has been made at rhetorical variation.

Neither is the choice of comparator determined solely by formal considerations, such as the requirements of rhyme. There are recurring collocations, certainly: "glas" and "was"; "mayde" and "sayde"; "goot" and "hoot," for example. But Chaucer is actually quite varied in the line position which his comparators fill, and thus they are not generally tied to rhyming needs. Even when they are in final position, the rhyme words vary: though "glas" and "was" usually rhyme, "allas" also appears (*Man of Law's Tale* 193); "stoon" (a frequent comparator) rhymes with "boon," "oon," "noon," and "anon."

Despite these sources of variety, it is important to acknowledge from the start that there is a strong element of the formulaic, the conventional, the clichéd in Chaucer's similes. Aural and semantic features seem to work together in some formulaic comparisons so that one is not even sure whether it is the range of meaning in a word or merely a phrasal tic that prompts the poet's use. For example, the Pardoner rings out his speech "as round as gooth a belle" (*Pardoner's Tale* 331). The image is of the sound of the speech, and this is supported by other instances of the image: when Pandarus sought to convince his guests of Poliphete's treachery, he "rong hem out a proces lik a belle" (*Troilus and Criseyde* 2.1615). But in the *General Prologue* to the *Tales* the comparator describes appearance not sound: the physical appearance of the Monk's semicope is described as "rounded as a belle out of the presse" (263). Although the two similes could not be formed unless the bell had the visual and aural characteristics to sustain them, one cannot discern whether Chaucer moves from one to the other because he is sensitive to the semantic range of the word "round," or because the sound of the phrase containing it has become formulaic for him and he adjusts it to the immediate context.

Similarly one can find things not worth the "montance of a gnat" at one point (*Manciple's Tale* 254–55), but the "montance of a knotte" at another (*Troilus and Criseyde* 3.1732). However, it is in this example of near repetition that the formulaic is transmuted into the truly creative. In the *Manciple's Tale* the comparison operates to intensify: it is part of the crow's forceful story that Phoebus has been cuckolded by a worthless rival. Its point is dramatic, coming at the climax of a speech which produces disaster for all including the crow. In *Troilus*, however, the idea of the knot has imagistic integrity in context: Troilus finds that other ladies' qualities "Kan nought the montance of a knotte unbynde / Aboute his herte of al Criseydes net." Here the "knot" is part of a "net," that association offering both tight semantic definition of "knot" and another example of aural association which goes beyond mere assonance towards *paronomasia*. These are striking witnesses to the juncture of formula and creativity in Chaucer, and to the mixed impulse of the aural and semantic which lies behind it.

Enough variation is built into the system for Chaucer's similes rarely to become irritating even if they are not contributing significantly to their poem. The point of greatest danger is when a simile recurs within the one poem, but even here disaster is unusual: within a dozen lines the Shipman tells us that people are glad "as fowel of day" and as "fowel . . . whan that the sonne up riseth" (38, 51), betraying his author on automatic pilot for once. However, repetition within the one poem can seem unobtrusive or mildly productive. Amidst the plethora of animal similes which appear in the Wife of Bath's *Prologue,* the battle of the Wife with her husbands reaches a delightfully heroic equality: they are like mad lions (429, 794); she is stubborn as a lioness (637). In the subromance battleground of the Wife's parlor these repeated images work well because they play off the genre in which the lion is most common as a comparator for the fighter and both sexes are involved. In the *Knight's Tale,* on the other hand, the same image is repeated but wider apart (1598, 2171), and simply marks, and preserves, the reader's generic expectations. Of course knights act like lions in romances. In the limited space of individual *Tales,* even, surprisingly, in the long *Knight's Tale,* the repetition with variation of particular similes does not form as subtle patterns of meaning as in *Troilus and Criseyde.* The *Knight's Tale* contains forceful individual comparisons, and it makes much of pairing and opposing similes, but it never develops a single similaic idea, changing its value through different contexts, as is done in the *Troilus.* Perhaps it is a feature of the poem's rather diluted style that, even when Palamon and Arcite, suffering the full anxiety of their jealousy, and explicitly compared by the narrator, are both described as looking like "asshen colde" (1302, 1364), the statements appear separate and conventional, and do not contribute to the opposition of the rival lovers. Their local context fails to give life to the similes' conventionality, and they fail to provide a context for each other.

V. A. Kolve says in *Chaucer and the Imagery of Narrative* that "Context alone turns a sign into a communication."[16] In one sense, that is a truism; in another it is the key to Chaucer's narrative practice, as Kolve perceived. It is the particularity of context that empowers Chaucer's creative use of conventional *similitudines.* Material which in its own right is not always promising is given a new life by the context in which it is placed. Admittedly, some of Chaucer's similes do remain conventional to the point of invisibility, and others, while less trivial, are stable in significance, whatever their immediate topic or context: for example, the image of the scorpion for a deceitful destroyer is found applied to Fortune in the *Book of the Duchess,* the Sultan's mother in the *Man of Law's Tale,* and the crow in the *Manciple's Tale* without any obvious difference in value. But against such an acknowledged background of conventionality and formula, Chaucer's creativity shows up in the relationship of simile and context.

Chaucer generally tends to juxtapose voices, details, tones, styles, sections of narrative, and so on, allowing one feature to form the context in which another is perceived, but often without defining for the reader what the juxtaposition means. Significance lies less in the individual parts than in the accommodation which the reader makes between them. Meaning is therefore something the reader contributes largely to fashioning. In this respect, Chaucer is primarily a contextualist rather than an overt ironist.[17] In keeping with this aesthetic his figurative skill does not lie so much in the complexity of his similes as in their deployment. Chaucer does not aim for similes of intrinsic depth and subtlety as does the *Pearl*-Poet; his own range of simile is quite narrow and conventional, and he repeats himself more than the *Pearl*-Poet does. But he can achieve a very wide range of effects by using similar material in contexts of varying narratorial, generic, and thematic complexity. The formulaic becomes heterogeneous; the conventional gets revivified.

This can be seen clearly in the contrasting values which one simile can have when put in different poems. Some extravagant contrasts emerge, and suggest that Chaucer was interested in contextuality itself, over and above the local effects which context could create. For example, in the *Book of the Duchess* Lady White's manner and comeliness are described as being like the torch "That every man may take of lyght / Ynogh, and hyt hath never the lesse" (964–65). Later, Chaucer was to give a version of this to the Wife of Bath, of all people, for her to justify promiscuity:

> He is to greet a nygard that wolde werne
> A man to lighte a candle at his lanterne;
> He shal have never the lasse light, pardee.
> (*Wife of Bath's Prologue* 333–35)

It is not the fact that the simile is used twice that suggests Chaucer's creativity is driven by context rather than by the intrinsic interest of a figure. Rather, it is the fact that when he reuses the simile, the new location gives it a diametrically opposite meaning. He seems attracted to the capacity of one idea to carry quite different significance just as the roundness of a bell could suggest either appearance or sound.

Comparisons can adjust or complicate tone, creating and changing contexts for each other and the narrative. As one might expect, the tonal range of the *Merchant's Tale* is reflected in its comparisons (both similaic and exemplary). The music at the wedding ceremony is humorously elevated to the point of bad taste as well as incredibility, by comparison with the melody of Orpheus or Amphion and the noise of Joab and Theodamas, these last comparisons bringing in warlike associations quite in keeping with a fabliau marriage.[18] We are told that May looks like Queen Esther but the narrator undermines the supposed ground of his comparison—Esther's meekness—by adjusting the topic: he starts the description as if May is actively eyeing up her surroundings and finishes it with a more playfully decorous emphasis on May as she is *seen:* "Queene Ester looked nevere with swich an ye / On Assuer, so meke a look hath she" (*Merchant's Tale* 1744–45). Similarly, when January deceives himself by a comparison with the lovemaking of Paris and Helen, space is opened up for the reader to consider the dissimilarities between topic and comparator. The actual lovemaking then takes place in a world where dogfish and magpies, rather than biblical and classical sources, however questionable, provide the similes.

A similar tonal shift affects the Host's attempt to be philosophical before the *Man of Law's Tale*. He says that time slips away from us like the stream "that turneth nevere agayn, / Descendynge fro the montaigne into playn (*Introduction* 23–24) but his discourse also descends when he exemplifies Seneca with the remark that time cannot be recovered any more than "Malkynes maydenhede, / Whan she hath lost it in hir wantownesse" (30–31). This tonal slippage foreshadows generic tensions in the narrative as a whole.

Generic expectations and associations function as a special kind of context which can shift the value of elements such as simile. They constitute a "known" with which, or against which, the simile can work. As far apart as the values which the *Book of the Duchess* and the *Wife of Bath's Prologue* gave to the "torch" simile are the romantic and mock romantic claims that Emily in the *Knight's Tale* and Chauntecleer in the *Nun's Priest's* both sing like angels. The Prioress is nudged away from spirituality towards sensuality by the remark that her eyes were gray as glass, and Simpkin's daughter in the *Reeve's Tale* is comically nudged from sensuality towards the romantic by the same simile. In each case, it is the context working against the generic associations of the simile which determines its force. Without a degree of conventionality in similes and an author willing to play with the conventionality of genre such effects could not occur. Chaucer's figurative conventionality and his unconventional playing with genre are sides of the same coin.

The traditional rhetorical goals of simile—to elevate or degrade the topic—are reflected in the modes of writing which most attract simile in his *Tales:* romance and fabliau. The description of Emily in the

Knight's Tale is an obvious example of the former. Simile is absent from the poem until this conventional romance subject calls for it, and then in conventional fashion four similes are clustered together to intensify the topic. Conversely, the remark in the *Reeve's Tale* that Simpkin's wife was "as digne as water in a dich" perfectly fits the degrading function of comparison to the contemptuous undercurrents of the fabliau genre. Chaucer appears to employ simile largely as a genre marker at the opening of the incomplete *Cook's Tale*. The three similes which occur in the first nine lines contribute to the rather over-anxious signaling of fabliau which goes on until the poem is broken off.[19]

Chaucer's comic armory includes undermining a character through similes which suggest sexual subordination. Perhaps only the Knight in his well-defined, and manly, context could get away with being meek as a maid. Elsewhere, the male sexual underdog is feminized or further subordinated by being shifted lower than the woman down to child level. In the *Miller's Tale* Nicholas promises that, once safely in his kneading trough, the carpenter will be able to survive Noel's Flood: "Thanne shaltou swymme as myrie, I undertake, / As dooth the white doke after hire drake" (3575–76). Nicholas's simile apparently asserts the married relationship of the carpenter to Alison but it also degrades the carpenter's sexual status to the duck, and elevates his wife to the "drake." Absolom, on the other hand, employs a putatively sexual simile which actually shifts him out of the sexual area entirely: he is like a lamb mourning for the teat. His attention is upon the teat; but the simile also conveys the notion that he is simply a baby. The narrator affirms this later by comparing him to a beaten child.

Chaucer also uses his knowledge of comparative stereotypes and common usage to create generic parody. Thus, in *Sir Thopas*, there are the clichéd tags of romance simile: as white as a lily, as red as rose, merrier than the nightingale, and Sir Thopas, like other errant knights, leaves on his horse like a spark out of a firebrand.[20] Chaucer also replicates the clustering of similes typical of romance *descriptio* (*Sir Thopas* 725–30), and which he uses again for comedy, though not generic subversion, in his description of Chauntecleer in the *Nun's Priest's Tale*.

Parody is a special type of context for simile since its significance lies in part beyond the poem. The precise generic target is not always evident to the modern reader. For example, when Chaucer degrades Sir Thopas by comparing his face to white bread he is classically diminishing the subject by simile but one also wants to know whether he is making a specifically generic point, commenting on what he considers to be failures of decorum in romance comparison. Is he pointing to similes which contain unacceptable dissimilarity between the topic and the comparator, or just employing one himself to make his hero comic? This is a difficult question, for it is clear that some English authors, developing hints in the French, but in a tradition which ultimately goes back to the *Iliad,* used domestic imagery for describing epic events. The author of the *Laud Troy Book* consistently and brilliantly familiarizes the mythical through such imagery, but does so within the framework of an unquestioning admiration for the heroism at Troy. In this text, the dissimilarity between the topic and the comparator is embraced in order to bring myth closer to the audience's perception. He says of warriors in single combat: "Echon on other ffaste doth bete, / Ryght as threscheres doth on whete" (9335–36) and that "thei fflowen ouer the hors tayl / Opon that playn, as it were two rattes" (6786–87). In these examples the domestication has a mildly reductive, but not a pejorative or critical, effect. One is not intended to explore precise points of similarity between topic and comparator but to appreciate the extreme cheapness of life and limb when great warriors come together. Thus a knight can ride about like a leopard or a fulmard after hens; men are cut down like sheep or split like logs, calves, or swine; they run away like a fox into its hole, or a hare from hounds; and they mass in battle like shoals of herring. This oft-repeated tactic does not amount to an undermining of the warrior ethic. An element of comedy may result, but it looks like deliberate witticism which is not intended to subvert the subject matter but, if anything, to raise it above the domestic experience through which it is viewed.

On the other hand, in *The Destruction of Troy* we are told that Helen of Troy had fingers with "nailes at the neþer endes as a nepe [turnip] white" (3076).[21] Since it is hard to accept the propriety of any part of Helen of Troy being compared to a turnip, perhaps this sort of simile supports the notion that Chaucer is poking fun at indecorum in poor narrative when he compares Sir Thopas's complexion to white bread. When he says that Thopas's bridle "as the sonne shoon, / Or as the moone light" (879–80), he is certainly making fun of the vagueness which can accompany intensifying simile in popular genres, so it may well be that there is a generic purpose behind his reductive simile for Thopas's complexion. However, it is tricky to move from local effect to generic parody.

Chaucer also describes Sir Thopas as being as "sweete as is the brembul flour" (746). This is not far from what Geoffrey of Vinsauf actually commended in the *Poetria Nova,* a work which Chaucer knew.[22] In his model *descriptio* Geoffrey said that a woman's eyebrows were to be likened to dark blueberries. The author of *Cleanness* employs, in all seriousness, a similar comparison for the two young men whose beauty attracts the attention of the Sodomites: their complexion was "as þe brere-flour" (791). It would seem possible, therefore, that Chaucer chooses the comparator as much for its feminine resonance as for any generic allusion. Its comic target is primarily Sir Thopas rather than poor romance. However, in the comic mélange of *Sir Thopas* such distinctions are perhaps misplaced.

Where genre is not a clearly marked aspect of context, the variety of effect can be greater, the shadings which context gives to simile more subtle. The Knight, the Clerk, and Jason in the *Legend of Good Women* are all described as being meek or coy like a maid. The first appears as the only simile in the *General Prologue* description of the Knight. Its figurativeness is thus more forceful for being seen against the different rhetorical device of listing the named battles at which he has fought. In this context of seriousness in style and content, it effectively implies the Knight's courtesy and modesty of demeanor. The second is developed into a sexual comparison: "Ye ryde as coy and stille as dooth a mayde / Were newe spoused, sittynge at the bord" (*The Clerk's Prologue* 2–3). This may reflect more on the speaker, Harry Bailley, showing his need to subordinate, and control by sexual comedy, the learning which he fears in the Clerk, and it thus contributes covertly to the richness of the pilgrimage frame. The third instance is actually used in a sexual context, and is poised between simile and factuality: Jason acts coyly in order to give Hypsipyle the impression that he is not a sexual threat, although he intends to betray her (*Legend of Good Women* 1548). Apart from the criticism that Jason is a deceiver, there is an implicit contempt for a man who behaves like a woman to further male sexual intentions. Basically the same comparator has been given different weight by different contexts and, in the case of Harry Bailley's simile, by an extension towards the sexuality of the wedding night. Although the dissimilarity between topic and comparator remains essentially that of gender, the meaning that the dissimilarity has, and the value placed on it, depend on context.

In a poem which does use clearly marked fabliau elements but, as a whole, is of mixed or uncertain genre, one finds that the same kind of derogatory simile has more complex effect through the contending forces of genre. It does not only work to characterize in a derogatory way but can complicate moral response. January in the *Merchant's Tale* is feminized at the point where he sees his wife having sex with her lover: "And up he yaf a roryng and a cry, / As dooth the mooder whan the child shal dye" (2364–65). In keeping with the ambivalent tone and attitude of the poem, this simile has the effect of making one criticize January as a sexual nonentity at the very point where one is supposedly disgusted by the actions of those who are not. The simile by its denigration of January, forces the reader to respond against the moral direction set by the deceit of the lovers and the violence of their copulating. The dissimilarity between the topic, which is January's observing the sexual act, and the comparator, which is the mother witnessing the death of a child, is extreme. The reader is evidently supposed to register both the feminizing of January and the gross indecorousness of the other association. However, what that indecorum is supposed to make the reader feel is harder to determine. One cannot be sure whether the link should inspire moral outrage instead of, or as well as, laughter. After all, cycle plays on the "Massacre of the Innocents" could involve the gendered comedy of the mothers beating the soldiers at the same time as the scene depicted the horror of soldiers killing children. One also cannot be sure whether the simile reflects on January's failure to discriminate; the narrator's complicity in that failure shown by his seeking a laugh where moral disgust is appropriate; or the narrator's, or Chaucer's, contempt for sexual obsession. Here the dissimilarity in simile constitutes a space for the moral and tonal confusion of the narrative to have full play.

The connection of simile to genre is sometimes made playfully indirect. The Miller is described with a cluster of similes whose grouping and content recall the topos of the outlandish beast in romance:

> His berd as any sowe or fox was reed,
> And therto brood, as though it were a spade.
> Upon the cop right of his nose he hade
> A werte, and theron stood a toft of herys
> Reed as the brustles of a sowes erys
> . . . .
> His mouth as greet was as a greet forneys.
>
> (*General Prologue* 552–59)

But here again, the significance of the similes extends beyond characterization. This gesture towards a genre higher than the fabliau, with which the Miller is supposedly connected by class, outlook, and narratorial choice, actually anticipates the nature of the *Tale* he tells. The elaborate, comic, and allusive description of the Miller in these romance similes adumbrates the intertextual, allusive, and elaborate style of his *Tale*, which quite outstrips the limits of the narrator's character and realistic capacities.

Even where there is no clear generic point to a simile Chaucer can take a conventional comparison and give it local visibility and life. The intrinsic dissimilarity of a clichéd simile will not be enough to make it noticeable, but Chaucer points it up with other elements, such as local tone and imagistic ambience. In the following example, it is the very commonness, even triviality, of the simile that he turns to use. The simile for happiness, "as glad as fowel of day," which was carelessly repeated in the *Shipman's Tale* appears to better effect at a key moment in the *Knight's Tale*. Arcite has just prayed to the God of Mars and has been promised victory: he leaves "As fayn as fowel is of the brighte sonne" (2437). Chaucer highlights the triteness of the comparison by using it in a context which is otherwise devoid of simile but crammed with powerful signs: rattling door handles, smells, flaring fires, ringing statuary. The tone of the simile seems inappropriate in such surroundings, and makes Arcite's joy appear ominously unfounded. Chaucer is using the conventionality of a comparison in context to create suspense and dramatic irony: one knows that things are to turn out badly for Arcite because of this inapposite lightheartedness.

Thematic context can also make a simile which is incidental in one poem contribute to the conceptual depth of another. In the *Legend of Good Women*, Dido's young knights ride about on "coursers swift as any thought" (1195). The fact that the comparator is used for horses, turns the simile into a mere intensifier. But Chaucer gives it quite different force in the *House of Fame*, where we are told that the House of Rumor went about "as swyft as thought" (1924). The topic is now sufficiently connected to the comparator by theme and allegorical style that the reader is invited to investigate the justness of a simile which does indeed add to an understanding of what rumor is: language which is produced with the speed of thought rather than under the control of reflection.

The previous examples have shown that, though some similes retain their meaning across context, other similes are given radically different meanings and force in different locations. There is another type also where Chaucer strongly associates certain themes with a simile but uses the figure in contexts which are themselves independently complex. This combination of determinative context with stability of thematic association challenges the reader to decide whether contexts are mutually informing. Each instance of the simile is fully embedded in its poem, and the poems are neither generically nor ironically related, but the comparisons derive from a deeper concern common to both. The most striking instance of this is the simile of the bird of prey catching a lark, which Chaucer uses both at the sexual consummation of Troilus and Criseyde (3.1191–92) and for the moment in the *House of Fame* when the eagle carries Geffrey aloft in his "clawes starke" (545–46). It seems at least arguable that this common terror of experience, which is implied for Criseyde and explicit in Geffrey, is intimately linked with Chaucer's attitude to language.

The narrator of *Troilus and Criseyde* does not offer the simile as an insight into how Criseyde *feels* when Troilus embraces her, though that is how we may take it. The lines actually read:

> What myghte or may the sely larke seye
> Whan that the sperhauk hath it in his foot?
> I kan na more
>
> (1191–93)

What the lark can say, or is allowed to say, is the issue. Language cannot defer the moment of experience, though it would: words fail or are somehow not permitted. Criseyde is unable to speak, though one is not told whether that is because experience supervenes over language or because the sparrowhawk, Troilus, imposes himself upon her will.

Geffrey in the *House of Fame*, silent, "astonyed and aswewed" (549), is also ravished into experience by the eagle which carries him "in his clawes starke" as lightly as if Chaucer were a lark (545–46). Despite his initial dumbfounded silence, the experience he proceeds to have is largely of the nature of language and, as I argued in chapter 2, the ravisher is linked by imagery to the irresistibility of language. But the experience is also one which Geffrey eventually constrains by not wishing to fly too high.

In the *Troilus* passage speaking is not just a problem for the lark or Criseyde or Geffrey; it is an issue for Chaucer. At the point of consummation, he comments on his own narratorial powers and responsibilities:

> I kan namore; but of thise ilke tweye—
> To whom this tale sucre be or soot—
> Though that I tarie a yer, somtyme I moot,
> After myn auctour, tellen hire gladnesse,
> As wel as I have told hire hevynesse.
>
> (1193–97)

It is a tangle of metapoetic gestures: the narrator is conscious of personal limitations in the face of his own simile for experience; he does not know what the lark can say to the sparrowhawk; he is aware that narrative takes up time; he thinks of his audience; he looks to his "auctour"; he justifies his narrative on the grounds that one must tell both sides of a story. The author's self-consciousness suggests anxiety, and constitutes a deferral of the sexual description. When that is under way Chaucer swings between radically different methods of coping with the challenge which the sexual act poses for the poet who might wish to transmute it into language but realizes he cannot.

These two passages are the only instances in which Chaucer uses the lark and bird of prey as a simile. Whatever their local significance, they indicate a deeper common concern: the nexus between experience and a language which tries to manage, express, and even defer it. However, one wants to ask how far this common theme runs between them. Both scenes link language and experience, but that experience is overtly sexual in *Troilus and Criseyde;* it does not seem overtly so in the *House of Fame.* Sex, death, flying, and the failure of language are certainly present in the *Troilus* but how many of them are also in the *House of Fame?* One might feel that, just as the context of the House of Rumor permitted a significant reading for the simile "swift as thought," a reading denied in the *Legend of Good Women,* so one has to set the sexual specificness of context in *Troilus* against the lack of any such guidance in the *House of Fame.* However, shortly after the eagle grasps Geffrey, Chaucer does indeed mention another *exemplum* for his experience which has sexual implication: Ganymede, who was ravished in the form of an eagle by Jupiter:

> I neyther am Ennok, ne Elye,
> Ne Romulus, ne Ganymede,
> That was ybore up, as men rede,
> To hevene with daun Jupiter,
> And mad the goddys botiller.
>
> (588–92)

His tone is comic and the comparison routed towards drinking; indeed, the comparison is denied; and it appears with others which have no sexual implication. Furthermore, Chaucer's penchant for extending an idea through *exempla* might be enough to explain his including Ganymede. One could further argue that *explicit* context is an important constraint on reading works of this period and particularly so for reading Chaucer, who creatively exploits the differentiating force of context. But it could also be argued that the reference to Ganymede actually imports a sexual reference into the ascent of the eagle with Geffrey which it otherwise would not have had; that it is the Ganymede reference which Chaucer puts last of the list of *exempla* and treats with narrative detail. And one could further suggest that it is made explicit and comic precisely in order that the deeper sexual resonance of the episode for Chaucer can be controlled self-defensively. If the context of interpretation is enlarged to include Chaucer's career-long obsession with writing about women, their sexual betrayal by men, or his own possible rape of Cecily de Champagne, one is left with the sense that the limits of explicit context should not constrain the critic in judging the sexual weighting of this metapoetically charged simile. In such cases, the interpretation of simile is bound up with the critic's general interpretative strategy for texts.

It is not my wish to offer a favored reading of the simile or to determine how far its intertextuality with Troilus and Criseyde should be allowed to run or to choose what depth of context is the appropriate one for reading it, though I should admit that I would be surprised if Chaucer's sexuality and his writing were not somehow both in play (I use the word deliberately) in these passages. Rather, one of the main concerns of this book is to show *how* such decisions are invited, and how they are ultimately qualified by the paradoxical structure of literary comparison. Reading a simile, judging its freight of similarity and dissimilarity, is something which the reader does driven by the reader's own goals. One of the chief attractions of comparison for Chaucer was its capacity to invite such response while ensuring that the response would be contestable by other readers who wished to select a different context for interpretation, or would differently judge the weight of dissimilarity in a simile.

Although Chaucer's creativity shows so well in his contextual deployment of simile, it should not be inferred that he was the only author with this ability, though he certainly shows the skill more generally and consistently than most. Admittedly, also, many writers of popular narrative lacked it entirely. They accidentally stumble into conventional simile and then repeat themselves because a phrase has stuck in the mind. But conventionality of comparator in medieval poems does not always mean conventionality in use, and the skilfully placed simile or the relocated cliché can be productive in the hands of less brilliant talents or writers with less complex literary goals. For example, a very common topos was the comparison of a soldier to a snail. It has its most conventional, though still comic, function in the *Tournament of Tottenham,* where a warrior is rousing himself: "he stirt up as a snaile" (177).[23] But such an obviously degrading use of comparison can create a subtler effect in a different context—in the following lines in the *Laud Troy Book,* for example: "He smot Paris, that he doun reled / Ouer & ouer, as were a snayl" (6742–43). Here the foreground of the simile is the motion of the unhorsed knight. But the image reaches beyond depiction to the convention of linking a failed or foolish knight to a snail. However, the reductive effect here is not primarily intended to create audience laughter. The context shows that the author is using a simile which reflects the shame felt by Paris at being unhorsed in full view of Helen. The simile is designed to characterize psychologically rather than simply to denigrate in line with its conventional function.

The image appears also in the *York Crucifixion* where it gains from the dramatic medium, being uttered by a soldier about himself. The executioners are trying to pull Christ's arm out to the hole already bored for the nail:

> *III Miles.* ȝa, þou comaundis lightly as a lorde;
> Come help to haale, with ille haile.
> *I Miles.*   Nowe certis þat schall I doo—
> Full snelly as a snayle.
> *III Miles.* And I schall tacche hym too,
> Full nemely with a nayle.
> (35.115–20)

The simile is intended by the soldier to declare his reluctance to work hard: he will draw the arm out swiftly ("snelly") as a snail. It may even be an aside to the audience.[24] But it also carries the conventional association with failed soldiery and rebounds on him at the very point where he thinks he is being clever.

Lesser writers than Chaucer can also link a simile's content to its ambience in order to give the conventional idea a new spark. In *Sir Degrevant*, for example, we find this apparently unenterprising simile: "Als þe dere in þe den / To þe dede he þam dyghtis" (339–40).[25] Context gives it much greater force, for those who are being killed by Sir Degrevant "like deer in the valley" are the men who actually killed his own deer illegally. They are being killed in revenge. The crime has just been described and attention drawn to it by the wry humor of the assailants: "Me thynke his hertys of grese / Berys na letters of pese" (265–66). The pointedness of the simile is enhanced by its being the only one used of the battle. The author clearly seeks to fashion a sharp irony out of a conventional description.

Use of simile by a character rather than a narrator can add significance to the comparison—as much in mixed voice narrative as in full drama. In *Susannah*, which is very light on simile, the accusing judges describe Susannah's clothing with a completely conventional simile: "ryche robys arayde reed as þe rose" (212).[26] In its semi-dramatic context, this romantic cliché is not intended by the author to ornament description but is used by the character to claim Susannah's sexual predilections and intentions. In fact it reveals the judges' own, in the same way as colloquial similes define register for the sinful characters in the mystery cycles.

In the *South English Nativity* Joseph is accused by the Bishop and Council of having defiled Mary.[27] The comparison they use for her to strengthen the force of their accusation is as follows "Milder þan any culuer in þe temple was þi wif" (283). But, of course, the image undermines their case with the reader by recalling the dove of the Holy Spirit, which did impregnate Mary, and by anticipating the offering of turtledoves which she later makes at her Purification.

The simile for Mary, the one used in *Susannah,* and by the knight in *York* all show writers allowing similes to subvert their users. In the first section of this chapter I drew attention to statements which, though couched as similes, permitted the audience to read them as literally true or true in a way different from that intended by the user. Because simile makes a claim, and makes it explicitly and without troping language, it offers a chance for the hearer to reflect, possibly to reject, what is said. It is therefore a perfect figure for creating narratorial or dramatic irony.

Sometimes a conventional simile gets new force from other aesthetic tactics in the poem. When the author of *Sir Gawain and the Green Knight* describes the ring which the lady offers to Gawain he uses a simile so ordinary that Chaucer makes fun of the comparator in *Sir Thopas*. The jewel in the ring "bere blusschande bemez as þe bryȝt sunne" (1819). However, one cannot ignore it as one might such a comparison elsewhere: firstly, because it is the only simile in the whole of Fitt 3, and secondly, because the poet has encouraged the reader to regard the few similes that the poem has as indicative of the character's perceptions, not the narrator's desire to ornament. Thus this simile does not so much describe the ring as reveal the beauty which it had for Gawain, who nevertheless turned it down. The bright sun, so clichéd elsewhere, is resonant in this poem of day, of life, of all that Gawain imagines he is losing. The simile is thus the condensed, figurative, version of the beautiful description of the passing seasons which opened Fitt 2 as Gawain contemplated his fatal journey.

Chaucer can use one simile to provide the context for another, so that two ordinary images form a more striking contrast. This is not always the result, of course, either for him or other writers. The *Laud Troy Book,* for example, goes through a phase of using paired similes which do not necessarily form any startling effect but are merely intended to emphasize. It is just one of the habits in using simile which this author, like others working at length, gets into. But *Sir Ferumbras*[28] uses two wholly conventional similes for the victim of an intended rape and her ravisher, and thus highlights the dramatic action and, one suspects, its titillating or horrific quality: "Pan liþ sche þer, þat swete þynge as whit as wales bone" and eight lines later, "Pe þef to hem þan tornd is fas þat was so blac so cole" (2429 and 2437).

All these examples show the authors employing conventional similes or adjusting them with a close eye to their value in context. One of the most successful instances of this is in *Émaré* where simile is deployed to elucidate plot.[29] All its ten similes are highly conventional and repetitive: white as whale's bone or foam or a flower; bright as a summer's day. The poem makes a virtue out of its neatly structured, highly conventional placing of simile. A character's change in fortune is marked by the use of contrasting similes: "She was wax lene as a tre" (365) and "She was bryʒth as someres day" (438). The same character's entrances and exit from the story are also marked by simile. When characters are first described, they receive one conventional simile. Most striking, however, is the fact that all these similes are used in description of women, except one. The simile "Whyte as flour on hylle" (729) is used of the heroine's son, described for the first time, in a work in which the link of mother and son will prove vital for the plot's conclusion. Both the use of simile itself and the comparator associate him with his mother, and we can guess the outcome through reading the strategy of comparison, however conventional the individual images may be. The security of knowing that there will be a happy ending is available to the reader who responds to the conventional rules of the game. Chaucer, however, tends to push at the constraints of genre, or to parody it, and therefore never creates a plot effect which, like that of *Émaré*, relies on convention having been strictly observed elsewhere in the poem. The minor semiotic pleasure which *Émaré* affords through the security of convention is far removed from the depth of suggestion that the lark and sparrowhawk image have in the *House of Fame* and *Troilus and Criseyde*.

This section has sought to show that Chaucer's skilful locating, contextualizing, and revivifying of conventional similes is measurable against the productions of other writers, but Chaucer clearly parts company from them in the complexity of the effects his ordinary comparisons can produce, and in the consistence of this achievement. He also parts company from them in that his deployment of simile has a larger poetic and philosophical significance for him. When he takes conventional and unremarkable *similitudines* and makes them creative through their use in context, he is generating poetry in the very place where he believes that that other form of comparison, *exemplum*, fails. While the conventional *similitudo* can take life from being placed in a new context, the conventional wisdom of *exemplum* cannot easily pass from one situation to another. The special features of the second context are likely to undermine the *exemplum*'s claimed relevance. Conventional similes are thus reborn from the very particularities which defeat the conventional wisdom of *exempla*. One might say that it is the force of particularity which empowers both Chaucer's use of similaic figures and his analysis of received wisdom, but that particularity affects these different aspects of the comparative process in opposite ways: invigorating the former and creatively undermining the latter.

Representing Otherness

Comparison has a doubleness of form and a doubleness in its dynamic which makes it particularly valuable for certain kinds of cultural mediation. It is double in form by having a topic and comparator, usually both expressed in verbal comparisons, and kept separate in a propositional statement which does not twist language from its normal usage. In the case of *imago* the original may not be present but is inferred or imagined. Comparison is double in its dynamic in that it proposes similarity while still leaving dissimilarity in play. We have already seen how different people responded to the possibilities offered by the range of possible dissimilarity, from those who played with the barely figurative to those who exploited greater dissimilarities. But whatever the extent of the dissimilarity, the doubleness of comparison was valuable in its own right. At the minimalist end of the cline of dissimilarity, the double dynamic of comparison allowed the author of the *Laud Troy Book* (otherwise a very creative exploiter of extreme dissimilarity) to convey the strangely double nature of the centaur by speaking of it in a way which both acknowledged the dissimilarity between a centaur and a horse, and yet affirmed that the centaur was a horse. At the other end of the cline, were the theologians who considered "dissimilar similarities" suitable for mediating between earthly and heavenly realms, because these were regarded as both like, and very unlike, each other.

When Chaucer told the eagle in the *House of Fame* that he did not wish to fly to the stars and, by implication, was restricting himself to the world of more ordinary human experience, he ensured that his comparisons would not serve such metaphysical ends. Unlike the *Pearl*-Poet, he does not exploit the inner dynamic of comparison, its similarity and dissimilarity, to represent otherness. He is not concerned with mediating between contrary worlds, unless these are the world of his fiction and the world of his audience. In this last section, I would like to show briefly how the doubleness of similaic comparison can serve such ends.

Any writer who can say that God pours out his gifts "as water of dyche" (*Pearl* 607) must be both confident about managing dissimilarity in comparison, and eager to embrace it. He expects not just to be able to control potential indecorousness while he keeps his eye on the ground of the simile, but believes that there is something positive to be gained by comparing things which are extremely dissimilar in value. Throughout his poems, and at all levels of style and theme, the *Pearl*-Poet reveals a delight in associating dissimilar things as a means of mediating between contrary conditions, values, and judgments. Pearsall and Salter, for example, write of the spiritual geography of *Pearl,* "the relationship between garden and Earthly Paradise is a web of reference and change."[30] We can see this fascination at its most extreme in the poet's account of what happens to the Cities of the Plain in *Cleanness* (1006–48). All that we would consider normal is reversed in their destruction: what was like Paradise became a pit "like of pich fylled" (1008); civilized life is replaced by water, the Dead Sea, and it also reverses the natural condition of water in a way which reflects the reversal of natural sexual law which has inspired the punishment: "lay þeron a lump of led, and hit on loft fletez, / And folde þeron a ly3t fyþer, and hit to founs synkkez" (1025–26). Behind the folksy fascination with horrible reversals of normality lies a basic structure of comparability. While we might in logic distinguish between relations of difference, dissimilarity, oppositeness, and negativity, this author explores the interface between things in all such relationships. All can be found in his poetry, and we must recognize the tension which lies at the heart of them all: the opposites of this section are the extreme manifestation of dissimilarity: the Cities are now as dissimilar to what they were as is possible; what replaces them is as dissimilar to the laws of God's creation as he can decree; what their inhabitants did was unlike what God required of them. It is the *connection* with what is normal that defines the sin and its punishment. The fabric of similarity has been loosened and dissimilarity enlarged through sin, but the connection, the comparability, still holds.

Even in *Sir Gawain and the Green Knight,* where the author is extremely selective in his use of simile, preferring a determined factuality except in key places where he can reflect the perceptions of his characters through the vividness of a comparison, this same pattern of linked dissimilars emerges: structurally, in the bedroom and hunting scenes; imagistically, in the red blood which sparkled on the green skin when the knight's head was cut off. The Green Knight and Bertilak are extremely dissimilar in their environments, cultural image, and methods but in another sense they are identical; the Green Knight is like men but unlike them also.

This poet's special interest in balancing, opposing, and mediating by means of similarity and dissimilarity explains his liking for similes which do not just compare two things directly but set up analogies, or double similes. As well as using similes with the form "a is like b," he uses similes of the form "as a is to b so is x to y." In such similes the relation of the items in a pair is the overt topic of the comparison, but the individual terms in each pair also are covertly compared. Though these similes can be quite brief, they serve to focus and express the larger contrasts of value upon which the poems are based and should be seen as the point at which rhetoric as ornament meets rhetoric as dialectic. Here the form of simile permits a balance which mediates between contrary values or judgments. Thus, in *Patience* for example, when Jonah, thrown into the jaws of the whale, is compared to a speck of dust in a cathedral doorway, the obvious topic of the simile is the vast difference in size between the man who has disobeyed God and the whale which is the instrument of his punishment (268).[31] But the comparator which is chosen to show the size of the whale (the church door), serves to remind us that Jonah is in God's care as much as if he were in church—an important indication of God's mercy when one considers that the whale was traditionally seen as an image of the devil, and his disgustingly devilish insides are lovingly described by the poet. In a poem about judgment and mercy, this double simile perfectly expresses both sides of the equation.

The poet uses the same device to similar ends in *Sir Gawain and the Green Knight*, where judgment and mercy, knowledge and understanding have to be balanced. At the climax of the poem an analogistic simile is fashioned for Gawain. It involves explicit and implicit comparison and it manages the issue of dissimilarity in such a way as to leave a gently ambivalent impression of Gawain's success in his adventure. The Green Knight says, "As perle bi þe quite pese is of prys more, / So is Gawayn, in god fayth, bi oþer gay knyȝtez" (2364–65). Explicitly, the poet does not say that Gawain is like the pearl, that image of perfection in his other poems. Gawain has not reached the pearl's spotlessness, and an overt simile comparing them might permit too great a sense of his achievement, diminishing that degree of dissimilarity between Gawain and the pearl which has emerged since he failed in "trawthe." Instead, the poet employs a simile which shifts the explicit area of dissimilarity towards the quantitative rather than qualitative, comparing Gawain to other knights not to the perfect pearl. Implicitly, however, within the structure of this analogistic simile, the comparison of Gawain to the pearl is still permitted: "As perle . . . So is Gawayn." The overt topic is the magnitude of Gawain's success within the limits of the world of human endeavor; the covert comparison of the terms permits a simile for Gawain which will compare him to the perfection which lies beyond the human, while still acknowledging, as all similaic comparisons do, that there is a dissimilarity. Consequently, the poet not only balances judgment of Gawain but keeps in play the relative and absolute criteria by which judgments can be arrived at.

The most powerful proof of this poet's ability to combine local similaic effect with larger issues comes in *Pearl* where the whole dynamic of the poem mirrors the tension in a simile between similarity and dissimilarity. *Pearl* joins dissimilar worlds, compares dissimilar value systems; explores changed states and identities. In their contrast of the poem's waking and dreaming landscapes, Pearsall and Salter see this exploration in terms of analogy: "The transmutation of natural and passing beauty into a durable form which mirrors or is analogous to 'the artifice of eternity' is a necessary and powerful prelude to the transmutation of human sorrow into spiritual acceptance."[32] Simile, which is structurally double and capable of playing with similarity and dissimilarity, is at the heart of this larger analogistic pattern as the following, almost emblematic, example shows. For this reason I cannot agree with Davenport when he lists the following simile as one of those "Evocative comparisons . . . mainly visual and enhancing in effect."[33] The dreamer is looking at the stones which lie in the bottom of the river which flows along the edge of the earthly paradise:

> In þe founce þer stoden stonez stepe,
> As glente þurȝ glas that glowed and glyȝt—
> As stremande sternez, quen stroþe-men slepe,
> Staren in welkyn in winter nyȝt.
>
> (113–16)

While the explicit emphasis is simply to describe the shining of the stones, this simile is remarkable for its controlled pattern of dissimilarities between all its constituents. The comparators reverse key elements in the topic, while still resting within a positive comparison, not a contrast. Firstly, while the dreamer is looking down into the water, he compares the stones to stars above in the sky. The context in which the comparison is made is a dream which he had in August, and during the day, whereas the stars are from a winter night's sky. Thirdly the dullness of earthly sleep referred to in the third line is being replaced by the vividness of spiritual illumination in the dream. Lastly, the stars are bright for "stroþe-men"—people of a low, dark, soiled world (the implications of "stroþe"),[34] but the stones they describe exist in an elevated, bright, crystallinely pure world. The comparison thus mediates between the earthly and heavenly by its positive form, yet also shows in its careful dissimilarities, that these worlds are distinct. It uses the elements of earthly perception to convey a hint of transcendent experience, and suggests thereby that the transcendent is communicable if one remembers also that human understanding of it will only be partial. Furthermore, it is wholly suitable that this studied arrangement of dissimilarity within similarity should happen where it does, for the simile is describing a river which runs through the dream countryside of the poem, and through the poem's thematic development, as both a barrier and a connection between the dreamer and Heaven: a river of life which can only be reached through death. The conjoining and separating forces of comparison are thus powerfully mimetic of the spiritual geography of *Pearl*. Theological, figurative, and wider literary values for dissimilarity seem to meet here harmoniously.[35]

Sir Orfeo is similarly creative, though on a more popular level, in the different genre of fairy tale, and with more of an interest in *representing* another world than in mediating between it and the earthly world.[36] One does not find, as in *Pearl*, that a dialectic of different values and the realms in which they exist is given formal expression and concentration in the doubleness of a particular simile. Instead, simile contributes to the poem's general interest in doubleness, an interest also expressed through action, plot and incidental detail.

Orfeo's Queen Heurodis is lost to the world of the fairies while sleeping under an "ympe" tree, that is a tree which has been cultivated by having one piece grafted onto another.[37] This dangerous location where two things become one is the point at which the fairy world and the earthly world meet, and the first communication between them is made in the ambivalent world of the dream, which is part of normal experience but is also isolated from that experience by its unusual nature and restriction to a single person. The passage from one world to the other is accompanied by grief which is perhaps the greater because the kingdom which is entered is not an obvious otherworld but rather a likeness of the earthly world which has been left behind. The nature of its likeness hovers between the relative similarity of *imago* and the relative dissimilarity of *similitudo*. There is a King to mirror Orfeo. He wears a crown, but it is made of a precious stone rather than silver and gold. There is a fairy Court and chivalry: men ride to the hunt, though the quarry, and the end of the hunt are never seen. The fairy land is recognizably beautiful, but flat and always bright. Dancing is perfectly, but silently, executed; the hunting horn is blown but is heard faintly. A queen in this world becomes a lady in the other. The power of love which draws Orfeo and Heurodis together has its dangerous opposite in the purely aesthetic values of the Fairy King who would keep them apart because Heurodis is beautiful and Orfeo is coarse and dark.

As part of this interaction between worlds the poem focuses on identity: Orfeo must change from king to harper to pass from one world to the next, and before he can return to his original position he must remain in the new identity in order to test his steward's loyalty to the man he was. His grief leads him to change from a creature of court to a creature of forest, and his appearance alters accordingly. The poet makes much of comparing and contrasting the two conditions. In a similar, almost symbolic way, the hollow wood of the harp must be returned to a hollow tree, in which it is hidden, before it can be reused to effect the salvation of the lovers.

Heurodis, on the other hand changes in subtler ways, unconnected with any disguise needed for plot purposes. She is recognizable at first when Orfeo sees her in the forest, but when he sees her in the courtyard of the fairy castle, he recognizes her by the clothes she is wearing. In a poem which turns on Orfeo's challenge that the Fairy King should be true to his word, and the steward's subsequent loyalty to Orfeo is shown by what he says to the "harper," it is significant that Heurodis loses her speech in her quotation of the Fairy King's threats and then never speaks after she has entered the fairies' power, not even when she returns from it. Other people who have been taken by the fairies remain the same as when they were on earth, but that is the very respect in which they are now different from what we know: Orfeo sees some standing without heads, or bound and mad, or in childbed, and in the courtyard is Heurodis sleeping under another version of the grafted tree.

The poem achieves its great effect through playing on our excited fear that the single may be double; and, conversely, that joining things, as in the grafted tree, warps the individual nature of things; that an identity is not a guarantee of continuity; that life is not single or continuous but a sequence of unsettlingly comparable states: that the world in the puddle can be entered if its thin skin is broken or that the mirror will turn to the consistency of gauze and we will be on the other side. Even if *Sir Orfeo* used no similes at all, it would succeed through the strength of its economic plot and the folk resonance of its central motifs. In that respect simile is more loosely associated with its movement between worlds than in *Pearl*. But simile also contributes significantly to representing the special nature of the fairy world in the following way.

The poem regularly employs those popular similes which constitute genre markers for the reader or hearer making them feel secure in a particular literary ambience. *Sir Orfeo* is highly conventional in the way that *Émaré* is, using the comparators "As white as milke" (146); "As briȝt as þe sonne" (152 and 352 and 372); "Gentil and jolif as brid on ris" (305); "clere and schine as cristal" (358). And, though it stands out from the others in context, the simile "yclongen also a tre" (508) is also fairly conventional. However, despite this conventionality, the writer has clearly thought about where the similes will be placed. All the similes except the last, are used of people with the fairies or aspects of the fairy world. The fairy crown, the fairy land, and the stones in the fairy castle all receive versions of the same simile (comparison with the sun).

The ladies who are with the fairies attract a simile when first seen by Herodis, and then again when seen by Orfeo. Consequently, the final simile is even more forceful. It is not of the fairies, but of Orfeo, a man who has been to their world. It is a marker of the change in his identity which has been necessary to pass from this world to the other. Not only is it the only simile which is not to do with the fairy world, it is the only one which is not laudatory in function, and it thus urges us, at a climactic moment, to consider the pathos of Orfeo's past suffering at his reentry into the normal world.

The author does not use simile heavily as a means of description, but he does seem to use it with selectivity: one can see in the conventional nature of his comparators the "naive" aspect of the poem, but his restricted use of the figure, and tactics for it in the text show more self-conscious artistry. The main difference between *Pearl* and *Sir Orfeo* is that in the latter it is not the internal tension of similarity and dissimilarity in the simile which conveys and mediates the otherness of the nonhuman world. Rather, the selective deployment of simile does this. But one could surely claim that it is simile's doubleness, its employment of what is known and, in this case, conventionally known, to throw light on what is unknown, that makes it a potent device in a poem of doubleness, even if its formal structure is not part of the poem's dialectic. One may feel that simile has a more complex role in *Pearl*, and, in intellectual terms, a more ambitious one. But *Sir Orfeo* suggests that less sophisticated literature can be attractive for similar reasons: by marking what is like and what is not like, simile's natural context is the point where worlds meet.

Medieval authors were evidently aware of the range of possible dissimilarities which could be present in a positive comparison, from the simile which barely escapes from apposition (or is ambiguously related to it) to the simile which can represent larger differences of world or experience by virtue of its combining similarity with dissimilarity. They were conscious too of how to exploit similes in relation to context and they do so in the service of different goals from the purely narrative trick through didacticism to more significantly analytical ends. Chaucer, though a powerful user of conventional similes, was not the only writer to exploit it with skill, and his special abilities in this area need to be seen against the perspective provided by contemporaries working in different modes and for different audiences. However, he was the only writer whose exploitation of it was part of a larger, and often explicit, concern with the comparative process as it could be used and explored at many levels of fiction. The chapters which follow look more specifically at Chaucer's achievements in this wider area.

4
Patterns of Comparison in *Troilus and Criseyde*

Troilus and Criseyde is a long and intricate work, and the comparisons which Chaucer uses in it are deeply rooted in their narrative context.[1] Though they are often set far apart, as often they seem to be related. They also recur frequently. Imagery of hunting birds, of fire, of trees and greenery, of a boat on the sea, of horses, of fishing, of sick men, of the passage of days or seasons, and others can be found throughout, sometimes given metaphorical expression *en passant* as events unfold, and therefore only implicitly comparative, sometimes overtly similaic in form and, consequently, more intrusively situated in the course of events. In the previous chapter I showed how Chaucer's skill lay in the deployment of similes rather than in their invention. I also claimed that this kind of literary skill exposes the interpretative predilections of the reader since the simile is only understood in relation to its context, and that context is defined largely by decisions on meaning arrived at by the reader. Individual comparisons quickly force one to recognize how critical preferences or prejudices are heavily involved in the significance given to figures. The same is true when one claims meaning, or the lack of it, in a sequence of comparisons. While it is relatively easy to spot the recurrence of a simile, it is more difficult to decide how far the lines of significance run between the separate occasions on which it has been used. If the image recurs in different poems, as in the lark and sparrowhawk simile from the *House of Fame* and *Troilus and Criseyde*, readers have to decide whether the fact that the poems are separate works gives a presumptive priority to local context, or whether the recurrence itself argues that the image has a deep significance for the author, requiring the reader to import into the interpretation of one context meanings more overtly present in another. But a version of this argument is latent whenever a simile recurs, even if it is within a single poem. The reader may judge that a comparison owes more to its local context, in which it might fulfil only a conventional function, than to any larger structural strategy of the writer's for developing meaning across episodes. However, literary comparisons provide context for each other, and are both fashioned by preceding ones and retrospectively revalued by subsequent ones. Their significance derives from the reader's wider associations of scene and image and from decisions to include certain comparators in a pattern; to downgrade some to local significance and upgrade others. Such decisions may link similes with the same comparator, or with similes which, though different in their comparators, are deployed in similar contexts and therefore invite interpretative association, comparison and contrast. Just as individual comparisons challenge the receiver to negotiate different degrees of latent dissimilarity so the receiver can form patterns of significance from images which are unlike but otherwise structurally related. Reading similes is thus not unlike the process of deciding on the value of *exempla*. It is a matter of relating contexts, defining salient similarities and dissimilarities, and judging the strength of particularity.

Furthermore, intertextual allusion is a kind of comparison. Though allusions may take a variety of forms from passing reference to full-fledged parallel, and may vary considerably in the overtness with which they are signalled, they appear to invoke a "known" to elucidate the immediate topic, in the same way as other comparisons do. However, as allusions, they often leave the reader to decide whether the "known" text which is invoked is an *imago* of the topic, or a *similitudo*, or an *exemplum*—in other words, whether the allusion is to something very like what is being discussed in the immediate text, or whether it contains a high degree of unlikeness, or whether its likeness is contestable. Such allusions may claim a minor point of similarity while covertly suggesting greater likeness in quite a different respect, or they may import features apparently dissimilar to the immediate topic, but which alter the reader's attitude to it. If such allusions are drawn from the same kind of source, or possess common features they may form a pattern as similes do and take on significance as a group as well as individually. In such cases of intertextual allusive comparison, one is faced with choosing the features of the original text which are relevant to the local context, but also with deciding how the pattern as a whole contributes to the poem.

The present chapter is concerned with recurring or apparently linked comparisons and allusions, the effects which they create, and the critical issues which arise when significance is claimed for them. It also develops these ideas so as to point up the contribution of comparison to the narratorial techniques of Chaucer's longest complete, single narrative poem, the centerpiece of the comparativist phase in his writing. The following section introduces some of the critical issues involved in judging a sequence of comparisons.

The narrator uses two versions of the same simile for Pandarus as

4: PATTERNS OF COMPARISON IN *TROILUS AND CRISEYDE* 121

he moves between Troilus and Criseyde: "But to his neces hous, as streyght as lyne, / He com" (2.1461–62); "And Pandarus, as faste as he may dryve, / To Troilus tho com, as lyne right" (3.227–28). On the face of it, these are formulaic similes with a merely intensive function to emphasise the urgency or keenness of Pandarus by showing how directly he went between the lovers. The same image is employed as a colloquialism by a soldier in the *York* cycle, who promises to hold a banner aloft "as even as a line" (33.244).[2] But, however conventional a comparator the straight line may be, the simile is given greater point if one links it to the celebrated comparison for Pandarus's work:

> For everi wight that hath an hous to founde
> Ne renneth naught the werk for to bygynne
> With rakel hond, but he wol bide a stounde,
> And sende his hertes line out fro withinne
> Aldirfirst his purpos for to wynne.
>
> (1.1065–69)

This comparison in its own context is emphasising the thoughtful prudence of the architect who first sends out in his imagination the builder's line for squaring walls and outlining the plan of a house. Nevertheless there is no reason why the same image might not be used also to show Pandarus's subsequent speedy activity in actually building the house of Love for his clients, Troilus and Criseyde. What appeared formulaic in the two "line" similes seems more significantly patterned when this earlier comparison is included. It could be objected that there is a gap of about 1500 lines between the housebuilder image and the first of the two "line" comparisons, but it is difficult to justify ring-fencing imagery if a reader has in fact made the connection. It would also be possible to argue that the comparisons are formulaic in the sense that one was merely sparked off by the other, whatever distant echo there might be from the housebuilder simile, but this becomes less easy to maintain if one includes narrative structure as part of the relevant context for analysis. These similes frame the plotted meeting between Troilus and Criseyde when Troilus is to offer support at her request and that of Deiphebus. The first occurs when Pandarus goes off to Criseyde to announce the renewed hatred of Polyphete, which will become the pretext for setting up the meeting, and the second when the lovers have met and all Troilus's visitors have gone. Admittedly, Chaucer does not often want to promote the sense that a particular episode or scene has its own narrative integrity. His emphasis is more frequently on proposing tendentious relationships between different sections of poems. Indeed he breaks this scene up with a

Book division. But one can still see the point of beginning and ending the episode with a pair of images which mark it as the deceitful creation of Pandarus. As devices for marking and characterizing such an episode these similes are far from formulaic. Their structural value further supports their association with the housebuilder image: they help to build the scene which is part of Pandarus's architecture of love.

Set against this claim that the comparisons form a pattern is Chaucer's style when marking changes of scene. The first "line" simile occurs in the following context:

> "Syre, al this shal be don," quod Pandarus,
> And took his leve, and nevere gan to fyne,
> But to his neces hous, as streyght as lyne,
> He com
>
> (2.1459–62)

Shortly after this, and before the second "line" simile, Pandarus has occasion to go to Troilus:

> Whan this was don, this Pandare up anon,
> To telle in short, and forth gan for to wende
> To Troilus, as stille as any ston
>
> (2.1492–94)

The final phrase shows a stylistic knee-jerk on Chaucer's part. The stanza has not gone well, even allowing for the dropping of temperature which Chaucer clearly builds in to mark the conclusion of one episode and the start of another. It is flabbily functional, and along with the change of scene comes a supposedly decorative, but actually line-filling, simile. Where Pandarus had gone to his niece's house straight as a line, he goes to find Troilus sitting still as a stone. The structure of the passages is very similar and suggests that both similes may be the result of a stylistic tic.

It is therefore the reader's decision to promote the structural function or imagistic connections of the "line" comparison over its status as part of a rhetorical formula for changing scene. As with individual instances of conventional similes, the reader prioritizes some features over others, and chooses some contexts rather than others in order to determine whether *sequences* of similes are creative or conventional and what special point they might have. While this chapter will now move on to look at some of the special effects and narratological advantages of linked comparisons it must also acknowledge that interpreting them is as open to argument as any other figuration in a poem.

The development of meaning which is possible when comparisons act in sequence can be shown from the following two similes which are immediately linked within the one speech. The imagery of love's fire is frequent in the poem and early in the poem, Troilus develops the narrator's hitherto chiefly metaphorical expression of it into two comparisons which invite analysis because of the overt, self-conscious manner in which they are proposed. Troilus is talking to himself and searching for an imagistic understanding of his condition:

> But also cold in love towardes the
> Thi lady is as frost in wynter moone,
> And thow fordon as snow in fire is soone.
>
> (1.523–25)

The mere fact of having used two linked similes for himself and Criseyde, rather than joining them in a single image, has the effect of formally acknowledging his separateness from her, while making the desired connection with her. But the pairing works in another way also, for it is embarked on with one apparent ground and another is suggested as it ends. The ground of the first comparison is stated to be Criseyde's coldness of feeling, but as the image of cold is carried through to describe Troilus also, the ground of the pairing turns out not to be amatory coldness, but the differing capacities of the two people to endure: Criseyde is cold in a cold world, Troilus like something cold in a hot world; Criseyde's coldness is natural and longlasting, Troilus's is instantly destructible. In contrast to Troilus's opinion, the reader can sense, and even approve, the integrity of Criseyde's condition as expressed in her simile, while also feeling sympathetic excitement for the passionate fragility of Troilus. Similes which work in relation to each other can thus be the medium of changing the reader's opinions, modulating between judgment and sympathy in a way not wholly unlike that found in the *Pearl*-Poet's analogistic similes. Though individual gestures of comparison, they are not bound to communicate only single, discrete ideas. This particular pair does describe the states of the two lovers, but works beyond Troilus's intention.

A recurring detail may work retrospectively to give meaning to an earlier allusion and thus to shape it as part of a pattern of comparison, a function not evident at the time. A well-known instance of this is found in the image of the "boar." Shortly before the lovers' union in Book 3, and in a passage not based on Boccaccio, Troilus prays to various gods and goddesses invoking their past amours (3.715–35). He starts the series by praying to Venus mentioning her love for Adonis, who was killed by a boar (720–21). All the allusions contain unpleasant detail or have unfortunate connotations, and this evinces Troilus's fearfulness in the face of his approaching meeting with Criseyde. At least, that is the dramatic meaning given to it by Pandarus's reaction, "Thow wrecched mouses herte, / Artow agast so that she wol the bite?" (736–37). Of course, they have another effect on the reader, not assimilable within the immediate interplay of the characters: they bode ill for the love, and prepare for its unhappy end. Troilus's allusions will prove to be comparisons grounded deeper than he thinks. But while this may be sensed at the time, it is only in retrospect that one sees the full literary irony behind the leading reference of the group: the mythic destruction of Venus's favorite by a boar.

Late in the poem Troilus dreams that a boar is kissing Criseyde (5.1241), and Cassandra interprets it as a reference to Diomede, who has the boar as his device. Although the mythic history of the boar which Cassandra employs to explain Troilus's dream is different from the myth of Adonis alluded to by Troilus in Book 3, a pattern of significance is retrospectively formed between the mythic and the dream boars. Though Troilus's reference to the gods is only suggestively comparative, the later boar reference changes its force and meaning. When Troilus alludes to the loves of the Gods, his focus is upon the desperation and strength of divine feeling. When the boar reappears as the rival lover Diomede through the ambiguous analogy of dream and Cassandra's interpretation, it shifts the earlier allusion towards *similitudo* and its ground towards the disaster of love rather than the strength of love. The analogy is now retrospectively changed from the strength of Troilus's feelings being like the strength of Venus's love to Troilus being killed by a boar just as Adonis was. The later, dream comparison is closer even than similitude: it is more an instance of *imago* formed through the physical identity of the boar and Diomede in the dream, and corresponding to the iconic identity promised by Diomede's badge. The poem does not acknowledge this retrospective effect, but the reader can hardly avoid noticing it: meaning in literary comparison is not simply a function of transferring what is known from earlier parts to the illumination of what is new. It works in the opposite direction also.

Linked scenes can create patterns of comparison, one providing a context in which to read the other.[3] In the following two pairs of scenes, one can see the very different effects created when the first scene is imagistically treated and the second is not, and vice versa. When the imagistically weighted scene precedes a more literal one the resulting narrative pattern lacks dynamism, though it may have other kinds of value and appropriateness. This effect is evident from the scenes in which Troilus first sees Criseyde, and Criseyde first sees

Troilus from her window. Both characters react similarly: Troilus is "glad his hornes in to shrinke" (1.300) and Criseyde "Gan in hire hed to pulle, and that as faste" (2.657). Although neither description is overtly similaic, the first implicitly compares Troilus to a snail, the comic simile for degrading a warrior which was treated in the last chapter. The second has no such imagistic content. Both episodes point up the privatising effect of love, but whereas one is comically rhetorical, in keeping with the heavily imagistic, even iconographic, presentation of Troilus's relation to love in Book 1, the second is comically naturalistic in keeping with the presentation of Criseyde's responses at this point in Book 2. The first could not be said to direct or prepare for the reading of the second, as is the case with the two scenes I will discuss next. There is no dynamic of significance linking the two; instead the comparable scenes provide a more formalized diptych of the lovers' reactions, signalling the decorum of Chaucer's chosen style to his subject matter: Troilus, the iconized lover; Criseyde, the more naturalistically perceived woman. This establishment of paired scenes for reflective comparison by the audience is found extensively in the poem, and will be discussed elsewhere.[4] In this case it creates at the level of event a pictorial patterning in accordance with the formal portraiture of the lovers in Book 5, but it encourages the reader to observe the characters rather than to judge or reflect upon them. Very different is the effect of the next pair of scenes which are linked by the motif of Criseyde looking from her window, and in which the literal is succeeded by the imagistic.

The two occasions on which Criseyde sees Troilus from her window in Book 2 are strongly contrastive.[5] In the first (2.610–51), Chaucer, seeing as it were through Criseyde's eyes, comically reveals the erotic effect which Troilus has on her, as he returns from battle basking in general acclaim and in the ludicrously heroic equivalent of muddy boots and torn football jersey. The key to the episode, however, is that it is not engineered by Pandarus, but has occurred by chance. In one stanza, Troilus goes a little red with embarrassment at the praise he is receiving (2.645).[6] In the next, Criseyde goes red on recognizing her growing attraction to him (2.652). Neither response is in Boccaccio. Though he balances these blushes formally against each other by their stanzaic position (each is the first line in its stanza), Chaucer is encouraging the reader to enjoy, and possibly to laugh at, natural reactions. The episode offers an exposure of complex feelings and of Criseyde's susceptibility to certain images. But her blush is presented within the fiction as natural, and the feelings of the protagonists are unguarded, and undirected by a sense that the other is watching.[7] Neither is presented imagistically.

When Pandarus later arranges that Troilus should ride below Criseyde's window (2.1247–70) the scene is rerun with significant differences. (Again, this is not in Boccaccio.) The reader is told that Criseyde responded to the vision of the manly knight, but this response comes last. The direction of sight has now been significantly altered: Criseyde, though seeing, is actually the object of sight rather than the independently sentient observer she was in the earlier episode. Pandarus forces her to stay in the window and be seen in the stereotypical position of the knight's lady looking down on him (2.1254–55). As the romantic object, it is not surprising that this time Criseyde goes red in a recognizably romantic way. Chaucer uses the standard romantic simile for her blush, and by this means subtly makes one feel that Criseyde is colluding in the romantic role which Pandarus has established for her; she is playing her part despite her apparent denial of it: "'Nay, nay,' quod she, and wex as red as rose" (2.1256). The natural blush is now a blush with many literary antecedents. Chaucer wishes to shift from the subtlety of unselfconscious but complex emotions in the earlier episode towards the more arch subtlety of conventional ones in the later version of the scene. He achieves this by using a conventional simile working against an earlier nonfigurative account of the same fact in scenes which, by their similarity, invite comparison. The combination of natural blush and conventional blush makes the simile for the latter more visible, and wholly unconventional in its literary function.

Just as she changes during the courtship from independent observer to beloved object, Criseyde's relationship to Troilus is fixed by a further shift in similaic comparison after they have consummated their love. At the end of Book 3 she is again mentioned as watching him from her window. Again simile is part of the structural development. This time the emphasis of the narrative is firmly on Troilus's achievement of chivalric and courtly perfection. In war, he is second only to Hector, and

> In tyme of trewe, on haukyng wolde he ride,
> Or elles honten boor, beer, or lyoun;
> The smale bestes leet he gon biside.
> And whan that he com ridyng into town,
> Ful ofte his lady from hire wyndow down,
> . . . .
> Ful redy was hym goodly to saluwe.
>
> (3.1779–85)

The line I have missed out introduces a different comparator into the recurring scene of Criseyde at a window. She is not "as red as rose";

now she is "As freshe as fawkon comen out of muwe."[8] In a kind of imagistic and scenic *entrelacement,* the simile weaves the male imagery of falcons used by Troilus and Pandarus in Book 1 into Criseyde's special location, her room and window. It also makes Criseyde into an extension of the courtly hunting which she is congratulating in Troilus. Stanbury writes of the lover's gaze and its penetration of seclusion: "The poem's ... fractures of private space seem to be mimicked as well in its ocular lines."[9] I would add that this fracturing is brought about powerfully through the patterning of *similitudo.*

The implication that Criseyde is Troilus's special possession is hard to avoid, and unattractive. The rest of the poem suggests that Chaucer would have found it at least problematic. But the simile of the hawk is a subtler one, more complex, and more representative of the ambivalent worth of the courtship. The ground of the comparison is not just ownership but a mutually willing intimate relationship which has only been achieved because one of the parties has been first deprived of will by the constraints of training and deprivation. Despite this harsh implication, it claims that that party has finally come to a fuller being, a nobler and more civilized mode of life through cooperating in the use which the other makes of it. The simile has considerable potential for making the reader review and evaluate the means by which Criseyde has now reached this state of courtly happiness.

It could be argued that the image of the hawk, far from representing the tension between achieved love and the means by which it was achieved, is actually suggested by the literal context, in which Troilus's hunting is being described. The use of the falcon is, perhaps, no more than one of those pleasant blurrings of the literal into the figurative which we encountered in the previous chapter. However, what prompts a more intensive reading of the falcon image under discussion is not just the demonstrable aptness of its grounds, when closely investigated, to the tensions and paradoxes of the love between Troilus and Criseyde, but also the fact that its narrative context clearly goes back, past the immediate description of Troilus as huntsman, to include previous instances of Criseyde appearing in the window.

One could argue further that the context also includes the next occasion on which a simile is used for Criseyde. That is well into the fourth book, for the opening of the book concentrates heavily on Troilus's response to the news of Criseyde's impending departure. But despite the 450 line gap, the first instance of comparison applied to Criseyde picks up the hunting falcon image again. However, this time it is ominous for overtly degrading her. In lines not based on Boccaccio, Pandarus is urging Troilus to turn to another woman for comfort. They all have their qualities:

> If this be goodly, she is glad and light;
> And this is fair, and that kan good aright.
> Ech for his vertu holden is for deere,
> Both heroner and faucoun for ryvere.
>
> (4.410–13)

There is an integrity of imagistic line passing through the three occasions when Criseyde is seen in the window and on to the point where she is absent. First the window motif shows her, uncompared, as an independent lover; then, with the conventional simile of the rose, in a conventional role as loved one; then figuratively as a falcon, an extension of her courtly lover's hunting; then as the window motif is lost, the falcon image takes over the continuity and shows her as just one of the specialized hunting birds men use, good for one thing, inappropriate for another. The existence of such a pattern carried on across many lines has considerable implications for our sense of Chaucer as an artist. It implies that he kept a clear sense of imagistic fields and their possible developments independent of the sheer weight of intervening narrative.

Even more revealing of Chaucer's narrative practice is the fact that this imagistic integrity cuts across the distinctions of speaker which modern readers tend to prioritize because of the realist novel, and the relatively greater place which dramatic tradition has in our culture over that of the late fourteenth century. It is Chaucer's narrator who uses the first simile of the falcon; Pandarus who uses the second, but the similes work both against and with each other. A study of Chaucer's comparisons reveals not only his penchant for neat associations of simile with context, but also a more revealing promotion of imagistic integrity over the aesthetic, quasi-dramatic, boundaries between different speakers. The result is an often ironic or poignant univocality which takes over at times from dramatic distinctiveness and dramatic perspective. Examples of this univocality are not hard to seek. The narrator's description of Criseyde as "She, this in blak" (1.309) is repeated a book later by Pandarus as if in quotation of Troilus: "so soore hath she me wounded, / That stood in blak" (2.533–34). The perspective provided by different levels of speaker, narrator, and character, is ironed out in this repetition of a striking phrase, and a degree of authority is conferred on Pandarus's mission when it so clearly represents the narrator's own description of events.[10] More than once Chaucer repeats, or develops, a particular similaic comparison across this aesthetic boundary. The following instance is Chaucer's creation, not based on Boccaccio.

When Criseyde is mulling over, between hope and fear, the possibility of loving Troilus, the narrator says,

> But right as when the sonne shyneth brighte
> In March, that chaungeth ofte tyme his face,
> And that a cloude is put with wynd to flighte,
> Which oversprat the sonne as for a space,
> A cloudy thought gan thorugh hire soule pace,
> That overspradde hire brighte thoughtes alle
>
> (2.764–69)

Chaucer then gives insight into what Criseyde is thinking and, indeed, it is the same simile which is operating in her mind as was working in the narrator's:

> For love is yet the mooste stormy lyf,
> Right of hymself, that evere was bigonne;
> For evere som mystrust or nice strif
> Ther is in love, som cloude is over that sonne.
>
> (2.778–81)

Unlike those authors who simply cannot get a simile out of their heads, Chaucer appears to embrace the extension of simile across boundaries of speaker, and he works with it. Here the device is at once sympathetic and evasive: it creates a seamless web of narrator and character, in which the caution of Criseyde has first been recognized and shaped in the imagery of the narrator, yet it also substitutes for narratorial judgment. It shows the narrator diluting his presence by merging into characters as, for example, the Manciple merges into the voice of his mother at the end of his *Tale*, and as he dilutes it in this poem and elsewhere by invoking false or real authorities, and by claiming ignorance.[11]

A study of how comparisons flow between narrator and characters argues that narrative poets, albeit writing in the "middle voice" where characters and narrator speak, did not feel bound to create dramatic perspective. Rather characters and narrator could be considered part of the same narrative, rhetorical, or imagistic cloth in which dramatic distinctions of voice might be allowed to appear as raised threads or, equally, might not. That is the light in which we must view Chaucer's creative, and to students often confusing, use of voices in the *Merchant's Tale*, where, for example, the narrator's ironic praise of marriage blends almost seamlessly into January's sincere but foolish praise of marriage. The "mixed voice" in which narrator and characters speak has obviously ambivalent potential. The conditions for the play upon voice which modern readers value as exposing the difficulties of communication were established by the contrary possibilities of narrative univocality and dramatic perspective.[12] The question must arise, however, as to whether the repetition of comparisons between speakers comes about simply because an image has stuck in Chaucer's mind. The problem in other, more popular, narrative poems is deciding on where depth of reading is not simply the critic's ingenuity. In general, however, *Troilus and Criseyde* supports the claim that Chaucer's linear effects of comparison are not just in the eye of the beholder.

When Troilus is told by Pandarus that a day has been set for the lovers to establish a more fixed relationship, he is overjoyed and Chaucer gives a long simile to expressing this

> But right so as thise holtes and thise hayis,
> That han in wynter dede ben and dreye,
> Revesten hem in grene whan that May is,
> Whan every lusty liketh best to pleye;
> Right in that selve wise, soth to seye,
> Wax sodeynliche his herte ful of joie
>
> (3.351–56)

Three lines later, Troilus assures Pandarus of his good intentions towards Criseyde, and he starts thus:

> Frend, in Aperil the laste—
> As wel thow woost, if it remembre the—
> How neigh the deth for wo thow fownde me,
> And how thow dedest al thi bisynesse
> To knowe of me the cause of my destresse
>
> (3.360–64)

Here, the simile of the reinvigorated greenery does not end with the narrator. One thinks that it has been employed simply to express the change in Troilus's spirits during this conversation with Pandarus, but it becomes larger in scope as the imagistic reference to May by the narrator is turned into a literal reference to April by Troilus, and this, together with the link between dead and dry hedges and the nearly dead Troilus sustains the simile beyond the point where it has been rhetorically closed down. The result of this extension of the simile is that, in a wholly covert manner, one is brought to see Pandarus, not as a vicariously sexual artist, but as the quickening force of Nature, the natural ally of love. He has been to Troilus as the force which clothes the hedges and woods in green.

I do not believe that Chaucer is responding unthinkingly to his simile in the earlier stanza, the conventional image of May suggesting the reference to April, which was in fact when Troilus went into the temple and saw Criseyde. In fact, although Chaucer is following Boccaccio in his simile of the greenery, it is Chaucer who adds the reference to May in the narrator's simile, and to April in Troilus's response. Admittedly, Troilus's description of himself as nearly dead for woe is highly conventional and does not necessarily argue a deliberate extension of the earlier simile's use of dead greenery. One of these stanzas is by the narrator, one by a character; one formally similaic, the other only suggestively linked to the simile by details which are themselves factually or conventionally authorized. However, this chapter has already shown how Chaucer exploits associations between imagistic and nonimagistic accounts of the same thing. Although the style shifts from the figurative to the literal, the latter is imbued with figurative resonance, and is assimilated into the figure which preceded it. The reading which results here is richly significant and in keeping with Chaucer's literary strategies elsewhere: it leaves us with a favorable view of Pandarus which cannot be solely ascribed to Troilus because it builds upon a narratorial simile, and yet cannot be wholly ascribed to the narrator either because it is the reader who has decided to associate the two statements. One feels closer to Chaucer's strategy of aligning his narrator with his characters when one reads in this way. The episode also reminds one that comparisons in a literary context do not necessarily end when their rhetorical markers appear to indicate this. To give a simile and then say "Right in that selve wise," need not end the influence of the comparison.

A more overt instance of simile developed powerfully between narrator and character occurs when the effect of Criseyde's letter on Troilus in Book 2 is described, a passage not based on Boccaccio. We are told,

> as an ook comth of a litil spir,
> So thorugh this lettre which that she hym sente
> Encrescen gan desir, of which he brente.
> (2.1335–37)

Following this account by the narrator, Troilus has recourse to Pandarus to talk about his growing longing, and Pandarus tells Troilus what he thinks must be going through Troilus's head at a time like this. The tree which was growing from a little shoot is now more mature: Troilus must be worried that "though she bende, yet she stant on roote" (2.1378). He shouldn't worry, but rather think,

> whan that the stordy ook,
> On which men hakketh ofte, for the nones,
> Receyved hath the happy fallyng strook,
> The greete sweigh doth it come al at ones
> (2.1380–83)

From sapling to timber, the oak tree comparison has grown between narrator and character across forty lines, changing its application as it goes. The small growing oak tree of Troilus's love has now become the stricken oak of "Daunger" in Criseyde. The subliminal cooperation between narrator and Pandarus in this image helps to impart that deterministic quality which one always feels is present directing the courtship despite the insight one gets into Criseyde's, apparently independent, decision making. This is one example of Pandarus's noted capacity to blend stylistically into a variety of situations.[13] But the effect in this case goes beyond the character, working across aesthetic levels and making the author and characters alike appear to be reflecting an inexorable reality beyond their words.[14]

The poem as a whole combines delicacy of subject, image, narratorial attitude, and audience response with intermittently brusque or shocking allusions, episodes or judgments, such as Criseyde's complaint about the falseness of the world, or the threatening discussion which Pandarus engineers about Polyphete, or Hector's letter about whether an unnamed man should be hanged, which is discussed to allow the lovers privacy in Troilus's bedroom, or indeed the narrator's own final fierceness about paganism. Chaucer's patterns of comparison contribute to this mixture, sometimes working in barely perceptible ways to link and shape characters and events, and to engage the reader's sympathetic cooperation with love's progress, and then creating quite brutal effects which distance the reader and invite judgment, even disgust for the means by which love is achieved. This mixture of strategies and its consequent mixing of responses helps create the ambivalent status of the poem as at once a noninstructive, unique experience, and also as a record of events which one could employ as an instructive "example."

This effect is well demonstrated by a group of comparisons which appear at a complex moment in the progress of love in Book 2. The section runs from Criseyde hearing Antigone's song after having seen Troilus riding beneath her window through to Pandarus's plan for Troilus to write a letter and ride past Criseyde's window again the following day. It includes a shift of narrative from Criseyde to Troilus, and a double account of the evening spent by them. It is also poised between night and promised day. Criseyde hears Antigone sing:

> What is the sonne wers, of kynde right,
> Though that a man, for fieblesse of his yen,
> May nought endure on it to see for bright?
> Or love the wers, though wrecches on it crien?
>
> (2.862–65)

The immediate effect of the comparison is to enoble love by its implicit association with the sun, and to make the activity of love seem

4: PATTERNS OF COMPARISON IN *TROILUS AND CRISEYDE*

immune from the judgment of lesser people who cannot feel it. All this is abating the fearfulness Criseyde feels about it. She goes on to dream of the exchange of her heart with a noble eagle. When the narrative shifts to Troilus, and back to the start of the evening, the narrator describes the joy with which he receives Pandarus's news that Criseyde is well-intentioned towards him:

> But right as floures, thorugh the cold of nyght
> Iclosed, stoupen on hire stalke lowe,
> Redressen hem ayein the sonne bryght,
> And spreden on hire kynde cours by rowe,
> Right so gan tho his eighen up to throwe
> This Troilus
>
> (2.967–72)

The earlier image was from a character's song to another character, this from the narrator directly to the reader, but they clearly work together despite the different dramatic perspectives in which they lie. Taken together, the reader's feelings are subtly controlled: the pairing affirms that Troilus is not a "wrecche" who cannot or dare not look on the sun of love, but it also implicitly makes Criseyde that sun, informing the episodes in which he sees her in Book 2, shifting the force of his first sight of her from "this in blak" (1.309) to a quite different image; developing also away from the comparison he drew earlier between her and "frost in wynter moone" (1.524). The narrator, rather than the character, makes these associations and shifts possible, and the reader is accordingly drawn into emotional sympathy with the change wrought in Troilus by Pandarus's action on Criseyde.

However, the second comparison also shifts the time frame, for it talks of flowers responding to the coming of day, and in doing this almost brings forth the day before the day is born. Criseyde is in the world of dream, but Troilus is imagistically, and in his eagerness, already waking up to the next morning. This playing with night and day is, of course, a recurrent interest of Chaucer's, most obviously expressed in the different values which night has for lovers before and at the time of consummation, but also part of the larger narratorial management of time which in Book 5 tragically takes the reader in Criseyde's and Diomede's company beyond her promised reunion with Troilus on the tenth day, before returning to an expectant and anxious Troilus. In this particular case, however, it encourages the reader's own emotional investment in the love-making, carrying the mind through to the next day's possibilities. One is seduced by the beauty of the flowers waking up to the sun into looking forward to the continued flowering of love.

At this point, Chaucer abruptly breaks up the pattern of imagery in a way which degrades Troilus's eagerness and chastens the reader. Troilus asks Pandarus,

> How shal this longe tyme awey be dryven
> Til that thow be ayein at hire fro me?
> Thow maist answere, "Abid, abid," but he
> That hangeth by the nekke, soth to seyne
> In gret disese abideth for the peyne.
>
> (2.983–87)

The urban realism of the image, which Chaucer recalls twice in the bedroom, through the sections on Polyphete and Hector's letter, brushes aside the natural imagery of flowers and morning sun, and Troilus, by his own image, appears more like the "wrecche" which the previous pair of images seemed to distinguish him from.

In addition to the immediate point of comparisons, it is clear, then, that much of their operation upon us derives from the patterns which they form and break down. One reads them in sequence and in combination, whatever their source in the fiction, and Chaucer evidently capitalizes on this to maintain a balance of judgment and involvement dissociated from a particular voice. Sometimes, however, a particular sequence of comparisons may be more deeply suggestive than its immediate contribution to the work suggests, and reflection may shift one's understanding of the imagery. The comparison of love with fire in various forms such as sun, the heat of fever, burning torment, etc., is ubiquitous in the poem, and is supported by a corresponding imagery of cold for emotional indifference or horror. But it also has its less elevated, more brutally realistic, variant in the idea of a house fire. Pandarus, as one might expect, gives it this dimension first, in urging Criseyde to act quickly towards Troilus's (feigned) jealousy as one would towards domestic conflagration:

> For whan a chaumbre afire is, or an halle,
> Wel more nede is, it sodeynly rescowe
> Than to dispute and axe amonges alle
> How this candel in the straw is falle.
>
> (3.856–59)

The immediate effect of this homely reduction of love's customary imagery is to point up the ignoble falsehood of the jealousy which the fire is ostensibly representing. But the image appears again with a rather different, and more significant, application in a context where one's sympathies are very much with the lovers: at the debate over whether Criseyde should be exchanged for Antenor. Hector opposes the exchange, but we are told, "The noyse of peple up stirte thanne at ones, / As breme as blase of strawe iset on-fire" (4.183–84).[15] The rush of flame, its noise, speed, and danger, is the more tragic for the worthlessness of its source. Resonant in the comparison is one's sense of the impending destruction of Troy by fire, which will follow on from the return to the city of the traitor Antenor who is here so fierily demanded. Behind the image of the comparison thus lies its literal correlative—a further instance of Chaucer exploring that mysterious relationship between the figurative and the "real" which we have already encountered several times.

Although both comparisons have a clear immediate function, one to denigrate Pandarus's work and the other to dramatize an ominous moment in Troy's history, the reason they both appear may have more to do with Chaucer's thoughts about language itself. If one recognizes this, Pandarus's comparison of Troilus's jealousy to a fire appears in a different light from that intended by Pandarus. When the narrator presents Pandarus's story of Troilus's jealousy, he makes the tenuous worthlessness of the claim evident through the tortured course of reported rumor: "He seith hym told is of a frend of his / How that ye sholden love oon hatte Horaste" (3.796–97). When Troilus later has to justify his pretended jealousy, the narrator, though now complicit with the deception in the cause of love, nevertheless also shows the cracks in Troilus's credibility, and introduces an idea not far removed from the straw on the floor mentioned in Pandarus's comparison:

> He seyde hire, when she was at swiche a feste,
> She myght on hym han loked at the leste—
> Noot I nought what, al deere ynough a rysshe
>
> (3.1159–61)

In the *House of Fame*'s more explicit account of language, rumor is described in familiar terms:

> Thus north and south
> Wente every tydyng fro mouth to mouth,
> And that encresing ever moo,
> As fyre ys wont to quyke and goo
> From a sparke spronge amys
> Til al a citee brent up ys.
>
> (*House of Fame* 2075–80)

The fabricated rumor which led to the conflagration of Troilus's jealousy; the speech of justification which tails off into something worth no more than a rush; the fiery roar of ignorant popular demand which threatens the lovers and the city—all emanate from Chaucer's sense of the potential threat of language, a threat he wants to expose in the case of Pandarus, ignore in the case of Troilus, and sympathetically dramatize from the point of view of the victims at the debate over Criseyde. Opinions, suggestions, claims, explanations, tidings all seem to partake both of the straw and the spark, because when the fire has started the two cannot be distinguished. It would be simplistic to say that the threat of language is felt by Chaucer to be external either to his class, or his study: that it is just the common people who threaten in *Troilus,* or the outside world of tidings on which, the eagle in *House of Fame* says, "Geffrey" shuts his door. The pattern of comparisons in *Troilus* suggests that the threat is inherent in language. But this also suggests that one should revalue Pandarus's comparison: the house fire which Pandarus suggests is taking hold is not really the fire of Troilus's jealous love, as Criseyde is intended to interpret it, but on reflection is simply the rumor-kindled fire of language used to further the lover's ends—dangerous, unreliable, worthless. The man who planned his love strategy as an architect plans a house, now includes the house burning down as part of that plan. One can't help feeling that Criseyde's appropriate response to this particular candle in the straw would have been a bucket of water, rather than acceptance of Pandarus's implied interpretation.

The close association which Chaucer forges here and elsewhere in his oeuvre between the imagery of conflagration and language shows that Pandarus's simile embraces the medium of the creative artist just as Pandarus himself has been seen as a quasi-authorial presence.[16] Chaucer's own hesitancies, evasions, and doubts about language form the deep structure of Pandarus's lie. If Chaucer feels that language is like a fire getting out of control, he employs various devices apparently to protect himself against responsibility for the fire he has started. Evasiveness, inconclusiveness, fragmentation of the authorial voice, the use of *personae,* parody, digression, ascribing opinions to characters, clerks, authors, and so on, all serve at once to give the impression of the rush of language on fire while preventing the reader from tracing it confidently to its real source. At the same time, however, just as the Pardoner in his *Tale* feels compelled to confess his own fault, Chaucer shows a compulsion to make this artistic deception evident. Chaucer reminds the reader of the true source of the creation precisely by employing narratorial stand-ins; he claims digression rather than simply digressing. The various masking activities in which Chaucer engages only serve to draw attention to the fact that the mask is not reality, that there is a face behind it. Throughout this book the metapoetic implications of comparison will tend to reveal this artistic paradox. Recognizing that language is untrustworthy does not lead Chaucer to abandon the medium. Acknowledging that particularity resists explication by general rules does not prevent him from formulating such rules. Flawed *exempla* are not abandoned but multiplied; ungrounded *imagines* are still teasingly offered as glimpses of reality; the extent of dissimilarity is not reliably mapped even if its contours are visible, and an inability to express the joys of sexual consummation demands more not fewer similes for it. Thus comparativist thinking is exposed while recurring nonetheless at all levels of his work. Even when he claims, through his narrator, failures of narratorial experience and the inadequacy of his sensibility for writing about love, the pattern formed by his comparisons may belie the statement.

Chaucer opens the *Prohemium* to Book 2 thus:

> Owt of these blake wawes for to saylle,
> O wynd, O wynd, the weder gynneth clere;
> For in this see the boot hath swych travaylle
> Of my connyng, that unneth I it steere
>
> (2.1–4)

Although he expresses it metaphorically, Chaucer clearly sees the image as functioning like a simile, for he proceeds to explain it to us (5–6). The sea is Troilus's tempestuous despair, and the boat is like the poem itself, in danger of being overwhelmed by its subject matter under the guidance of an unskilled pilot who cannot cope with, or perhaps even understand, the emotions of love. However, while the narrator appears modestly to distance himself from the material, the comparison tends in a different direction, for it develops imagery already employed by the very lover whose experiences are so taxing the narrator. These comparisons develop the "Canticus Troili" of Book 1 in which Troilus described himself thus:

> Al sterelees withinne a boot am I
> Amydde the see, bitwixen wyndes two,
> That in contrarie stonden evere mo.
>
> (1.416–18)

The *Prohemium* imagery does not merely express the sympathy of the author for his character; it covertly asserts an imagistic identity between the progress of the poem and the progress of the lover. Both narrator and lover are steersmen of their vessels in difficult conditions. Thus, while the content of Chaucer's Book 2 *Prohemium* is saying one thing, the imagistic link of his opening comparison with an earlier one, is asserting the opposite: demonstrating that total control over the progress of the poem which he claims to lack, and an emotional affinity with the lover which he frequently denies, implying the closeness between the business of the lover and the business of writing about love.

The patterns of comparison discussed so far have depended on identifiable similarities either between the images themselves or between the contexts in which they are being used. The last group of comparisons in this chapter are linked by similarities of this kind, but their most obvious common characteristic is that, whether implied through allusion or overtly presented as comparison, they involve the reader being directed to other texts, mostly Boethius, Ovid, and Dante, and hence carry with them the possibility that some features of these texts, though unmentioned in *Troilus,* may nevertheless valuably inform understanding of Chaucer's poem.[17] It is in these features, rather than in the stated reason for their use, that one can often see patterns of meaning emerging. Chaucer lets individual comparisons have their own local force, such as the gentle irony with which Pandarus is implicitly associated with Boethius's Philosophy, when he applies to Troilus her image of an ass unable to appreciate music (1.731–35). But this chapter is concentrating on the meaning that comparisons may have by virtue of their relations with each other. The allusions in question are those to Titius (1.786–88), Procne (2.63–70), Tantalus (3.592–93), Alcmena (3.1427–28), Oedipus (4.300), Proserpina (4.473–76), Myrrha (4.1138–39), Athamas (4.1539–40), Ixion (5.211–12) and to a lesser degree, Amphiorax (2.100–05).[18]

Readers of Chaucer are used to the tenuous or specious manner in which he often links successive sections of his poems together. This is particularly evident in the dream poems, and is implicit in the pilgrimage frame of the *Canterbury Tales*.[19] Whether one believes that this comes from a desire to mask or to facilitate his dialectical line depends on what one believes the point of the poems to be. A corresponding tactic is evident in Chaucer's use of intertextual comparisons: the dialectical possibilities of opening up a textual link can be obscured, even flouted, by the trivial or explicit manner in which the link is suggested. For example, the stated ground for Pandarus's alluding to Titius is the comic claim that Troilus is suffering from love pangs as severely as Titius suffered from the vultures tearing his liver. The reference to Procne comes as part of a romantic topos of birds singing on May morning. Tantalus is someone whose deep position in Hell Pandarus would be worthy to match if he betrayed Criseyde's trust. Alcmena's importance is the length of time she spent in the embrace of Jove; Oedipus's the fact that he ended his life blind; Proserpina's that she lives in hellish misery. Myrrha is mentioned for the bitterness of her tears; Athamas for his madness, and Ixion because when Troilus tosses and turns on his bed, he is like Ixion turning on his wheel. All these stated grounds for comparison or allusion work effectively within their immediate context, but it takes small acquaintance with the stories alluded to to realize how much additional depth of meaning they might have as applied to *Troilus and Criseyde,* and how much similarity of meaning there is between the allusions themselves, suggesting an overall strategy for them as a group.

Firstly, they frequently convey suffering and punishment in a pagan world, and this prepares the way, though perhaps not with the reader's complete emotional assent, for the *Palinode's* rejection of paganism, and of the gods as "rascaille" (5.1853): Titius, Amphiorax, Tantalus, Proserpina, and Ixion are all in Hell; Procne, her ravisher Tereus, and Myrrha were all metamorphosed; Athamas, punished by Juno through the agency of the Furies, was sent mad; Oedipus, pursued by Furies, blinded himself. Secondly, there are acts of sexual criminality: Titius wanted to rape Latona; Procne's sister was raped by her husband Tereus (a point made relatively unobtrusively by Chaucer); Alcmena was deceived into having sexual intercourse with Jove, who came to her in the shape of her husband; Proserpina was ravished by Dis; Oedipus unknowingly committed incest with his mother; Myrrha tricked her father into incest; Ixion sought to seduce Juno. Thirdly, the tragedy is often familial: this is evident in the case of Oedipus, Myrrha, and Proserpina, who was taken from her grieving mother. Athamas and Tantalus both killed their sons, and this led to the suicide and death of Athamas's wife and other child. Procne revenged herself and her sister by making her husband unknowingly eat their son, and Amphiorax was sent to his death by means of his wife. Fourthly, deception, either perpetrated or suffered, recurs. Although Myrrha and Athamas are both in Ovid's *Metamorphoses,* they appear within 300 lines of each other in *Troilus,* and this is probably because Chaucer found them closely associated in Dante's *Inferno* 30, where they are examples of falsifiers, albeit Myrrha's deceit was deliberate, and Athamas's frenzied perception that his wife and children were a lioness and cubs was inspired by Juno.[20] Tantalus's crime was also a form of falsification, for he cut up his son and cooked him in a stew to see if his divine guests would spot the deceit. Alcmena was subject to the deceitful shape-changing of Jove. Ixion was frustrated in his attempt to woo Juno by being supplied with a false Juno made from cloud.

These broad contours establish the potential of the comparisons to work as a group. It is easy to see the broad relevance of such material to *Troilus and Criseyde.* Paganism, suffering, sexual content, and deceit can all be found in the poem. There is even an element of the familial involved: Troilus carelessly, and paradoxically, offers his sister to Pandarus to prove that he believes Pandarus's motives were not those of a bawd (3.407–13). And a mere twenty-five lines before Troilus refers to Oedipus, he wishes that Fortune had killed his father or brothers rather than taking Criseyde (4.274–81). Certainly, in neither case is the familial insult unqualified: he also offers Helen to Pandarus, and his own life to Fortune, but there can be no doubt that one is expected to judge the enormity of his emotional dislocation by these gestures towards his family.

The problem for readers is deciding how far these features of the classical comparators can be mapped onto the poem. A pattern of comparisons has been set up; relatively trivial grounds for making the individual comparisons in their immediate context are stated. However, large-scale similarities between the allusions, and between them and the interests and themes of the poem, can be found if the stated ground is regarded merely as a local device rather than a hermeneutic control. Consequently the usual challenge of comparison is posed. The reader can either stay with the stated ground of comparison or enlarge it to include other similarities and dissimilarities. The choice of these reflects the reader's own interpretative preferences. Implicit in the choice is the reader's decision about what the relevant context of interpretation should be: whether the local context of their use should control reading, or whether the mechanics of the poem should be left behind to discover those issues Chaucer might, perhaps unconsciously, have found empowering his work. Having found such deeper issues it is then open to the reader to carry them back into the interpretation of the immediate context. For example, one could look to the familial tragedies of his classical comparators and the occasional articulation of familial matters within the poem itself, as in the speeches by Troilus mentioned earlier, or the tension of Calchas's parental love with his daughter's sexual desire, or the narrator's pointed ignorance of whether Criseyde had children. One might support this interest by studying Chaucer's literary use elsewhere of the parental relationship.[21] Children do not seem to be part of the Wife of Bath's world, and it is possible that the lines in which she learns her woman's tricks from her mother actually testify to editorial interest in the mother-daughter relationship.[22] Chaucer does not seem to include parents among the authoritative or influential forces on "Geffrey" in the *House of Fame*, but children are important devices of emotional intensity in poems like the *Man of Law's Tale*, the *Clerk's Tale*, where the tension of the amatory and parental is again present, and the *Prioress's Tale*, where the innocent child has a transcendent religious function.

4: PATTERNS OF COMPARISON IN *TROILUS AND CRISEYDE*

The scope and point which Chaucer gives to parent-child relations seems as significant in general terms as any other social, literary, or political issue which he might be masking, hinting at, or forcing along particular channels for self-serving ends.

Chaucer's pattern of classical allusion makes the familial dimension a possible area for interpretation of *Troilus and Criseyde*. If the reader thinks it insignificant, it is the reader's *decision* to exclude it when managing the comparisons which Chaucer has opened up, for there is enough evidence to suggest that this is an important area of Chaucer's work. The prominence of the family in the classical conception of disaster is not in itself enough to explain the frequency with which it is found in *Troilus* or to foreclose studying the significance such matters might have for the author. On the other hand, the falsification and deceit present in several of the comparators do seem more immediately relevant to the poem, where moral condemnation is a problematic issue. The comparison with Tantalus is reported as part of intense, and therefore suspect, avowals of trustworthiness made to Criseyde by Pandarus (3.589–93). Chaucer does not state the obvious, literal support for making the comparison: that Pandarus is inviting Criseyde to supper, and it was also at a meal that Tantalus attempted to deceive the gods, though that detail may have formed part of the analogy which attracted him into the allusion. If the reader recognizes this ground, it will bring along with it the deceit being practised at the two meals, as part of a narratorially unstated criticism of Pandarus.[23] One may also ask whether the analogy goes further, suggesting that Criseyde, no less than the gods, knows precisely what is going on.

In contrast, it is hard to believe that the Myrrha comparison, however authorized by Dante as a hellish instance of falsification, is working in its immediate context to encourage criticism. It is applied to both the lovers at their meeting after the impending separation has been determined on:

> The woful teeris that they leten falle
> As bittre weren, out of teris kynde,
> For peyne, as is ligne aloes or galle—
> So bittre teeris weep nought, as I fynde,
> The woful Mirra thorugh the bark and rynde
>
> (4.1135–39)

The lovers have our sympathy, and though self-deception about their future actions may be imminent, deceit designed to lead to sexual intercourse, as in Myrrha's case, is not part of the current concern of the poem.

Although an interest in falsification probably led Chaucer to follow Dante in locating the Myrrha and Athamas references close to each other, it does not follow that he wanted the references read with a precise attention to falsification in the context in which they appeared. Indeed, the Myrrha comparison forms a pattern with others in quite different ways. Like Troilus's allusion to Proserpina (4.473–76), it conveys the idea of imprisonment: Proserpina is imprisoned in Hell, Myrrha is imprisoned in a tree, through whose bark and rind she weeps. This particular form of powerlessness is all the more poignant following the earlier images of natural growth which we have already discussed in this chapter, and it further renders explicit the stanza in which the impending loss of Troilus's love was like the destruction of greenery by the force of winter, leaving Troilus "Ibounden in the blake bark of care" (4.229). The lovers are now figuratively imprisoned in the very images which marked the flowering of their joy. These interests, rather than a deeper interest in falsification, are more likely to be determining the local use of the comparison. Locally, Chaucer seems to use Myrrha in an Ovidian rather than Dantean manner. The same is true of Athamas.

The comparison with Athamas is also ambiguous in its relation to the theme of falsification. It is made in a context not unlike Pandarus's avowal of trustworthiness: Criseyde swears that she is made of truth with an intensity made all the more suspect for the reader's knowledge of the eventual outcome:

> For thilke day that I for cherisynge
> Or drede of fader, or for other wight,
> Or for estat, delit, or for weddynge,
> Be fals to yow, my Troilus, my knyght,
> Saturnes doughter, Juno, thorugh hire myght,
> As wood as Athamante do me dwelle
> Eternalich in Stix, the put of helle!
>
> (4.1534–40)

The difference between her and Pandarus is that Criseyde does not intend to deceive Troilus. Although she does in the end betray him, and one knows this as she speaks, the Athamas reference brings in the notion of someone almost innocent of culpability for the falsification in which she is involved. Athamas did not deceive, but saw falsely because he had been sent mad. The comparison, as Criseyde makes it, overtly suggests that the madness is a punishment; as the reader takes it, however, it is significant as a measure of exoneration, reminding one of the tragedy which can arise from the pressure of outside forces. Here again, the Dantean condemnation latent in the reference may be allowed to work in a general way preparing for the exemplary function which Chaucer gives to his poem at the end, but it is not working thus in the comparison's immediate context.

The Ixion comparison is Chaucer's addition to Boccaccio, and its relevance to the theme of falsification is enhanced by its being the next instance of classical *comparatio* after those of Athamas and Myrrha, though a few hundred lines and a Book division separate it. The falsification involved, that is the fabrication of a false Juno from cloud, was not part of Ixion's crime, but the strategy used by Jupiter to frustrate his sexual assault. Nonetheless, one could read the analogy as anticipating the narrator's final criticism of earthly love, implying that Troilus sought a "feynede" love and his suffering at its loss was deserved and inevitable. However, this is to supply a very specific alternative significance to the one actually given. Much more salient than the theme of falsification is Ixion's physical punishment on the wheel. It is this which gives Chaucer an image for Troilus tossing and turning on his bed. This visual image does actually bear a significance deeper than the stated ground, but in accordance with it: Chaucer has chosen the comparison as an image of Fortune's wheel, appropriately transmuted into an instrument of torture for a man who foolishly claims to have honored fortune all his life (4.267). This meaning is consistent in all respects with the narrator's final criticism of earthly love, but is more directly derivable from what the poem actually says than is the analogy of Criseyde with a false Juno.

In its context of use, the destructive power of Fortune seems a much more convincing resonance for the Ixion comparison than others. Yet it is hard to avoid the sense that sexual misdemeanor is a prominent feature of this and other classical comparisons in the poem, and that the predatory aspect of that behavior is but an unspoken parallel to some of the imagery used of the lovers, admittedly without overt criticism but opening such possibilities for the reader. Again, however, local context serves to determine how far the sexual dimension will be particularized into specific judgments. For example, Ixion's intended seduction of Juno seems only indirectly relevant to the specific context in which the comparison is made, that is, Troilus's loss of Criseyde. On the other hand the allusion to Procne and Tereus's rape must surely be acting as a covert invitation to criticize Pandarus's ensuing seduction of Criseyde on Troilus's behalf. Conversely, the rape intended by Titius does not seem as important in Book 1.785–88, as the pain he is famed for suffering, and Oedipus's incest, though it parallels that of Myrrha, must surely, like that of Myrrha, be irrelevant to the local context of its use in *Troilus*, however generally relevant to the poem misplaced desire might be.

These ambiguities can be explained, if not resolved, by recognizing that Chaucer's engagement with classical comparison is on two levels. Broad thematic considerations which inform the poem and his work generally direct him to particular comparisons, and thus one finds patterns emerging between them: patterns of sexual criminality, falsification, paganism, punishment, and so on, all of which he understands as part of the larger "sentence" of his work. But these themes are not necessarily determining the function of the comparisons in their local contexts, and the poem's subtler forces would be misrepresented by a reading which drew on the larger thematic patterns of the images for local interpretation. This pattern of mythical comparison offers the interpretative extremes of local specificness and general suggestiveness and the consequent challenge that the reader negotiate between them. If anything, the myths duplicate the problem of all *exempla:* that the particular and the general cannot quite marry up but cannot be wholly divorced either. Latent dissimilarity is a condition of the allusions as it is of comparisons, but the extent and force of that dissimilarity remain to be determined by each reader, shaping and limiting context in the light of the reader's own goals. The mythical stories thus offer an exemplary backdrop against which the particularity of the poem is defined, but like all *exempla* constitute a body of "known" and supposedly authoritative ideas which it is hard to ignore, and which color any thinking which employs them, but which force through a claim for similarity which the local topic may wish to resist. Consequently, they provide an excellent transition between this chapter's focus on the effect of grouped comparisons and the dangerous world of persuasion by comparison which will be the subject of the next chapter. In that chapter we will find that the person who receives comparisons in this poem does not always *seem* in such a strong position as the reader of a poem, but may *in fact* have similar freedom to accept, reject, and revise the comparisons they receive.

5
Persuasive Comparisons in *Troilus and Criseyde*

ATTEMPTING TO UNDERSTAND THINGS BY COMPARISON WITH other things is essentially amoral, being nothing more than a reflection of what the user already knows directed by the user's desires or existing assumptions. However, comparison can shift toward immorality when used in persuasion and, as Barry Windeatt has written, "*Troilus* is a poem supremely of talk, of conversation, and of argument and persuasion."[1] In such a context comparison is fashioned from the user's limitations and may run up against the principles, desires, and interests of the person being persuaded. For example, Pandarus, with more good intention than moral principle, counsels Troilus to love another when Criseyde is no longer there, and uses the same kinds of persuasive example as he employed during the course of the love affair:

> For also seur as day comth after nyght,
> The newe love, labour, or oother wo,
> Or elles selde seynge of a wight,
> Don olde affecciouns al over-go.[2]
>
> (4.421–24)

Here the narrator casually condemns the argument as foolishness (431). Although comparison can be used for good as well as bad purposes, the effect of the passage is to taint the comparative method with the promiscuity which it is being used to commend: if comparison can support quite contrary positions it becomes suspect as a way of thinking. It is not a means of arriving at truth; only of arriving at a position to which oneself and others may or may not accede.

This chapter considers Chaucer's fascination with the process of persuasion by comparison, as it is evidenced in the use and abuse of the technique by characters. Though the immediate function of comparisons may be probative within argument, the arguments they serve are intended to persuade, and their ultimate function is thus a rhetorical rather than logical one. Sometimes, the rhetoric is directed at others; sometimes reflexively at the speakers who make the comparisons; but it is always itself made subject to analysis. Because Chaucer believes that comparison is a natural and inevitable way of thinking about the world, he is concerned to show the errors which people make in analogistic thinking because of self-seeking, or emotional necessity, or other pressures. Indeed he gives such error a mythical, almost an aetiological, status in the poem when he has Troilus reject Cassandra's claim that Criseyde has betrayed him. Troilus counters with a mythical comparison, which shares the problematic of all such allusions:

> As wel thow myghtest lien on Alceste,
> That was of creatures, but men lye,
> That evere weren, kyndest and the beste!
> For whan hire housbonde was in juperty
> To dye hymself but if she wolde dye,
> She ches for hym to dye and gon to helle,
> And starf anon, as us the bokes telle.
>
> (5.1527–33)

Chaucer could have had Troilus reject Cassandra's views, in accordance with the mythic necessity that she was never believed, without further demonstrating his blindness by employing a classical comparison so patently at odds with the truth. Furthermore he has Troilus narrate the story of Alceste beyond mere allusion to emphasize what is, in Chaucer's view, the archetypal, and inescapable, folly of the human condition: the transfer of meaning across the gap from the known to the new. It is just this transfer that readers engage in when they believe that their understanding of life gives them purchase on the meaning of a book and, conversely, when they wish to claim that a book permits greater understanding of the nontextual world. In each case, a comparison is claimed because of a preexisting desire for the relationship, its latent dissimilarities being occluded or revised according to the lights of the reader. The readings made of the text have to find support in the context of the text as a whole. Umberto Eco writes, "How to prove a conjecture about the *intentio operis?* The only way is to check it upon the text as a coherent whole."[3] But the coherence of the text will be shaped by the same desires as are framing the text's comparative relationship with the nontextual. Troilus makes the text of Alcestis fit the text of his life with Criseyde. He is completely wrong in his choice of comparison as the details of its narration reveal, but what he does is usual, inevitable and, from the reader's point of view, metapoetically significant. As each narrative detail of Alceste's sacrifice succeeds the other, far from intensifying his point, Troilus opens up space for the reader to acknowledge that people believe what they want, or are prepared, to believe, and call upon the resources of texts, authorities, the natural world, personal or common experience to justify themselves to themselves and to others. Troilus puts the narrative of the myth in the place of truth as if the very detail could press the comparator closer to its topic. Thus the "sentence" of the *exemplum* gets hidden beneath, or is even replaced by, the "solaas" of its narration.

Equally, a comparison, whatever its source, is only as effective a persuader as the capacity of the hearer permits. Earlier in the poem, Troilus, bewailing the impending loss of Criseyde, resolves to die because he is convinced that there is no free will but all is determined. To support this position he employs, of all arguments, Boethius's *exemplum* of a man sitting on a seat, an *exemplum* which Philosophy used while persuading Boethius to accept that God's divine prescience could coexist with human free will. The value of the *exemplum* is limited by the user's paganism (4.1023–43). Troilus can see no further than the inexorability of events because he has chosen no higher goal than what the world of events can offer. Thus his *exemplum*, though from the loftiest of spiritual sources, cannot bring him any illumination but only the misery of determinism (4.1076–78). He is left with the hopelessness of a prayer that Jupiter will have pity on him or cause his speedy death. Comparative persuasion, whether to good or ill, brings the known world to illuminate the new topic, but it is still constrained by the limits of the person who seeks the illumination.

With varying degrees of overtness, Chaucer scrutinizes the mechanics of comparative persuasion, and sometimes has his characters anatomize it explicitly. But as is clear from the Alceste allusion the implications of this analysis can run far beyond the immediate context of use to encompass his attitudes to poetry, itself a rhetorically and argumentatively dense medium of persuasion. Criseyde describes Pandarus's arguments as a "paynted proces" (2.424) and the same could be said of poetry: both are painted with the colors of rhetoric, and, in Chaucer's poetry, painted heavily with those colors which fall under the general heading of comparison. This chapter will look at some of the metapoetic implications which arise from Chaucer's account of comparison in use.

We order our world by the comparative judgments which we make. Correspondingly, the limitations which our lack of experience imposes on understanding are shown in the comparisons which are open to us. It was for this reason that classical rhetorical manuals frequently required the rhetorician to develop a fecundity in the range of the comparators which could be called on. Nor was this wholly a matter of intellectual display. The point of a comparison is that it should draw upon the known in order to elucidate the unknown. To enlarge the sphere of the known is thus not merely to acquire knowledge, whether that acquisition be conceited or disinterested; it is to empower oneself to educate and persuade. However, as one's comparators become more arcane, one either limits the audience able to be educated rationally by them or increases the degree to which the audience is wholly in the power of their persuader, dependent both for understanding of the topic and the comparator which is to illuminate it. There is thus a paradox built into the process. It is intended to enlighten, but unless the comparator used to do this is in the realm of common knowledge already, the enlightenment may be more dependent on the claims of the user than borne out by the comparison made.

There is often a reciprocity in the management of topic and comparator: the hearer is required to draw on partial knowledge of both to arrive at a conclusion, or at the least, to draw on what appear to be the salient features of the topic, as prompted by the particular context of the comparison, in order then to select from the comparator what features are supposed to be adduced to illuminate the topic. Chaucer was evidently fully aware of the hidden trickeries of persuasion by comparison for he exploits and exposes them through the dynamic exchanges of the characters. One of the first things which the persuaders, Pandarus and Diomede, do is to challenge Criseyde's sense of relative worth based on her existing judgments and experience. They attempt to reshape the world of the known through revising normal quantitative comparisons before embarking on figurative comparison or using argumentative *exempla*. Pandarus tempts Criseyde with a piece of good news. In fact it is Troilus's love for her, but her judgment, based on the relative values of the world known to her, naturally leads her to the notion that the siege has been lifted. Pandarus responds that his news is five times better than that (2.125–26). The claim is outrageous, and Criseyde says so, but it is so outrageous that merely by making it, Pandarus challenges existing canons of judgment and opens up the possibility that there could be a radically different way of looking at the world. He then moves on to assert the equivalence of Troilus and Hector, moving from the modest, figuratively guarded, idea that Troilus is "The wise, worthi Ector the secounde" (2.158) to the disingenuous factual description of them as Priam's "sones tweye" (2.170), and then to evaluation, claiming that Troilus has the "same pris" as he describes for Hector (2.181). From the outrageous revaluation of things earlier, he has moved to a more insinuating, seductive revisionism in comparing Troilus to Hector. Again Criseyde responds honestly, trying to retain the comparative values that she knows are true while also being generous in judgment:

"By God . . . of Ector that is sooth. / Of Troilus the same thyng *trowe I*" (2.183–84; my emphasis).

In neither case is Criseyde tricked out of her judgment, but in both cases that judgment has been challenged in the area of quantitative comparison. This is an important pressure to bring upon Criseyde for she is, in a sense, an isolated woman, living in a world within a world, understanding the state of things by what "men tellen" (2.185), viewing it from windows and, with the exception of Troilus's first glimpse of her in church, seen herself within rooms rather than at large until her passage to the Greek camp. She is challenged first in the constrained realm of what she knows before Pandarus moves on to the potent and more deceptive persuasions of figurative or exemplary comparison. Diomede employs the same technique at the start of his courtship urging her to abandon the relative inequality of worth in which she has held the Greeks and Trojans. He claims that the Greeks can be as respectful, faithful, and kind to her as the Trojans (5.124–26). This assertion is not easily dismissable even by the reader. This is not Henryson's or Shakespeare's version; Criseyde is not discarded by a succession of Greek lovers, and there is almost as much to despise in Troilus and Pandarus's joint enterprise of persuasion as there is in the self-taught and self-knowing Diomede, who cites proverbial comparisons to himself and acts on them. The essential difference between the two is that the reader cooperates with the first in an expectant mood and observes the second in the perspective of tragic defeat, seeing it as a speeded up version of the earlier courtship by someone who is sexually aware of love as competitive in a militarily competitive environment. When Criseyde has her sense of comparative worth challenged by Diomede, not even the reader is wholly confident about rejecting his claim. Criseyde herself is hardly in a position to do so, as she did when Pandarus tried the technique. She does not have the evidence to judge its veracity. She seems to be at the mercy of the comparisons of the persuader because the world of the known has paradoxically shrunk for her even as she has moved outside the constraints of Troy's walls, its rooms and its window seats. If Troilus's paganism limited his capacity to use an exemplum of his own citing, so Criseyde's isolation limits her ability to deal with those she is offered. In a similar way, the reader of a poem like the *General Prologue* is only progressively empowered to deal with the meaning of the words which Chaucer ensures will recur: for example, we are permitted to understand a word like "worthy" in more precise ways as we pass from its appearance in the Knight's portrait to that in the Squire's and then the Friar's.[4] The *General Prologue* is, in this sense, an exercise in contextual comparativism in an expanding textual world: a practical literary introduction for the reader to a problem which Criseyde is constantly faced with by her suitors.

When comparison is figurative, the possibility of its operating below the level of rational discussion is increased. A comparator is adduced to make a claim which is amenable to enquiry and discussion. But the choice of comparator may communicate independently of the ground of the comparison, carrying suggestions, or directing discussion, in ways which contradict the general argument which the comparison is supposed to be supporting. Such an ambivalent analogy is given to Criseyde by Pandarus when he senses that she is afraid of public opinion should Troilus be seen visiting her house. Pandarus rejects the idea that people will interpret Troilus's visit in the way she fears: "What, who wol demen, though he se a man / To temple go, that he th'ymages eteth?" (2.372–73). It is a figuratively radical, even confusing, conflation of Criseyde's house with a temple. The point of the comparison is that the mere fact of Troilus's visiting Criseyde would not lead people to suspect the two were in love. The argument is obviously flawed in that the two parts of the comparison are too dissimilar: people who saw Troilus visiting Criseyde would not be restrained from suspicion as they would be if they saw him, or anyone else, visiting a temple. Pandarus is trying to force a point of similarity in the *similitudo* where the other latent dissimilarities actually disable it. But the main function of the comparison is not its overt claim. That would hardly stand up to scrutiny. It is to import under the cover of that claim the implicit comparison of Criseyde's house to a temple and, by implication, Criseyde herself to the *imago* of a Goddess. The choice of comparator thus permits Pandarus to assert the amatory at the very point where the argument he is making denies it. It is not clear whether Criseyde is conscious of the trick, or is affected by it: her reaction to Pandarus's "paynted proces" seems to suggest that she is aware of the trickery in general, and has not been emotionally seduced by it, but Chaucer's interest is as much in subjecting the reader to the subtle workings of comparison. He may wish to have Criseyde preserve her distance and integrity at this point, but he wants the reader to enjoy the persuasive blandishments of comparison and be seduced into complicity with Pandarus's use of them.

Similarly, when Pandarus describes Troilus in battle, he presents a picture which is redolent of conventional romance battle descriptions: "For nevere yet so thikke a swarm of been / Ne fleigh, as Grekes for hym gonne fleen" (2.193–94). It is part of his enterprise to present Troilus to Criseyde as the perfect knight. But it is the genre of the comparator, rather than the claim, which acts on the reader's mind, helping to shape Troilus as the conventional literary lover. It may be acting on Criseyde also to make Troilus seem like the knights she hears of from books, though one does not know. It would not be going beyond the bounds of Chaucer's depth of characterization to imply that Pandarus is seeking to blur the boundary between reality and Criseyde's book knowledge, just as he tries to do when joking that the book she is reading with her maidens is about love, and as Chaucer himself does when blending the literal and figurative to give a realistic power to his imaginary world.

Pandarus also persuades Criseyde by using groups of comparisons to reshape the world of the known. In the following stanza the multiplicity of comparators serves to create an alternative reality, not wholly unlike the effect created by the many similes for Alison in the *Miller's Tale*:

> Wo worth the faire gemme vertulees!
> Wo worth that herbe also that dooth no boote!
> Wo worth that beaute that is routheles!
> Wo worth that wight that tret ech undir foote!
> And ye, that ben of beaute crop and roote,
> If therwithal in yow ther be no routhe,
> Than is it harm ye lyven, by my trouthe!
>
> (2.344–50)

Jewels, herbs, beauties, tyrants, a woman who represents the whole flower of beauty—it is a stanza which delights by its variety as it harps upon complaint. But the variety is intended to do more than support the rhetorical intensity. It fills up the poetic unit of the stanza in the way it is supposed to fill up the space for argument. (Pandarus does the same thing with Troilus at 1.946–52.) One of the similes would have made the point adequately, but when one analogy is propped up by others, they advertize themselves not as discrete similarities but as a reflection of the way things are. This is important, for Pandarus's argument is all about what is *natural* to the individual. The argument is stronger because it can find various correlatives elsewhere binding the world of nature. The argument, of course, misses any consideration that what is being counselled might be wrong or unwelcome or untimely, or inappropriately or deceitfully introduced, but in the persuasive enterprise part of the trick is to select out the damaging considerations and force discussion to address, if anything, only the justice of the specific claims made. So much of the effect of persuasion lies in the fact that the issue in question is talked about at all, as opposed to other possible subjects. Just as comparators can direct thought by shaping the world of the known in a particular way, for example, towards romantic matters, so the persuasion is on the way to success by getting itself on the agenda of discussion, and edging out other subjects.

Pandarus's early attempt to set the agenda by asking if Criseyde's book is about love comes to comic disaster when it proves to be about Oedipus killing his father and the fall of Amphiorax to Hell. Amphiorax was brought there, if one follows up the allusion, by his wife, who betrayed him for a necklace, as Criseyde later shows her betrayal of Troilus by a brooch. But even without bringing this information into the interpretation of the local context, the tonal incongruity of Pandarus's question with the actual subject matter serves to expose his machinations. But in the stanza I have been looking at, the density of multiple comparison succeeds, as does Pandarus's insistence on discussing things with Criseyde in private, in giving an impression that the world of experience is limited to that defined by the persuasion itself. It is all the more startling, therefore, when Criseyde not only rejects what Pandarus is saying as falsehood, but proves herself to have the freedom of mind to fashion his suit into a comparison of her own:

> Allas! I wolde han trusted, douteles,
> That if that I, thorugh my dysaventure,
> Hadde loved outher hym or Achilles,
> Ector, or any mannes creature,
> Ye nolde han had no mercy ne mesure
> On me
>
> (2.414–19)

Criseyde still has control of the world of her experience; it has not been supplanted by the world of books channeled through Pandarus's romantic comparators or the world of nature as shaped by Pandarus's multiple analogies; her capacity to compare the truths of her experience with those being offered to her is unimpaired at this stage.

By Book 3, Criseyde is apparently less in charge of the argumentative process, however much she may be fundamentally in charge of what she is prepared to allow. She is trying to insist that she should not meet Troilus to cure his feigned jealousy until the morning. Her mistake is temporarily to leave the high ground of absolute principle and descend to the treacherous terrain of comparison where Pandarus can argue the case. Pandarus says that she must never have loved Troilus if she lets him remain outside all night. She replies "Hadde I hym nevere lief? by God, I weene / Ye hadde nevere thyng so lief!" (3.869–70). The triumph of finding himself on familiar territory is audible in Pandarus's response, and shows up not least through his explicitness about the comparative persuasions in which they are now engaged:

> Now by my thrift . . . that shal be seene!
> For syn ye make this *ensaumple* of me,
> If ich al nyght wolde hym in sorwe se,
> For al the tresour in the town of Troie
> I bidde God I nevere mote have joie.
> (3.871–75; my emphasis)

Pandarus can then map out the rest of the argument, again through using comparative contrasts: Troilus is not like a fool in a jealous rage; his jealousy is more noble and life threatening (3.899–905); Criseyde is not like the slothful or vicious wretches who won't understand the propositions of Euclid; she knows what is going on (3.930–38). Pandarus has thus used comparison to adjust Criseyde's view of himself, herself, and Troilus, something which was immeasurably aided by her imprudent shift from a known world defined by fixed principles into one negotiated through comparison.

However apparently successful, and however intrinsic to the human condition, comparative thinking is tragically limited in its capacity to cope with the unforeseen changes of life, because it depends on utilising the known. Pandarus's comparisons begin to self-destruct after he is no longer in charge of the progress of the love affair. Chaucer builds into them elements which undermine their persuasiveness for the reader and accordingly charts Pandarus's decline in importance. These failures do not seem to be appreciated by Pandarus, or even yet by Troilus, but they create in the reader an underlying pessimism before the events justify it.

Thus, when Pandarus is urging Troilus to leave his sorrow until he can hear if Criseyde has a plan, there is all the old readiness with example, but the example chosen is ominous: "A man may al bytyme his nekke beede / Whan it shal of, and sorwen at the nede" (4.1105–6). There have been other uses of the comparison with a condemned man, but not one which argued for good cheer and yet assumed that the execution would take place nonetheless. Similarly, when he asks Troilus to compare his life before Criseyde with that now likely because of their separation (4.1093–94), the result is to affirm the loss not its survivability. These gestures are being made when it is not clear to the characters that the loss will indeed be permanent, but they are already undercutting in the reader's mind any future plans which the characters have for changing their fortune.

Part of the problem is that Pandarus's line of argument is not single, but varied. He thrashes about in the face of circumstances; argues for the possibility of a saving plan, but only after he has urged Troilus to accept Fortune's destructiveness through seeing love as like the chances of a dice game (4.1098–99). It is typical of this part of the poem that assertions by characters are undermined by details in the comparisons used to support them. This can be seen in the following cases. In the first, Pandarus tries to bring Troilus to a sense of reason by urging him to compare his situation with that of other lovers whose ladies have been absent for a fortnight (5.333–35). The parallel is appropriately courtly, and the argument persuasive. One's knowledge of the final outcome prevents the comparison from seeming more than wishful, but it is fundamentally disabled by the casual, idiomatic detail of the length of time the knight and his lady will be separated. This ominously shifts the period of Criseyde's analogized absence beyond the ten days she has promised, and anticipates the agonised realization of Troilus later that the appointed hour will not be met. Similarly, when Pandarus seeks to emphasize his advice that sorrow in love must be borne by citing the case of lovers who see their friend wedded and bedded without consent (5.346), he unconsciously imports the spectre of Diomede and gives it a base in the argument, wholly subverting the support he offers.

Such a subtle cruelty in analogy is neither Pandarus's fault nor evidence of his insight; it should not be understood at the level of character at all. It amounts to a determined assault by Chaucer on the efficacy of comparative arguing in the world of unpredictable fortuitous circumstances. If Chaucer's aim were merely to discredit Pandarus, there would be no need for him to do more than show how the character's arguments and efforts came to nothing; instead he wants to build the failure into the very details of the comparative argument itself; to let the pressing circumstances of the world in which comparative argument is being made intrude on the examples through key details, and thus suggest the weakness of analogistic argument in the face of particularity. By using the reader's knowledge of the fiction's future, Chaucer exposes the tragic complicity between the form of comparison and its failure. But it must be added that such comparison also operates on the reader's emotions accustoming them to the betrayal before it takes place and thus accommodating Criseyde's failure into the reader's sense of what is and must be. Although Chaucer reveals failures of thinking, he is not concerned that they should swamp sympathy. It is wholly typical of him that when he is at his most forensically analytical, he can be setting up the means by which sympathy can be evoked.

It is not just the self-serving use made of comparison by the characters which is at fault, this method of thinking itself eventually gets displaced by unforeseen facts which no analogical thinking could accommodate. One of the most noticeable features of Book 5 is that comparative argument by characters tails off and is replaced by a brutal, tragicomic, signifying by objects: Troilus's pillow (224), the sparred doors on Criseyde's house (531, 552), the Greek tents (670), the bay steed (1038), the brooch (1040), the sleeve (1043), her glove (1013), the "fare-carte" (1162), even the places they had visited, or through which Criseyde passed (564, 603, 610), the letters as physical manifestations of their relationship, and so on. These things persuade more powerfully than any comparison could do.

This shift from similes to facts reveals the supervening of circumstantial, fortune-driven reality over the management of life by a comparativist thought which is dependent on life repeating itself enough to allow inference from examples. It is Criseyde who constantly urges present loss to gain future advantage on the evidence of past instances:

> Lo, Troilus, men seyn that hard it is
> The wolf ful and the wether hool to have;
> This is to seyn, that men ful ofte, iwys,
> Mote spenden part, the remenaunt for to save.
>
> (4.1373–76)

But it is Criseyde herself who falsifies these proverbial assemblages of analogistic reasoning when she is subdued by the unexampled particularities of the Greek camp. While in Troy, the world of the known offers many examples by which she can predict and think to control the future, as one sees in her lengthy arguments with Troilus about what action they should take or avoid to cope with her impending departure. When she is in the world of the new her imagination can only fashion particularities, the scenarios of threat. From the false illumination of what "men seyn" she moves to the isolated imagining of "what if . . . ?"

Although characters spend so much time attempting to persuade each other and themselves by comparative reasoning, Chaucer suggests that there is a point beyond which the persuasive force of comparison cannot go. When emotion or principle is too strong, it is impossible to employ this technique successfully. The attitudes of the auditor are fundamental to the success of persuasion, as Pandarus discovers when he tries to argue Troilus, by examples, out of his grief for the impending loss of Criseyde and into the love of another (4.400–427). Troilus points out that such persuasion could only work if it fell on the ears of a "fend" (4.437), and in what is his first substantial use of exemplary comparison in argument, Troilus rejects Pandarus's use of the technique:

> Thow farest ek by me, thow Pandarus,
> As he that, whan a wight is wo bygon,
> He cometh to hym a paas and seith right thus:
> "Thynk nat on smert, and thow shalt fele non."
>
> (4.463–66)

This is a dramatic reversal, for Troilus attacks Pandarus in the form which Pandarus has made very much his own, and even uses Pandarus himself as an *exemplum* against his own persuasions. Criseyde also tried to do this but at a time when the real course of events was not running against Pandarus. Troilus challenges him:

> But tel me now, syn that the thynketh so light
> To changen so in love ay to and fro,
> Whi hastow nat don bisily thi myght
> To chaungen hire that doth the al thi wo?
>
> (4.484–87)

Troilus considers Pandarus's argument as not grounded in reality, which is the source from which must flow the persuasive force of comparison. Pandarus can only argue theoretically (4.497). Troilus's attack is not on comparative persuasion as such, but on that method when it is divorced from realities of emotion, principle, and other example.

The last assault on Pandarus's use of the technique follows quickly. Pandarus taunts Troilus: "Artow in Troie, and hast noon hardyiment / To take a womman which that loveth the?" (4.533–34). The moment is all the more forceful because Chaucer has the reader and Troilus interpret a comparison which Pandarus only hints at: that Troilus should act towards Criseyde as Paris acted towards Helen. This is the ultimate *exemplum* Pandarus can use because it draws upon the fact which most defines the "known" world of the Trojans. But its very experiential authority disables it for the rape of Helen is what has led ultimately to the tragic loss of Criseyde. Troilus dismantles the comparison openly with reference to the violence and dishonor of such an act, and the war which resulted from it (4.547–53). After this failure, Pandarus tends to get stuck between using brief pejorative similes for intensive effect to goad Troilus to action (4.595, 626, 629), as he did in Book 1.731–35, and using himself as a hypothetical example by saying what he would do in Troilus's position (4.582–86), neither of which techniques are very persuasive, particularly since Troilus is fully conscious of what Pandarus is trying to do and will not be incited by these means.

Although persuasion by comparison may sometimes involve an element of trickery, as any rhetorical language does, Chaucer gives the impression that characters in this poem are never really persuaded unknowingly or beyond what they will permit. Their own feelings, perceptions, and decisions appear to circumscribe persuasion. Although Troilus tells Pandarus in Book 1 to abandon his old examples (760), Pandarus again explicitly offers "Ensample" (1002–8) because Troilus is a willing listener. Pandarus and Criseyde are aware of using example in their argumentative fencing, and Criseyde intermittently shows complete awareness of the end towards which Pandarus's trickery is tending, and her conscious yielding of herself to it. Although persuasion by comparison often appears to be successful, that success depends on the inner assent of those being persuaded. It is a strategy which does not, in the last analysis, convince the unconvinced, a trickery which does not really trick, but is a ritualized communal activity by which contrary desires or opinions can be asserted as expressions of what has been proved natural to the world. The power of rhetoric shown through persuasive comparison is thus implied to be limited, though its use seems an essential part of social intercourse.

This is an insight with substantial significance for Chaucer's own writing for it implies that the success of fiction depends upon the readiness of the reader to be directed by its various forces, to respond to its semiotic code, even to accept its fictionality as worthwhile, and it also acknowledges that the fiction supplied is the product of a mind no less subject to the pleasures of selectively persuasive comparison than the reader's. The painted process of Pandarus's comparisons and the painted process of poetry both ultimately depend on the receiver's willingness to be seduced. In the remaining part of this chapter I will look at some other instances of comparative persuasion which seem to have metapoetic significance.

One of Chaucer's major achievements in the poem is evoking our sympathy for Criseyde at the same time as he reveals how her betrayal of Troilus is likely to come about, all within the context of the reader's prior knowledge that the betrayal will indeed happen. He does this by almost dividing Criseyde into two people, one of whom attracts sympathy, and the other of whom is already thinking in ways which will make betrayal possible. This is achieved by subtle management of persuasion by comparison, and by an ambiguity which is built into one of the linguistic markers of comparison. When Criseyde hears of her impending separation from Troilus, her distress and lamentation are extreme, unfeigned, and provoke sympathy in us, as in the narrator. Her choice of imagery which has already been heavily used in the poem seems to link her closely with the narrator and characters who have employed it previously, thus embedding her in the past joys which she must now give up:

> How sholde a fissh withouten water dure?
> What is Criseyde worth, from Troilus?
> How sholde a plaunte or lyves creature
> Lyve withouten his kynde noriture?
> For which ful oft a by-word here I seye,
> That "rooteles moot grene soone deye."
>
> (4.765–70)

The problem is that her lament here takes the form of a set of comparative *exempla,* a device of persuasion, uttered through rhetorical questions which are actually left unanswered until the last line, though an answer is implied in the tone of the speaker. There is no question of her sincere belief that she will die without Troilus but the form chosen for expressing it has a much stronger tradition of use in this poem for persuasion than certainty. It comes to sound as if she is persuading herself towards death without Troilus rather than asserting a natural consequence of their separation. It must also be said that this occurs after the comparative method has been substantially discredited by Troilus's rejection of Pandarus's advice earlier in the Book.

In addition, the *exempla* she employs do not quite hold together. Firstly, the opening image of the fish dying without water is deflected into an image of worthlessness which does not actually assume death: "What is Criseyde worth, from Troilus?" Secondly, her examples imply a natural, inevitable death following upon lack of sustenance. But she then shifts this towards death as a willed act in which the means depend upon her choice:

> I shal doon thus—syn neyther swerd ne darte
> Dar I noon handle, for the crueltee—
> That ilke day that I from yow departe,
> If sorwe of that nyl nat my bane be:
> Thanne shal no mete or drynke come in me
> Til I my soule out of my breste unshethe
>
> (4.771–76)

Chaucer maintains the notion that she will kill herself for love, and will do it in a manner similar to the natural examples of death without sustenance, but Criseyde herself recognizes the possibility that the separation may not actually constitute a natural loss of necessary sustenance, and that the coming of death depends on the sufferer's decision—a decision which one knows she will not take. Suicide by violence is rejected; death by grief is only a possibility; self-starvation is a decision rather than an inevitability. The *exempla* do not quite carry the point though they are given the illusion of doing so by her choice of death by starvation. Again Chaucer manages comparison in context so that it has an effect independent of the argument which it serves.

Just as one hears the persuasion beneath the assertiveness of her comparisons so one hears the attractions of imagined narrative in her *exemplum* of Orpheus:

> For though in erthe ytwynned be we tweyne,
> Yet in the feld of pite, out of peyne,
> That hight Elisos, shul we ben yfeere,
> As Orpheus and Erudice, his feere.
>
> (4.788–91)

It is a touching comparison, but also a narrated one, with a little narratorial gesture in the naming of Elysium, and worrying narratorial selections such as her skipping over Orpheus's attempt to recover Eurydice. Her fatalism is implied in the diversion of grief into narrative comparison; her particular case into the authoritative exemplar; and it is built into her presentation of the story. However, such passing inconsistencies and digressions do not produce one's sense of impending disaster as much as does her deictic presentation of herself. She projects herself into the figure of Euridice, but the process has already begun before this. She did not ask "What am I worth, from Troilus?" but "What is Criseyde worth, from Troilus?" In lamenting her plight, she externalizes, rhetoricizes, and to a degree fictionalizes herself. She envisages herself as seen by others, as a sign or token:

> And, Troilus, my clothes everychon
> Shul blake ben in tokenyng, herte swete,
> That I am as out of this world agon
>
> (4.778–80)

She is the visual image of sorrow, she claims to Pandarus: "Whoso me seeth, he seeth sorwe al atonys— / Peyne, torment, pleynte, wo, distresse!" (4.841–42). She is certainly grieving, but the grief is expressed in ways which create a fictive double: the double which can form part of a comparison, the double which is observed, an *imago* which stands in for the original Criseyde. Though an *imago* is very close to its original, it is not the same. Thus, at the very point when the integrity of the individual is most asserted, and most needs to be, Criseyde imagines another self, and so compromises that integrity.

This deixis is supported, and made more explicit, by the narrator:

> She was right swich to seen in hire visage
> As is that wight that men on beere bynde;
> Hire face, lik of Paradys the ymage,
> Was al ychaunged in another kynde.
>
> (4.862–65)

The narrator says that she who was an *imago* of one thing has now become an *imago* of another: she has changed her "kynde," from the angel to the corpse. Chaucer wants to present Criseyde as she would like to be seen. He supports her self deixis, but his pictorializing of Criseyde has a slightly different effect from hers. From him, it enforces sympathy; from her, it makes one aware of a doubleness: real pain and projected pain, felt anguish and observed anguish.[5]

That Chaucer is consciously employing the device of a double Criseyde, is supported by his exploiting ambiguity in one of the linguistic markers of comparison in order to leave unresolved alternative views of her. After Diomede's lengthy wooing speech at the start of Book 5, Chaucer describes Criseyde thus:

> Criseyde unto that purpos lite answerde,
> As she that was with sorwe oppressed so
> That, in effect, she naught his tales herde
> But her and ther, now here a word or two.
>
> (5.176–79)

It is left open whether that "as" in the second line is the "as" of apposition or the "as" of comparison.[6] Does the "as" assert the minimal dissimilarity of *imago* or the substantial dissimilarity of *similitudo*? One does not know if Criseyde was indeed someone so oppressed with sorrow that she heard little of what Diomede said, or said little in answer "like" someone oppressed with sorrow? The ambiguity cannot and should not be simplified since it is intended to unbalance any straightforward reading, and is backed up by the ambivalent force of the next line, "Hire thoughte hire sorwful herte brast a-two," which once again combines grief with Criseyde's reflection upon grief. This is one of the limited number of occasions on which Chaucer can be found playing with the minimalist dissimilarity exploited by the romance writers and, in this case it is part of a much more complete assertion of the doubleness in comparison. While the author of *Guy of Warwick* wishes to play tricks directly on the reader, Chaucer prefers to locate ambiguity at the level of character. And while the romance device depends on an eventual resolution of the ambiguity, it is clear that Chaucer does not want the ambiguity of Criseyde's character to be *resolved*.

Although comparison is used to persuade, it is in essence an intellectual device. It opens itself up to scrutiny by its propositional form and its avoidance of the tropological. It encourages reflection and consideration on the part of the hearer, and implies those activities in the mind of the person forming the comparison. To have Criseyde use comparative methods is to import the reflective into the dramatic, the intellectual into the emotional, and to a degree, the artificial or fictional into the real. This does not make one question Criseyde's sincerity; instead it leaves a sense of two Criseydes: the one grieving, the other representing grief to others and herself. It constitutes in her a demonstrating of the self to the self, which has the effect of keeping the self private by offering a public copy. The parallel with Chaucer's own use of narratorial substitutes and "Geffrey" *personae* is obvious. This doubling of the self is a way of insisting that the reader or hearer respond consciously to the demands of comparative analysis. When Criseyde doubles herself, it is unavoidable that one will ask whether the two Criseydes are really alike, and if so, whether they share sincerity or artificiality. When the author doubles himself into the work, it is inevitable that the reader will ask how much similarity exists between "Geffrey" the narrator and Geoffrey the author, and it is inevitable that the answer will lie in an amalgam of similarities and dissimilarities, selected to serve the critical ends of the person investigating the matter. In this respect I agree with Judith Ferster when she says that our difficulties in trying to identify Chaucer through his poems are not to be avoided but acknowledged: "this is a frustration we are invited to feel: that we are constantly directed toward Chaucer the man, and constantly unable to find him . . . His work stimulates awareness of the necessity and the insufficiency of interpretation of people (including writers) as well as of texts."[7] In not resolving such questions Chaucer is being no more than realistic. He is not seeking wilful ambivalence or inconclusiveness. He is simply conscious of the fact that two things cannot be one thing, and that we live our lives in the constant negotiation of comparative judgments, whether they involve the parts of a simile, Greeks and Trojans, poems about love and love experienced outside poetry, the self-image of a grieving woman, or a narrator standing in for an author. In the immediate context of Book 4 of *Troilus and Criseyde* his doubling of Criseyde is the means by which he is able both to show her sincerity and prepare us for her ultimate betrayal of Troilus. It would be a mistake to attempt to resolve this into a complex characterization of Criseyde as unknowingly self-dramatizing, or naively and unconsciously insincere. It is a narratorial sleight of hand which does not require to be explained at the level of character because it is already so firmly embedded in the narratorial techniques and hermeneutic concerns of the poem.

One feels that a critical sympathy for his own art and his role as an artist is implicit in Chaucer's presentation of Criseyde as grieving and yet making images of her grief. The artificial is not allowed to supplant the real, or to imply the insincerity of the user, but these possibilities are recognized nonetheless. He lets the two sides effect, within the poem, a delicate balance of sympathy and judgment which does not call for a unitary resolution. He is not being consciously metapoetic but, given the fundamental role which comparison plays in his work and his thought, it is hard to miss the significance for his own poetic enterprise of Criseyde's foray into the world of *imago,* her projection of real grief into a comparable, but alternative, image of herself.

This kind of metapoetic significance is also evident in the treatment of Pandarus. He is the first character substantially to use comparative *exempla* for persuasion. He hopes by this means to convince Troilus at the start of the affair that someone who is unsuccessful as a lover in his own right, can be useful to another lover (1.628–70). With varying degrees of explicitness, he compares himself to a blind man, a whetstone, a fool, bitterness, the color black, shame, sorrow, and the god Phoebus, who was able to cure others but not himself. He then contrasts himself to the soaring hawk, which is implicitly the courtly image for Troilus at this point (1.670–71) though it is shifted to apply to Criseyde later. In effect, Pandarus is engaged in the traditional opening rhetorical technique of gaining the *benevolentia* of his audience, and is doing so by comparative arguments which will assert his value to Troilus's enterprise of love despite Pandarus's own failure in the field. By these *exempla,* Pandarus promotes not just his own vicarious desire to be taken into Troilus's confidence in amatory matters, but also a whole way of learning through the analysis of dissimilarities between things (and, by logical implication, analysis of their similarities). He claims "By his contrarie is every thing declared" (1.637); "Ech set by other, more for other semeth" (1.643); "of two contraries is o lore" (1.645); In all cases, the efficacy of the "other" is being argued. Although Pandarus's accent here is upon the *contrast* between things—upon their extreme dissimilarities—this is no more than an emphasis within the larger comparative method. If one sets aside for a moment the individual comparisons which Pandarus raises, the relationship which he implies could exist between himself and Troilus is actually that traditionally seen to work between the two parts of a positive comparison: illumination is gained from the comparator, though it is the topic which is the important object of our understanding. Troilus should look to Pandarus for assistance in his more important amatory enterprise in the same way as one looks to the comparator to elucidate a more important topic. Chaucer is creating an analogy between Pandarus and the helpful narrator, servant to love's servants. The law of mutually informing contraries applies both to the lover and his friend and to the audience of lovers and their narrator: as Troilus could benefit from the disappointed Pandarus so, it was suggested, could lovers from their unsuccessful would-be brother, the narrator (1.51).

What makes this claim especially intriguing is that it comes from someone whom, it is frequently argued, Chaucer offers to us as an image of the artist.[8] The first analogy between Pandarus and the narrator supports a higher analogy between Pandarus and the artist, with whom, of course, the narrator also enjoys a similaic relationship. Pandarus's lengthy speech is full of persuasive comparisons in a way which mimics Chaucer's own poetic dependence on comparison; it is invigorated by the sheer narrative power which comparative *exempla* provide in a way which recalls Chaucer's attraction to the device. Thus the speech draws together his activity with that of the verbal artist even more forcefully, though perhaps less obviously, than does the famed "housebuilder" image (1.1065–71) by which Chaucer links his Pandar to the rhetorician envisaged in Geoffrey of Vinsauf's *Poetria Nova*.[9]

A web of similaic relations emanates from the speech to cover all aspects of the fictive process: the artist may be to the reader as Pandarus is to Troilus, the narrator to the fictive audience of lovers, and as the comparator is to the topic: of lesser stature and "other," but also the source of illumination and assistance. The analogy suggests that poetry is part of a common enterprise between author and reader; that the role of the former is supposedly to illuminate the latter from a real or pretended position of inferiority; that what poetic fiction shows is recognizably similar in some sense to the world of the reader and that it is the world of the reader which is the important thing to understand. However, it also implies that there are inevitable dissimilarities and areas of mutual incomprehension between the author and reader, differences of motive, feeling, and understanding, gaps between the poem's world and reader's world, and so on. Pandarus is not the same as the narrator, nor the author; Geffrey in the *House of Fame* is not the same as Geoffrey Chaucer. The author is like, and unlike, the reader, and the poem does, and does not, adequately address the reader's situation—just as there are dissimilarities which Pandarus says separate him from Troilus and, one could argue, just like the dissimilarities which separate the two parts of an *imago, similitudo,* or *exemplum*. Poetic fiction is a world of comparison in which dissimilar things are brought into an analyzable and arguable relationship of similarity. In framing the various analogies between the terms of a comparison, the quasi-artist Pandarus and the author, love activity and poetic activity,

Chaucer has been opening up an argument which links *Troilus and Criseyde* with the oeuvre as a whole, and with the process of writing.

It is when one considers what immediate reactions one is encouraged to have to Pandarus's mode of argument, that its resonance for Chaucer's work in general becomes most notable. Perhaps surprisingly in view of the argument I have just set out and the instances we have studied earlier in this chapter, it is neither the inadequacy of Pandarus's individual examples nor of his comparative method which is most strikingly at issue at this early point in Book 1. The very number of comparisons adduced militates against their being open to individual analysis, and therefore to rejection as flawed analogies. It would certainly be possible to argue philosophically that they do not all support the central thesis in the same way: the functional relationship of a whetstone to that which it sharpens is different from the conceptual relation of the color black to its contrary, white. Both cannot support comparison with the lover and his guide in the same way. The analogies are vaguely suggestive rather than logically tight. But this quibble is beside the point in the context of frenzied persuasion. It seems, rather, that Chaucer has deliberately exploited a range of comparative relations in a range of styles, and has done so, not to bring discredit on them, but rather to demonstrate the variety of comparison available to support an argument. Thus there are common saws such as "A fool may ek a wis man ofte gide" (1.630) mixed with the same proverbial material adduced as personal experience: "I have myself ek seyn a blynd man goo / Ther as he fel that couthe loken wide" (1.628–29). There is the supposed "proof" of *ex cathedra* theoretical statement, such as the claim that "of two contraries is o lore" (1.645) together with analogy embedded in a mininarrative within the story, as when Oenone's complaint, following her abandonment by Paris, is quoted to bring to the present case her own example of Phoebus. Comparative proof seems to come from various sources: text, personal and reported experience; it is enshrined in authoritative utterance, and is communicable between people; it is both proverbial and narrative. In other words, it is the richness of the comparative *method,* not the propriety of individual instances, which is on show.

Neither is the comparative method which Pandarus employs undermined by the claim it proposes. Admittedly, one knows the eventual outcome of the love story: the final incapacity of Pandarus to help Troilus when the mishaps of baleful Fortune predominate. In the long term the comparisons do prove inadequate and the argument flawed. But what Pandarus says at this point in the poem is actually true: he does assist Troilus to amatory success, albeit helped on the way by chance events.

The aspect of comparison which Chaucer chooses to draw to one's attention most forcibly is not the accuracy of the individual example, nor even the partial truth of what is being claimed by Pandarus. It is the fulsomeness of the manner in which it is conducted. Citing a multiplicity of examples is not an inevitable aspect of arguing from comparison, but it is frequently found in this poem and elsewhere in Chaucer's oeuvre. It cannot be claimed that the number of examples cited by Pandarus is necessary to the proof of his case, and one wonders why Chaucer has engaged in such supplementarity. Dramatically, it appears to characterize Pandarus's enthusiasm, perhaps even his desperation to be involved, possibly his garrulousness.[10] And maybe bringing together a fool, a god, and a whetstone to prove the same point produces a lack of rhetorical decorum which suitably prepares for the lack of moral control shown at the end of the argument, where he says that he would not even restrain Troilus's love if it were directed at Helen, the wife of Troilus's own brother (1.676–79).[11] But to limit response to the plot or characterizing functions of Pandarus's speech is to ignore the association which Chaucer implies between Pandarus and the artist and, specifically, to undervalue the flamboyant demonstration here of Chaucer's own poetic style. Though the metapoetic implications of the speech are not highly signaled by Chaucer, and its dramatic function is clearly predominant, nevertheless it is hard not to be carried by the speech towards consideration of the author's poetics.

Behind Pandarus's cascade of example ultimately lies Chaucer's rhetorical delight in the plenitude, ornament, and creativity of listing.[12] Different kinds of list are constantly on show in his work from the packed stanzas or reiterative sections of early dream poems through the lengthy, repetitive speeches of characters such as Dorigen, the Merchant, the Knight or the Manciple, to the formal multiplicity of his pilgrims' tales. The plethoric quality of list is given different values in different contexts: sometimes it suggests the author's own inexperienced exploitation of learning; sometimes word-spinning by the character using it; sometimes its plenitude is a feature of irony, as in the Merchant's praise of marriage, or fatuousness, as in the excesses of Chaunticleer, who fails to act on what he so conclusively proves by multiple *exempla* and numerous authorities; sometimes it seems to facilitate allegorical density, as in the trees or mythical figures of the *Parliament;* sometimes it complicates one's judgment of the speaker, as in the cases of Dorigen's list of classical *exempla* for suicide, or Criseyde's many sincere arguments that the lovers' final happiness will be served better by giving up a little of it through temporary separation.

What one would consider overargument in any nonpoetic context, and can sometimes feel is excessive even in a poetic one, often results in a foregrounding of the verbal medium itself, in addition to any value such speech might have in its immediate context. The fulsomeness of speech, frequently shown, as in Pandarus's case, through a plethora of comparisons, can have the effect of drawing "poetry" into the argument of the individual poems. It is not always clear whether its presence there has real metapoetic implications in a particular context or is simply a concomitant of the author's style and general interests. However, in the present case, the strong characterizing aspect of Pandarus's speech, even although it comes at an early point in the poem when one is forming views of the protagonists, should not deflect attention from the fact that he is elsewhere hinted at as an image of the artist, and is speaking here as so many of Chaucer's characters and narrators speak. Metapoetic considerations are more appropriately entertained in *Troilus and Criseyde* than in some other poems, even if they are not pointedly signaled in the text at this particular point.

The dramatic point of the speech is that it fills up the space of Troilus's refusal to speak to Pandarus. But this is the fictional expression of a larger issue in Chaucer's work: the possibility that communicative richness and verbal control substitute for, or even defer, reality rather than articulating it. Although they are drawn from different sources of human experience, and map so many aspects of human intercourse, Pandarus's comparisons as a group nevertheless serve to put words in place of the world; monologue in place of the dialogue he is arguing for. In the same way it might be argued that, however appropriate they are, and however attractive their speaker, Dorigen's examples defer her wished suicide; or the Friar's multiple examples against anger in the *Summoner's Tale* substitute for his actually mastering his own passion; or the Monk's many tragedies supplant his recognition of the spiritual context in which earthly tragedy must be viewed; or the rhetorical lists in the *Parliament of Fowls* displace the harmonised view of love which the narrator appears to desire; or the many projected tales of the pilgrimage defer, and ultimately make impossible, the conclusion of a return to the inn at Southwark. The condition of poetry as potentially substitutive, superfluous or, at least supernumerary, words is thus bound up with the way in which Chaucer presents comparative argument in the mouth of his quasi-artist, Pandarus.

However, it would be a misrepresentation of Chaucer's variety in using lists to claim this as its constant metapoetic implication. In this particular case, the conviction that Pandarus is like an artist is one which grows as the poem develops, and the metapoetic implications of his method of argument at this point, 700 lines into Book 1, are not part of the immediate dynamic of the poem. They are sensed in retrospect and should not swamp one's reactions to the speech, which are actually of wry delight in the enthusiastic prolixity of the argument, and in the dramatic situation of one character trying to convince another who knows precisely what is being done and is inviting it by failing to respond. Chaucer himself sets up a shimmer between immediate poetic context and its possible metapoetic significance, and it is better to respect this than to translate one into the other. The same is true for the possible significance one might attach to the opposite end of the spectrum of words: silence.

Just as Chaucer dramatizes verbal fulsomeness with intermittent metapoetic implications, so he dramatizes its opposite: the moments when the pressure of present forces bears upon the speaker and chokes off the flow of words. Criseyde, after her many and extended arguments for separation, leaves the poem with a cruelly curtailed letter, arguing that "Th'entente is al, and nat the lettres space" (5.1630). After Pandarus's numerous *exempla* to prove his usefulness to Troilus, when he is faced with the truth of Criseyde's betrayal, he is left motionless, astonished, and silent (5.1728–29). The Pardoner, whose tale has been but a record of his most successful *exemplum*, is silenced dramatically by the Host; the Monk and Chaucer the pilgrim are both cut short by others, Chaucer to speak again with the *exemplum* of *Melibee*, the Monk to refuse speech beyond the *exempla* he has given.

Coming to the end of words seems to be a powerful, though polysemous, *topos* for Chaucer. It reflects upon the intensity and possibly self-defeating nature of multiplied speech, shown in such devices as rhetorical lists, groups of *exempla*, or numerous arguments. Barney writes, "Logic will not rest content with multiplicity; hence the numerousness of wisdom-lore, whose sign in Chaucer is the list, undermines its efficacy. A man learned only in wisdom can be cunning, even practically efficient, but not true."[13] The metapoetic relevance of silence is obvious, though varying meanings for it are given in the foreground of the poem in which the *topos* appears. The most overtly metapoetic expression is that of the *Manciple's Tale*. There Chaucer paradoxically combines verbal fulsomeness with silence by having his narrator expatiate on silence using words which are not his own. One may or may not wish to see this as a final bleak turning aside from poetic communication,[14] but whatever value one gives it, it is a late, mythicized expression of a tension which has always been present in his work: between a world of words and the end of that world. Here again, it is through his management of comparison that Chaucer shows his deeper poetic concerns, for the paradoxically verbose demand for silence is built upon an *exemplum* which has offered two images of communication: one through the crow, in which truth is spoken and brings punishment and the other, through the Manciple himself, in which what is spoken is constantly denied to avoid punishment. Speech and silence meet most forcibly in the world of comparison: in the *Manciple's Tale* at the end of Chaucer's career and formatively in his midcareer masterpiece, *Troilus and Criseyde*.

The extravagance of Pandarus's argumentative comparisons is thus part of a larger recurring tension in the oeuvre. But it has its own specific counterpoise in the poem. Pandarus's vibrant wordiness may give way in the end to silence, but his assertive argument by comparison has its contrast, not in silence, but in a morally sensitive refusal to narrate the comparisons he could deploy.[15] This occurs at the key moment when he is showing insight into what he has become: "swich a meene / As maken wommen unto men to comen" (3.254–55). He tells Troilus what his responsibilities should be to the woman who has now permitted his suit (3.239–343), and he shows responsibility in his own control over comparative argument. Chaucer has Pandarus aver at this moment of moral insight that there is a large body of exemplary support for the moral argument he is making. But pointedly he refrains from the attraction of narrating the examples themselves.

Comparison is not *per se* an illegitimate tool because it can be used to persuade someone to actions they would not independently desire, or because it can be used to deceive, though its inadequacies are fully displayed in this poem. It can also be employed for good, and the narrator's desire to present the poem as an "example" implies this. But a delight in the narrative possibilities which the comparative method opens up is more suspect. Comparison diverts one from the topic to the comparator, supposedly to permit a more enlightened return to the topic, but the wordiness of narrated comparative argument could be seen as a verbal diversion which might easily become a substitute for that which it seeks to prove or illuminate. In lines added to Boccaccio, Chaucer has Pandarus reject the "diffusion of speche" which *exempla* can cause, whether proverbial or anecdotal:

> And nere it that I wilne as now t'abregge
> Diffusion of speche, I koude almoost
> A thousand olde stories the allegge
> Of wommen lost through fals and foles bost.
> Proverbes kanst thiselve ynowe
>
> (3.295–99)

Comparison seems susceptible to rhetorical and narrative indulgence which divagates from the argument it is supposed to sustain or may delay its claims being put into effect. It opens up an imagistically and narratively rich, beguiling, and substitute world full of comparators. It can serve the truth, but it can also be meretricious. By avoiding narrated *exempla* in Book 3 Pandarus holds fast to the moral truth he is wanting to promote. But by his list of *exempla* to prove that Troilus should speak to him, Pandarus effectually shuts him up for a considerable part of Book 1. These two instances of comparative argument by Pandarus, one cited without elaboration in the course of serious moral argument, the other attractively detailed and expatiated upon to gain amatory confidences, reflect as a pair Chaucer's ambivalent attitude to persuasive fictions which can serve both "sentence" and "solaas."

This chapter has argued that Chaucer dramatizes comparison in use, and reveals errors of belief, understanding, or principle through the characters' use and abuse of comparison. But it has also claimed that, through this dramatic exploitation of comparison in the fiction itself, Chaucer metapoetically suggests a comparative model for the process of reading poetic fiction. Through opening up the process of comparison, and in particular its metapoetic significance, to scrutiny, Chaucer showed that his poetry was resistant to totalizing readings. Carolyn Dinshaw has argued that this resistance is discovered best through feminist reading: "Troilus and Criseyde only hints—through the reading action of Criseyde—at alternatives to totalising strategies."[16] This may well be true of the alternative to male readings, but both consciousness of the danger of such strategies of reading and resistance to them is signaled at a more fundamental level in Chaucer's own rhetorical epistemology of comparison. In the next chapter I will develop this idea with attention to the status of the poem itself, and the question Chaucer poses as to whether *Troilus and Criseyde,* and his other poems, can constitute *exempla,* illuminating comparators from which the hearer or reader can benefit. However, such a question cannot be answered without bearing in mind Chaucer's sustained dramatizing of comparison in use, its flaws, and advantages, and, of course, his insight that the hearer must be receptive or all comparisons will fail to persuade.

6
The Poem as *Exemplum*

CHAUCER AND HIS CONTEMPORARIES HEARD OR READ COUNTLESS NARratives which contained or constituted *exempla*. Such texts were offered as part of a comparison: they provided the comparators; the lives of their audience constituted the topic which the comparators could illuminate by their transferred meaning. The duty of the writer who wished to teach was to provide such instructive analogies. Consequently, writers who had this intention were always shaping for others the world of the "known" by their writings, whether they left behind translation, version, compilation, imitation, or creation. They expected that their readers or hearers would draw upon this body of "known" truth to elucidate their own experiences, and guide them through life's unpredictability.

The root assumption involved in promoting or using *exempla* was that meaning could be transferred intact from one context to another: from the exemplary story to the hearer's life. The particular was thought to contain a generally valid truth; that general truth could then illuminate other particular contexts. This book has shown that Chaucer's skill in figuration lay precisely in his exploiting different contexts to give a range of value and significance to conventional *similitudo*. An author with such a sense of the particularity of context in one aspect of comparison could hardly avoid questioning the efficacy of comparative *exempla*.

The present chapter looks at some of the ways in which Chaucer's poems problematized the exemplary function which they themselves seemed to promise. For several reasons, it is not an account of all the places in which it was done. Firstly, comparison was consistently explicit in the poetic agenda of the Boethian years, but the heuristic problems which Chaucer exposed then through his analysis of comparison became diffused into the fictionality of the later poems. Consequently, in the later poems it is often more appropriate to study how Chaucer problematizes all meaning than to attend specifically to comparison. Secondly, four of the later *Tales* for which the status of *exemplum* is clearly proposed and undermined have been studied by A. C. Spearing, and I do not wish to go over the same ground: these are the *Friar's, Pardoner's, Nun's Priest's,* and *Manciple's Tales*.[1] Thirdly, I wish to retain an emphasis on Chaucer's longest narrative, *Troilus and Criseyde* because it shows his scrutiny of comparison at its most developed and complete. Nevertheless, I will also be looking at several ways in which Chaucer extended the insights of his middle years into the later poems, and made them resistant to any claim that they provided a "known" body of exemplary wisdom which could then be applied in instructive comparison to the lives of the readers. The chapter begins by discussing the possibility that *Troilus and Criseyde* might itself constitute an *exemplum* for its readers or hearers, and looks at the ways in which Chaucer promotes and undermines this function for his poem.

In a passage not found in Boccaccio, Troilus's sudden falling in love is commended to the audience in this way: "Forthy ensample taketh of this man, / Ye wise, proude, and worthi folkes alle" (1.232–33). The narrator then expands this injunction, adducing the example of wise, great, and worthy people from books and everyday life. The audience is encouraged to find in these people a relevant lesson about not scorning Love:

> Men reden nat that folk han gretter wit
> Than they that han be most with love ynome;
> And strengest folk ben therwith overcome,
> The worthiest and grettest of degree:
> This was, and is, and yet men shall it see.
>
> (1.241–45)

But the narrator does not name these important *exempla*. There were indeed many instances of wise, proud, and worthy people who had fallen in love and whom Chaucer's narrator could have mentioned by name. When one considers Chaucer's penchant for listing names, and in particular named exemplary individuals, it is striking that he eschews such rhetorical expansiveness at the very point in Book 1 where he is operating independently of any source or parallel. A clear instruction to learn from the *exemplum* of Troilus is thus qualified by imprecision masquerading as the forceful persuasion of common knowledge.

Before attempting to explain Chaucer's reticence on the matter of *exempla* here it might help to watch the same process as the reader has just been involved in, played out by a character. As Criseyde walks through the garden with Antigone, her friend begins to sing (2.825). The song is a thankful celebration of happy and fulfilled love by a woman who did not suffer socially as a result. When Criseyde asks whose song it was and, by implication, who experienced in actuality this love match, she is told "the goodlieste mayde / Of gret estat in al the town of Troye" (2.880–81).[2] Again, the person is not named though in terms of the fiction this runs against one's expectations of what knowledge Criseyde and Antigone might have shared: if the maid was as notable as Antigone suggests, she would surely have been known by name to both of them, or could have been named. But, of course, maintaining a consistent fictive world is not Chaucer's aim. What he wants to do is to show how the song is fashioned into an *exemplum*. The name of the maid is not given so as to avoid particularizing the song too much.

One infers from Criseyde's subsequent sighing, her questioning, her refusal to comment, and her changing the subject that she has chosen to find in the circumstances of the maid in Antigone's song an example relevant to her own state, and has let love sink deeper in her heart as a result. The unnamed maid is described in a way which easily permits an analogy with Criseyde herself. Indeed, she appears as the original of whom Criseyde is the *imago,* and Criseyde subconsciously supplies her own name in finding the description appropriate to her condition. Chaucer wants the reader to make the same inference, and mentally to supply Criseyde's name in a way which will make the reader complicit with her framing of the analogy. Covertly, Criseyde has turned the song into a full-fledged *exemplum* in which the "goodlieste mayd" and her experiences clarify and illuminate Criseyde's confused feelings about love.

As we have seen, framing *exempla* and naming, or not naming, the comparator are activities which people engage in with their own private agendas, narrators and authors no less than readers. In the earlier example, in which the narrator commended Troilus as an *exemplum* of how people are unable to avoid falling in love, the narrator was evidently enthusiastic about the benefits of love:

> For alderwisest han therwith ben plesed;
> And they that han ben aldermost in wo,
> With love han ben comforted moost and esed;
> And ofte it hath the cruel herte apesed,
> And worthi folk maad worthier of name,
> And causeth moost to dreden vice and shame.
>
> (1.247–52)

The narrator has an agenda at this point, and even as he is introducing the reader to the business of taking the poem's events as exemplary, he is also protecting his current preferences by failing to name the examples which he urges the audience to accept. The reason is clear. When a named example is imported into a text, the whole story of which it is a part extends the comparison, and can import potentially damaging dissimilarities, or even details which cut against the meaning which the *exemplum* is supposed to promote. The great and good lovers of the past come trailing messy details, tragic endings, traditional evaluations (and sometimes conflicting traditions). To name them would be to open up the narrator's stridently optimistic commendation of love to the ferreting interpretation of the reader or hearer. By giving no names to the examples, Chaucer achieves three things: he protects his narrator's enthusiasm for the amatory process at a point where the reader is to be made complicit with it; he reveals, at the start of the poem, the special pleading which exemplary comparison supports; and he creates a space in which the reader, without apparent encouragement from the narrator, can reflect upon the *exempla* which the narrator does not name, perhaps supplying examples of great and wise people who have fallen in love to their manifest *disadvantage*. Although exemplary comparison is described here by the narrator, with characteristic Chaucerian duplicity, as "other thing collateral" (1.262) to the actual narrative of Troilus, it is actually the area in which the author negotiates with his readers about meaning, altering his own emphases as he goes, and encouraging them to reflect on the adequacy or clarity of the meaning being offered.

The events of *Troilus and Criseyde* are intermittently presented by character and narrator as potential *exempla*. At points, the narrator feels able to draw general, instructive, conclusions about the state of his and the readers' world, claiming that the experience of the tragic lovers is not unique. A ground of similarity is established; a common truth seems to cover the poems' characters and its readers. At such points, the poem is offered implicitly as a comparative example. He states what illumination it brings to us:

> Swich is this world, whoso it kan byholde;
> In ech estat is litel hertes reste.
> God leve us for to take it for the beste!
>
> (5.1748–50)

However, this is supposedly the same narrator who enthusiastically conveyed more buoyant attitudes to love earlier. His exemplary teaching too often seems like a simple generalizing of the stage the poem's events have got to, without an overall, consistent, point of view. When all is exemplary, nothing is especially illuminating for what is claimed is merely a reflection of what we do anyway: cling to past events as a comparative guide for the future.

Chaucer's artist persona Pandarus also offers the events of the poem as example and tries to draw significance from them. When disaster has finally occurred, Pandarus gives this summation of meaning:

> For in this world ther is no creature,
> As to my dom, that ever saugh ruyne
> Straunger than this, thorugh cas or aventure.
> But who may al eschue, or al devyne?
> Swich is this world! Forthi I thus diffyne:
> Ne trust no wight to fynden in Fortune
> Ay propretee; hire yiftes ben comune.
>
> (4.386–92)

Pandarus's speech is paradoxical. He implies that the catastrophe of the lovers' separation is so extreme that no prior case of destruction by chance is an adequate comparator. This response reveals the crushing particularity with which disaster impresses its victims. When one is on the receiving end of unpredictable chance the first casualty is one's sense that there is an illuminating "known" whose comparative *exempla* will explain the event. However, Pandarus moves quickly to reestablish the comparative scheme, implying that *because* this story is unexampled it can act as the ultimate comparator for others—an *exemplum* so signal that it is really the exemplar. He draws wisdom from what this case tells him, and implicitly sets it up as the example to which all should turn when trying to understand the chance disasters of their lives. If one is confused by disaster, this poem will prove a suitable guide: "swich is this world."

However, Pandarus's claim is inherently paradoxical, for the essence of Fortune's operation is that it can always escape the judgment of predictability which one would make for it. There is no guarantee that this story, tragic as it is, will indeed remain the most signal instance of Fortune's operation, or will do more to illuminate than other disasters of Fortune which one could use for comparison. In claiming as much as he does Pandarus reveals the measure of personal investment which everyone has when deciding about uniqueness and comparison: he is trying to dignify the situation of the lovers; perhaps trying to accommodate the ultimate failure of his own amatory enterprise; and to a degree trying to control an essentially uncontrollable force in the world by claiming to have established the foundation for all future comparativist thinking on the issue. He wishes to fix the events and their meaning. The story is to be plucked from the flux of events, and made stable through transmutation into a series of "saws" which can be drawn from it. Pandarus is using life to make proverb, hopelessly asserting the value of wisdom based on comparison when the events themselves have run away from any practical wisdom he can offer. The

6: THE POEM AS *EXEMPLUM*

world of chance is a world of particularities which are resistant to illumination by previous events and will never be repeated exactly again, so that they cannot themselves elucidate the particular events yet to come.

When Chaucer shows his narrator espousing different exemplary meanings for the events as they unfold; shows Pandarus's attempt to fix the "known" on which later comparisons will be built; and shows Criseyde privately shaping a song into an *exemplum*, he is offering the reader salutary paradigms for the reading process. The narrator and characters all try to read exemplary meaning in the events of the poem, and in doing so are turned themselves into *exempla* of the unreliability of exemplary thinking.

For the poem to be entertained as a source of possible *exempla* the person who is going to draw upon it has to consider it comparable with the world it is to illuminate. Events which could be considered unique, or wholly "other" lose their capacity to instruct because the dissimilarities between the comparator and topic are too great. For a poem to sustain an exemplary function, its constituents, its characters, its events and its cultural milieu, have to be recognizable enough to make the comparison worthwhile, and dissimilarities from the world of the hearers have to be clearly delineated so that contrast can form part of the instruction. Consequently the reader's judgments about similarity and dissimilarity are the basis of any claim that the poem is didactic in effect.

Sometimes the experiences of Troilus and Criseyde are presented as recognizably like those of the audience; sometimes their foreignness is asserted. This ambivalence extends to the location of the poem in a medieval walled city.[3] Sometimes also the role of *exemplum* is claimed for the poem on the basis of its constituents sharing the world of the reader, and yet at other times Chaucer presents them as either too past or too pagan, or unique, or too emotionally appealing, or too much part of an unpredictable world in which no analogies can be helpfully drawn, to permit its comparison to the readers' lives. These shifts are particularly marked in the *prohemia* to Books 2 and 3 and in the introductory lines to Book 1 which function as a kind of *prohemium*.

> The double sorwe of Troilus to tellen,
> That was the kyng Priamus sone of Troye,
> In lovynge, how his aventures fellen
> Fro wo to wele, and after out of joie,
> My purpos is, er that I parte fro ye.
> Thesiphone, thow help me for t'endite
> Thise woful vers, that wepen as I write.
>
> (1.1–7)

Far from promising general significance, the poem actually opens with a narrow narratorial focus, and the extreme stylistic introversion of wordplay. Chaucer links the names of hero and city, and in doing this compresses the notion of the "doubleness" of the sorrow to be narrated into a *traductio* which is almost the punning of *adnominatio:* the poem will tell of the "double sorwe of Troilus . . . / That was the kyng Priamus sone of Troye."[4]

As the stanza develops one finds that the emotions which the story can arouse do *not* depend on its being brought into the public domain: the narrator already has a private emotional engagement with it. Certainly, there is a generically determined declamation in the opening, and a direct address of the poet to his audience, but these are supplanted by a more powerful image of private weeping. Despite the directness, public telling actually means "writing."

From this point, however, the poem begins to swell again into the realm of function, of comparison, of public service.[5] The narrator becomes an instrument to assist others in their lamentation, and he situates decorum in the world of analogies which link the reader and himself, the subject matter and the style in which it is delivered:

> For wel sit it, the sothe for to seyne,
> A woful wight to han a drery feere,
> And to a sorwful tale, a sory chere.
>
> (1.12–15)

Wordplay now creates extrinsic links, in lines which by their very chiasmic repetitiveness assert that the narrator and lovers are comparable even if there is dissimilarity etched into their likeness: "For I, that God of Loves servantz serve, / Ne dar to Love" (1.15). This close relationship becomes almost substitutive when the chiasmus intensifies to reverse our expectations about action. The poet thanks the lover whom he is serving, and whose labor he takes over

> if this may don gladnesse
> Unto any lovere, and his cause availle,
> Have he my thonk, and myn be this travaille.
>
> (1.19–21)

The effort to compare must also be made by the supposed audience: the narrator canvasses the sympathy of happy lovers by asking them to recognize similarities between the unhappy lovers of his story, and themselves, and other, supposedly nonfictional, lovers. Others may "ben in the cas / Of Troilus" (1.29–30). The narrator's avowed aim is to demonstrate a condition unlimited by place or time, to show "Swych peyne and wo as Loves folk endure" (1.34). Consequently, he seems to expect that the poem's likely reception will involve comparison and the identification of similarities between the events of the poem and the experiences of the lovers who listen to it, or read it.

However, the comparability proposed is at least complex and also slightly oblique. A four-way comparison is set up: between the lovers in the poem, the lovers in the fictional audience, other lovers who are suffering as Troilus did, and the author, whose analogy with lovers is tenuous and ambiguous. As the function of the poem is enlarged from the initial specificness of its reference, it proves to be dependent on a difficult set of comparisons shot through with potentially disabling dissimilarities. For example, the narrator asks lovers to sympathize with unhappy lovers like Troilus. But the ones he addresses are those that "bathen in gladnesse" (22). To do this they are expected to make comparison either with their own past experiences remembered (from a condition of joy not wholly conducive to accurate memory), or that which they can recognize in other people. It would be possible, therefore, for the audience of happy lovers to feel at this stage that, if it has status as an *exemplum,* the poem does not have it directly for them. The condition of love which the narrator is proposing to outline does not have direct similarities with their own present one.

Furthermore, when the narrator sets up the different classes of Love's servants for whom his audience should pray, and for whom he writes, one is struck as much by their radically different fortunes as by their similar status as lovers: prayer must be made for those like Troilus; those who will never recover from their despair; those that are falsely slandered; those that are at their ease. The condition is happily homogenized under the single term "love" but the single stanza contains such a great diversity of experience as to subvert the community of similarity which the narrator is proposing and thus undermine any comparisons one might want to frame.

A kinship relationship, implying similarity between the narrator and lovers, is set up but even that is qualified by the ambiguities of the statement: the narrator is to have compassion on lovers "as though" he were their own brother (1.51). Ambiguity here draws dissimilarity after it, and both similarity and pretence to similarity are implicit in the phrase "as though."

In fact, despite the opening web of comparisons through which the narrator seeks the benevolence of his audience, the poem offers a different view of the world. The uniqueness of all experience and, hence, the problematic status of example, is a recurring insinuation in *Troilus and Criseyde* and is present at the start in what we might think of as merely an instance of rhetorical modesty. The narrator says that he can only show the pain and woe of Love's folk "in som manere." If we read the statement closely it proves not to be about stylistic inadequacy for which the poet might be held responsible. It is a variant on that idea which actually locates the potential for failure in the exemplificatory function of the poem:

> And ek for me, preieth to God so dere
> That I have myght to shewe, in som manere,
> Swich peyne and wo as Loves folk endure,
> In Troilus unsely aventure.
>
> (1.32–35)

The aim is to exemplify general pains through (or "in") the particular events narrated. But the phrase "in som manere" already envisages that the result will be partial, individual, limited in its representativeness and, therefore, in its capacity to function as an instructive comparison for our own experiences. Chaucer signals here the disabling of comparison which he believes undermines much of our received wisdom, be it literary or existential, but which, as I have suggested, also empowers his writing. He suggests such disability at the same time as urging the reader towards the thinking which is vitiated by it. The phrase is another example of Chaucer keeping in play both failure and success in communication. One is reminded that "Geffrey" only saw lies and truth mingling "sometyme" on their way to the House of Fame (*House of Fame*, 2088).

Fractures in the similarity upon which the exemplificatory function depends are thus hinted at, though not openly acknowledged, from the start. The passage as a whole (1.1–56) is a *prohemium* which is deliberately not signaled as such, so as to allow complexity of poetic function and application to arise with apparent naturalness out of the opening narratorial gesture.[6] The apparent simplicity of an historical enterprise is progressively caught up into widening circles of potential comparison which join to Troilus a fictional audience, the narrator as narrator, and as would-be lover, and lovers of different kinds outside the poem. The past event is not discrete, but part of present perceptions; the past lover not isolated but joined to present lovers; the unhappiness that is done with is prolonged fictively by its capacity to act as an example. But the poem in which it will do this acknowledges the complexity and failure of the enterprise.

The formal, extranarrative, *prohemia* elsewhere in the poem also require us to be conscious of the tension between inscrutable particularity and the matrix of comparison within which we try to understand

6: THE POEM AS *EXEMPLUM*

it. The *prohemia* to Books 2 and 3 express this tension with different emphases. While the narrator of Book 1 asserted the positive comparability of the story to the lives of the hearers, and set up Troilus's experiences as an example for us, the *Prohemium* to Book 2 moves away from any sense that the comparable includes a high measure of similarity which might lead us to draw positive instruction from the story. The substantial dissimilarities at the heart of the *similitudo* now predominate; the particularity of all experience now denies the capacity of the individual case to act as example for another. The narrator who was hoping to be treated as though he were the brother of lovers now hides behind lack of "sentement" (2.13). Comparisons which operated positively in Book 1, get reused to assert the opposite: whereas Pandarus thought a blind man could sometimes achieve what the sighted could not (1.628–29), now the blind man's deficiencies are emphasized as Chaucer argues for his own dependence on the Latin of his "auctour" rather than any personal insight. Similarly, love itself is seen as more individual, less a matter of common practices: there are hardly three people listening to the poem who have acted or spoken in love exactly alike (2.43–44). Linguistic idiom changes through time, and behavior appropriate at one time or to one lover seems inutile out of its context. The possibility that the audience will not unanimously recognize a common experience with each other let alone with the poem's hero is openly acknowledged. Both writing and loving now prove to be very individual activities: some men carve wood, some stone; some write out of knowledge, others are translators; some love one way, some another. By implication, the capacity of Chaucer's poem to offer *exempla* is substantially reduced after the buoyant comparisons of the first Book, which were proposed by Pandarus and narrator, and which were intended by the former to direct the emotions and actions of Troilus and by the latter to convey the story to the reader as exemplificatory of general truths. The sense one had of similarity, of positive comparability now leads to an emphasis on dissimilarity and on comparability which can only issue in contrast.

Of course, what the assertions of the Book 2 *Prohemium* do is to alert one anew to the issue of comparability and to the need to explore the dissimilarity and similarity at the heart of the narrative's relation to its hearers. In effect, comparability is all the more strongly on the agenda for Chaucer's having stressed the dissimilarities which would emerge to frustrate its issuing in example. While this *Prohemium*'s emphasis on mystery may owe something to the characteristic rhetorical modesty which Chaucer displays when discussing women (engaged in here because the narrative is now switching to Criseyde), it is not actually the enigma of woman's reception of a lover which is overtly presented; it is the enigma of the lover's actions and the writer's conveying of them which exercises the narrator. By doing this, the *Prohemium* ensures that the reader's judgment is not subordinated to emotional interest in the courtship but is focussed more earnestly about the lines of similarity which run between the poem and extratextual experience.

The narrator does actually raise a specific instance of dissimilarity between the lovers in his audience and his characters: the claimed contemporary English practice of courting openly (2.38–42) but, while the secretness of the affair is indeed a major issue for Troilus and Criseyde, it seems unlikely that this concern would appear alien to the poem's audience; the claim smacks of wry disingenuousness. In any case, it would be a mistake to think that the argument about similarity and dissimilarity in love's practices comes down to this particular issue. It is typical of Chaucer to offer an instance (which I suspect is here ironic, anyway) without saying clearly whether the instance is one of many possible props to his argument or, in fact, wholly constitutes the argument. It is thus left to the reader to diminish the problem by believing it wholly encapsulated in the particular instance. The effect of the *Prohemium,* taken as a whole, is to insist that readers judge the courtship as a representation of behavior more or less like their own, with all the attendant moral reflection which such a recognition should carry, and with all the disabling hermeneutic circularities and interpretative prejudices which are involved in such judgments.[7]

To summarize, the *Prohemium* to Book 2 demands that readers should not wonder at the dissimilarities between Troilus's road to love and their own. The gap between different individuals, societies, and ages is explanation enough. At the same time, however, the stress of the *prohemium* is heavily comparative; the depiction of the lovers in the succeeding Book often recognizably contemporary rather than historical; and the aim is precisely to make the readers compare the courtship in the Book with their own sense of how love's process might be carried out. By making the question of dissimilarity overt in a context where similarity is undoubtedly present, Chaucer promotes both judgment and empathy in the reader and, if anything, suggests the relevance of one's own experiences for feeling, understanding, and evaluating the process by which Troilus and Criseyde are brought together.

In the *Prohemium* to Book 3, however, the emphasis has shifted markedly. It stresses the universality of love, and says that there is a general law of love for all, namely, that defeat awaits any who oppose love. But it also asserts that only at the divine level is the particularity of things understood. Here the poem agrees, though in a less pessimistic and less explicitly pagan way, with the plot of the *Knight's Tale.* There the success of Palamon and the disastrous failure of his near identical brother-in-arms, Arcite, are decided upon by Saturn. Whatever explanations the characters themselves offer, the poem's plot argues that the mysteries which make two similars so dissimilar in fate are only explicable at the divine level.[8] Addressing Love, the narrator says:

> Ye knowe al thilke covered qualitee
> Of thynges, which that folk on wondren so,
> Whan they kan nought construe how it may jo
> She loveth hym, or whi he loveth here,
> As whi this fissh, and naught that, comth to were.
>
> (3.31–35)

Enigma, mystery, and incomparability are at the heart of love's apparently analogous actions despite all the space given to exposing Pandarus's machination, and Criseyde's ratiocination, and all the comparisons one might implicitly frame with one's own lives in trying to understand the course of events in the story. Explanation and application have to admit their incompleteness before the enigma of love. If love is so enigmatic, so unpredictable, its capacity to produce usable *exempla* must be limited.

The *prohemia* are the places where the narrator is overtly on show, and the contrasting emphases of those which preface the first three books reveal his anxiety about his role as medium for a tale of love; about the reader's drawing comparisons between the extraliterary world and the poem, and about the potency of argument from comparison in the face of love's mysteries. As so often, however, Chaucer is using love as the focus of issues which are fundamental to the human condition: issues of learning, writing, understanding, and exerting power over our own and other people's experience, through transferring meaning from one context to another. The heart of the problem for Chaucer is the tension he perceives between the particularity of things and general meanings, which have themselves derived from other particular contexts. This anxiety cuts across the solace of the poem, which Alfred David claims "comes from the pleasure of feigning the ancient world after the image of the modern one so that ... we, too, may imagine that we are experiencing identity with its fiction and feeling both its pleasure and its pain."[9] Understanding the particular seems to demand quite contrary modes of thought: employing the known and acknowledging the unknown. This tension lies behind the promise of exemplary meaning for his poems and their consistent failure to deliver that exemplary meaning in a convincing way. One can see the tension reflected in his account of the lovers' sexual consummation.

After very many lines in which Chaucer has built his imagery into dynamic, metaphorical phrasing which operated *en passant* at the level of narrative, he begins more substantially to employ simile when the lovers embrace in bed. One thinks of these similes as descriptive and as carrying the reader into the love, but they are also gestures of distance which insist on judgment rather than feeling, and which paradoxically recognize the unknown quality of love by using comparisons from the known world to illuminate it, and by doing so repeatedly. The sparrow hawk and the lark, the aspen leaf, the woodbine and the tree, the startled nightingale, the condemned man suddenly rescued, and of course the bitter medicine which heals, and the distress which can be a necessary preliminary to joy—these comparisons are all used within fifty-five lines (3.1191–245) to ornament the episode, explore its action, and to fashion some kind of understanding of it. They fit into and extend existing patterns of imagery, such as natural growth, the condemned or executed man, the bird of prey, and the use of examples to argue for changes of fortune from bad to good.

However, the choice of overt comparison betrays the narratorial, and perhaps authorial, struggle to understand while it seems to demonstrate authorial power over the reader: it shows the speaker's separateness and reiterated search as much as his involvement and achieved narration. It is not hard to sense a similarity between this urgent examination of the known world to permit a similaic grasp of the ineffable, and the frantically committed courtship activity of Pandarus, who draws on *exempla* to harry Troilus into speech and Criseyde into bed. Pandarus's problem is represented in the narrative as a personal failure in love which leads him both to vicarious involvement in Troilus's courtship, and to a limitation of vision, ultimately revealed in the tragedy of the lovers' separation. Chaucer's problem, though often similarly fictionalized through his narrators' ignorance of love and perhaps carrying some of the sexual anxieties which Pandarus shows, also has a more philosophical dimension, lying in the gap between the individual event and the world of events within which the individual exists and from which it has a multitude of potential comparators.

One sees at the highest level in this narrative project a tension between the particularity of the lovers' story and its role as a possible *exemplum* for others; correspondingly one finds Chaucer in this passage swinging between extremely different ways of understanding the event: first by comparisons, in the similes already alluded to, and then immediately afterwards by a determined factuality which offers instead the physical details of Criseyde's body, as Troilus discovers it, as a complementary way of understanding the experience of love. If the wider lens employing comparison from the known won't do, perhaps a lens focussed on the particularities of the body will:

> Hire armes smale, hire streghte bak and softe,
> Hire sydes longe, flesshly, smothe, and white
> . . . .
> Hire snowissh throte, hire brestes rounde and lite.
>
> (3.1247–50)

Chaucer thus replicates by a simple juxtaposition of points of view the deep problem of understanding which underlies most of his work: whether the individual can be understood by comparison, or whether the comparative enterprise has to give way before the particularities of the individual. The practical answer is, of course, that they both contribute to understanding, but they contribute by their tension, not by offering an area of overlap or common truth which one could arrive at by looking at the issue from either direction. The simile of the aspen leaf and the immediate factuality of her white flesh don't really amount to a whole representation of Criseyde, but exchanging one for the other gives an illusion of wholeness, even if it leaves the heterogeneity of things unresolved.

The description of the lovers in bed thus offers a version of the larger problem which is seen elsewhere in the dissimilarity at the heart of the simile; the fracture between the individual instance and the *exemplum* one would comparatively adduce to understand it; even between the *imago* and its source; between the genre and the particular piece of writing one would assign to it; between a sexual tradition for describing or judging women and an individual woman; between the final exemplary ends of the author's fictional project and his capacity to see more in a particular case than he can explain. Of course, there is a further paradox in that the description which Chaucer gives of Criseyde's body, though it asserts the particularity of experience, is actually here of a conventionally beautiful woman. While Chaucer is moving between the extremes of comparison and particularity and is thus revealing what he believes is a fundamental difficulty of understanding, he is also, as a narrator, promoting a generically determined appreciation of Criseyde's beauty and Troilus's feelings, and is inviting the reader to share the joy of the consummation through conventional detail. His artistic commitment in the consummation scene is double: to recreate the experience of joy, and yet also to show the difficulty of understanding that joy. This is best achieved by speaking in a conventional mode which purports to convey, but actually denies, the individual experience.

It is because of this doubleness that one emerges from the scene of the consummation with a puzzling sense of beauty and of unease; of involvement, and distance; with room left both to applaud the acme of the lovers' pleasures and to judge them. It is not just modern insight which allows one to object to the predatory or threatening implication of the sparrowhawk or condemned man images, nor is it simply that these images could have carried such implications at the time they were written.[10] Rather, all such responses are permitted because Chaucer has left space in the narrative to permit judgment, and interpretation. And he has done this partly by adopting the overt, self-consciously, comparative form of simile, and partly by representing in the sequence of the narrative an anxiety of understanding, his own anxiety in my view, albeit one structurally ascribable to his narrator in this case.

The *Palinode* is the fullest development of the claim that the poem can function as example, and the most assertive statement of the value of comparison as a means to enlightenment, but it also shows the limitations of those views.[11] In urging young, fresh folks to turn from the transient, pretended love offered by this world, the narrator's argument is based on the priority of the close likeness between humanity and God over other kinds of relation. His readers are supposed to feel the strong pull of a higher likeness, coupled with a recognition of the essential dissimilarity between Christ's love and earthly ones: its faithfulness to death. The comparisons between earthly loves subtly urged at the opening of the poem and in the *Prohemium* to Book 2 give way in the *Palinode* to a comparison in which the dissimilarity of heavenly from earthly love is both identifiable and fundamental. All people should love the one who died on the cross for love of humanity, rose again, and ascended into heaven, for he will not be false as earthly lovers may be (5.1842–45). Despite its flaws and dangers, Chaucer has not turned away from comparison as a mode of thought at the end of the poem. Rather he embraces it, transferring it to a higher sphere of operation in which the grounds for conducting it are more certain, and the dissimilarities contained in it are more predictable. While he draws an obvious contrast between the betrayal he has narrated and Christ's faithful love, Chaucer also asserts a close, even dramatic, confrontation of similars in our human relation to God.

> And of your herte up casteth the visage
> To thilke God that after his ymage
> Yow made
>
> (5.1838–40)

Does Chaucer mean that figuratively our heart looks at God or that from our hearts we look at him? In either case, the face sees a near reflection of itself. The structure of the spiritual universe is predicated upon a deep and positive comparison between us and God, and this gives salvific potency to comparison as a mode of thought, and underpins the author's didactic enterprise to use the story of the lovers as an example for us.

Chaucer does leave the poem as an example in important respects. One can sympathize with the notion that the story of these unhappy lovers will always be exemplary of the unpredictable condition of the world: "Swich is this world, whoso it kan byholde; / In ech estat is litel hertes reste" (5.1749–50). It is an adequate "ensample" of betrayal and of life's fortuitous disasters, and of the common human failure to choose the proper object of love. However, the shift in tone and fragmentation of discursive line which characterise the end of the poem suggest the author's concern about the claim that his poem can operate successfully as an *exemplum*.[12] In making the comparative process difficult at the conclusion of the poem, Chaucer is developing the dynamics of this process as he has seen them from the beginning. These final slippages accompany particular details which bear heavily upon the poem as *exemplum* and cannot be easily accommodated by it. If the poem is to be a comparator in future comparisons, how significant are the lovers' paganism and the fact that it was a woman who betrayed a man?

The first detail is not satisfactorily accommodated. Chaucer chooses to tie paganism into the argument about contrasting earthly and heavenly lovers but his tone in doing so is extreme, emotionally confusing and distances the reader from the argument. On the surface, paganism seems theologically part and parcel of the narrator's direction that young fresh folk should look to God. However, the story's exemplary force is partly undermined by its implying that the paganism of the lovers is a significant feature. A disabling dissimilarity between the lovers and Chaucer's contemporary Christians, who are supposed to be taking illumination from them, is thus built into the comparison on which the exemplary function of the poem depends. The assertion that the lovers were pagans may well strengthen one's spiritual rejection of them, but it does not make the comparative enterprise from which wisdom is finally drawn more personally convincing, for it directs the spiritual argument into a specific contrast of Christian and pagan, whereas the paganism of the lovers is supposedly only the extreme instance of life lived separately from God. By reminding his readers of this, Chaucer shifts their awareness away from the similarity between the lovers' earthly condition and their own towards perceiving their dissimilarity. The poem would otherwise be acceptable as an "ensample" of the painful, transient, fortune-dogged nature of earthly love. However reluctant one might be to release emotional commitment to the lovers, one would have to recognize the justice of the comparison drawn to distinguish between earthly and heavenly love. But one is not permitted this clear significance. It is, in fact, the citing of their paganism which *prevents* their experience from being directly exemplary for a Christian audience.

The second detail exposes a major difficulty in adopting the story as an example. Chaucer addresses this explicitly when he requests that women will not blame him for having written of Criseyde as he has (5.1772–85). The problem is whether, within an exemplary poem, Criseyde is specifically to constitute an "ensample" of women's behavior towards men. The problem would not be so great if the narrator were not arguing so strongly for the story's being exemplary as a whole. His general didactic intention is creating localized problems of interpretation just as all claims for similarity have to cope with particular dissimilarities. *The Book of Troilus* is hopefully to be one of the comparators which will frame the lives of everyone, one of the "known" things by which the unknown will be understood. But if that function extends to detail such as the sex of the betrayer, it may be damaging to women, unacceptable as an example, and indeed inaccurate. The fact that the story already has this status is used by Chaucer to defend himself for having told it. He is not bringing a new misogynist comparator into the world for other books have been written about her betrayal (5.1776). Chaucer wishes to alter the tradition which he finds by making it less misogynistic, yet also to defend himself by its prior existence.

He is wholly conscious that to make a poem is to reinforce or alter the matrix of comparison which will structure the thought of readers to come, establishing the known literary comparators for them to apply in understanding other events or tales. Writing requires authorial responsibility because it is a potentially dangerous thing for the people receiving it.[13] He shows the Wife of Bath circumscribed, in the literal and political senses of that word, by the examples contained in Jankyn's "Book of Wicked Wives." Perhaps it is evidence of Chaucer's deeper sympathy for his lovers that Criseyde is not one of Jankyn's examples, though he acknowledges in *Troilus* that she had become one and takes steps to avoid leaving her gender as part of the exemplary thrust of the poem. Christine de Pisan recounts an instance, comparable to that of Jankyn and the Wife, which involved the *Romance of the Rose* and a jealous man

> who, whenever in the grip of passion, would go and find the book and read it to his wife; then he would become violent and strike her and say such horrible things as, "These are the kinds of tricks you pull on me. . . ." At every word he finds appropriate, he gives her a couple of kicks or slaps. Thus it seems clear to me that whatever other people think of this book, this poor woman pays too high a price for it.[14]

Part of the difficulty one experiences when reading Chaucer's defence of himself for telling the story is that one finds him elsewhere playing with just those features of the comparative process which he now wants to clarify. Setting up potential comparisons only to deny their salient, and obvious, ground of application is a technique which he seems self-consciously to acknowledge as his through his portrayal of the Manciple. The Manciple presents three "ensamples" with obvious derogatory application to women, and then outrageously applies them instead to men (*Manciple's Tale* 162–88). On the face of it, this is not too different from writing a poem which ends in a woman's faithlessness and then trying to obstruct the gender implications at the point where the poem is offered as *exemplum*. However, in raising the issue of Criseyde's betrayal of Troilus, and rejecting it as part of the example, Chaucer does appear to me to be sincere. It is consistent with his narrator's sympathy towards Criseyde elsewhere; it is less shocking than the Manciple's volte-face. And he is more truthful in his claim: he simply argues that men also betray women, and that there are authoritative counter examples of women's faithfulness to men. However, the extent to which one accepts this limitation on comparison will depend ultimately on the desires which govern one's reading. Readers are no more free from preference or prejudice in responding to Chaucer's definition of the poem as example than Troilus, Criseyde, Pandarus, or the narrator in their attitudes to comparison.

With the exception of the Retractions, the *Palinode* is the final place where Chaucer addresses explicitly the terms in which the poem should or should not be seen as a comparator by his future readers, and hearers. In it he negotiates with them about the comparative mode of understanding which he has employed, exploited, and even thematized in the poem itself, and of which he knows the poem, once heard, will become a part. Though he acknowledges, and creates through his narrator, fractures in the exemplificatory conclusion to the poem, that does not mean that the claim for the poem as didactic example is fatally flawed or unacceptable; rather that its acceptability is a product of the reader's managing of comparison, the reader's selection of similarities, choice of priorities, and analysis of dissimilarity.[15] Chaucer knows that the poem is cut adrift when written; he is explicitly concerned lest it should be miswritten by its copyist, and he is evidently anxious to prevent certain readings by its audience, but he also recognizes the continuous contestation of reading which his own poem most deeply exemplifies.

Chaucer developed in later poems some of the methods by which he problematised *Troilus and Criseyde* as an *exemplum*.[16] The *Clerk's Tale* is a case in point. It is offered to its audience as an *exemplum*, a "known" for future illumination, but it is an uneasy comparator.[17] The Clerk first has to take gender out of it, as the narrator of *Troilus and Criseyde* tried to do, and he has to change the salient virtue in the story to accommodate his moral, preferring to make it more like the *Man of Law's Tale,* a story counselling constancy in the face of earthly adversity:

> This storie is seyd nat for that wyves sholde
> Folwen Grisilde as in humylitee,
> For it were inportable, though they wolde,
> But for that every wight, in his degree,
> Sholde be constant in adversitee
> As was Grisilde
>
> (*Clerk's Tale* 1142–47)

Readers are to strip away from the *exemplum* its most prominent features, and understand it not in its own terms but by the meaning assigned for its application. The exemplary point is shifted away from what the fiction sustains, away from the features which the Clerk thinks would disable it as a suitable moral comparison for our own lives. The story's failure of credibility is thus transmuted into a purely quantitative dissimilarity between its action and action with a higher spiritual value:

> For sith a womman was so pacient
> Unto a mortal man, wel moore us oghte
> Receyven al in gree that God us sent
>
> (*Clerk's Tale* 1149–51)

Having made this shift, the narrator then has to strip away more of the fiction and encourage the reader to do it: what God sends us is not sent for the reasons that Walter visited pain on Griselda; God is not like Walter; he does not have psychological obsessions to work out; He does not tempt us; as our Creator He has every justification to test what He made; He has already redeemed us; the benefits of this spiritual exercise to us are implicitly greater than Griselda's recovery of what was hers anyway (1152–61). This sequence of adjustments to the comparison is not unlike that which problematizes the *Palinode* of *Troilus and Criseyde.* There the narrator shed features of the fiction; condemned what he had commended; culturally revalued his lovers; and embraced a higher comparison between humanity and God, forcing his audience to perceive a simple contrast between God's love and earthly love, rather than permitting them a more complex negotiation between their own lives and those of the lovers. Both poems find that the exemplary function threatens fiction, and it does so because inevitable dissimilarities between the comparator and the topic have to be elided to make the comparison stick. The fictive comparator carries with it details which are embarrassments to the application of the story as an *exemplum*. But the *exemplum* could not be so disrupted by details if Chaucer were less committed to grounding his fictions in a world of recognizable emotions and to using naturalistic techniques on material which might otherwise be kept distanced and abstract. Because Chaucer eschews a purely exemplary world and intermittently naturalizes his narratives he both opens up the fiction as a potential comparator for the lives of his readers, and yet limits its capacity to operate as pure *exemplum*.

The *Man of Law's Tale* shows these contrary tendencies. The story is drawn, on the one hand, towards proving moral truth through a mythic narrative and, on the other, towards moments of real emotionalism which ground the truth in recognizable experience. Each dimension actually has its supportive form of comparison (though it is the larger comparative function of the story itself with which this chapter is concerned). The moral superstructure is constantly upheld by historical and biblical *exempla* among which, one feels, the narrator would like his *Tale* to be placed.

> Who yaf Judith corage or hardynesse
> To sleen hym Olofernus in his tente,
> And to deliveren out of wrecchednesse
> The peple of God? I seye, for this entente,
> That right as God spirit of vigour sente
> To hem, and saved hem out of meschance,
> So sente he myght and vigour to Custance.
> (*Man of Law's Tale* 939—45)

On the other hand, the impulse to realise the story shows itself in the emotional scenes and direct speech of Custance which Chaucer adds to his source. Passages such as that in which Custance covers her baby's eyes with a scarf, and says "Pees, litel sone, I wol do thee noon harm" (836), may seem to the modern reader too sentimental to give the story a naturalistic grounding, but they are clearly intended to do so. It is also impossible to ignore the immediate effect of this supportive *exemplum*:

> Have ye nat seyn somtyme a pale face
> Among a prees, of hym that hath be lad
> Toward his deeth, wher as hym gat no grace,
> And swich a colour in his face hath had
> Men myghte knowe his face that was bistad
> Amonges alle the faces in that route?
> So stant Custance, and looketh hire aboute.
> (*Man of Law's Tale* 645–51)[18]

Whether or not we wish to associate the comparator in this particular comparison with the professional experience of the Man of Law, it remains at the opposite experiential extreme from the text-based *exempla*. It imports its "known" not from books but from life, from the contemporary world in which the virtue of constancy must be practiced, and the poem is being read. The poem does not sustain this effect for long: the narrator immediately turning to a different audience of queens, duchesses, and ladies (652–53), but the extremes of style and reference which are revealed in these comparisons affect the total exemplary character of the poem.

With both naturalistic and textual *exempla* working together Chaucer seeks an overall balance between the exemplary force of the *Tale* and a naturalistic base for responding to it. However, the balance between these in the *Man of Law's Tale* is struck on the side of the exemplary. Consequently its naturalism is accepted as an intermittent vivifying of a fundamentally unrealistic, though exemplary *Tale*. The opposite is true for the *Clerk's Tale* in which the exemplary agenda is a strain upon the intense emotions aroused by the naturalist elements in the poem.

One's first difficulty in accepting the exemplary programme of the *Clerk's Tale* is not caused by the need to excise important details to make it into an *exemplum*. Rather it is the emotional effect which these details have been allowed to have during the *Tale*. Chaucer here carries further than in the *Man of Law's Tale* the project of mixing features which are conducive to exemplary narrative with those which command emotional recognition and compassion. At one point the *Clerk's Tale* seems like a rags to riches fairy tale; at another it seems sociopolitically aware. The heroine is glimpsed through the lens of biblical allusion at one point: "hye God somtyme senden kan / His grace into a litel oxes stalle" (*Clerk's Tale* 206–7), but appears later as a woman shaping her own comparisons: "Lat me nat lyk a worm go by the weye" (880). She is bound by a strict vow which in other works might constrain one's response, but here one cannot avoid questioning her adherence to it in the light of its apparent consequences for her children. Patient Griselda sometimes looks like Complaisant Griselda.[19] The repetitive structure seems determined by folktale tradition, but the violence of its incremental quality challenges the idealist action as much as it expresses it. The poem blends schematic, idealist, and quasi-allegorical features with strongly naturalistic ones. The former prepare the ground for the exemplary claims of the end, but the latter involve readers in prior comparisons between the situation described and their own lives. The more naturalistic the poem the less susceptible it is to exemplary constraint because the dissimilarity and similarity which has been managed by the readers during the poem is not that enjoined on them by the moraliser at the end. One is emotional and to do with the reader's sympathies and recognition of the emotions in the story, the other is intellectual and to do with framing a workable *exemplum*. Because the *Clerk's Tale* employs both styles throughout the appropriate method of responding to it remains unclear, and the *exemplum* is accordingly undermined.[20]

The main advance which the *Clerk's Tale* makes upon the exemplary project of *Troilus and Criseyde* is that the narrator is now characterized as a Clerk. The dramatized environment of the *Tales* permits the reader to transfer the failure of *exemplum* in a given instance to another social realm, explaining the tension of fiction and its exemplary point in terms of the supposed professional limitations and predispositions of the narrator. The Wife of Bath claims that clerks cannot speak any good of women and one can read the *Tale*'s uneasy shift to an exemplary type of meaning as a product of clerkly failings. In *Troilus and Criseyde* the narratorial source also contributed by its ambiguity to making the exemplary project fragile. But the narrator himself remained an individual, a "particular" source, albeit a complex and changeful one. In the *Canterbury Tales*, however, Chaucer chooses to use narrators whose social location makes them only ambiguously individual. His analysis of comparativism had hitherto exposed the difficulties of transferring the general meaning of *exempla* to a particular context; now he situates that difficulty in the source of narration itself. By giving his narrators professional names, like Knight or Clerk or Man of Law, which inevitably have reputational "names" associated with them, Chaucer extends to the source of narrative itself all the problems of classification which he had exposed in the *House of Fame,* and further compromises the notion of transferred meaning. He locates the tension of general and particular in the source of the communication itself. In the dream vision poems he had played with the minimal dissimilarity latent in *imago*, using a narrator with his own name and with a set of characteristics which were intended to suggest the originating author. In the *Tales,* although he still plays this game through the pilgrim "Chaucer," his other socially rather than personally rooted narrators have their *imagines* imbued with that larger tension between the general and particular which leads to the disabling of *exemplum*. Because the narrator portraits of the *General Prologue* are part of the complex web of poetic and intellectual comparison that this book has charted, I cannot here follow David Wallace's advice "to forget the master metaphor of the art gallery and focus attention on the cultural institution . . . the *felaweshipe* or *compagnye* of pilgrims."[21]

For example, Chaucer does not make it clear whether his Clerk is to be seen solely as a representative of clerkly views or a particular speaker in whom such views may be present at points. With this lack of direction, it is left to the reader to claim similarity between a particular feature of the Clerk's narration and the general character which he or she believes clerks to have. Reading the *Tales* becomes a management of comparison whereby the reader decides on similarities which tie the particular *Tale* to what is "known" wisdom about a teller, and dissimilarities, where the particularities of the *Tale* seem unable to be accommodated within what is supposed to be the general character of the teller. In this aesthetic of reading we all become Pandaruses, drawing from existing assumptions, preferences, and prejudices about types of people such wisdom as we hope will illuminate the particular narration before us. The process is as inevitable as it is bound to be inconclusive and contested. Coming from such unknown sources, sources which are to a degree constructed by the very readers who are receiving the narration, it is impossible for the *Tales* to have a clear exemplary effect. The undermining of *exemplum* is thus built into the origin of the *exemplum*.

But exemplary fragility does not simply derive from the difficulty of accommodating the particular within the general. The wild card in the hermeneutic process is the poet's own love of style. For example, Chaucer prevents a generalized definition of the Clerk and hence a socially determined reading of his *Tale* by disrupting the Clerk's manner of speech at the very point where he might be thought to be expressing clerkly misogynist views. This occurs with the Clerk's final comic descent into a song which replaces all the high comparativism of the preceding *Tale* with the coarse battle similes of the gender war: archwives are strong as camels; weaker women must be fierce as tigers, and scold on and on like the clapping of a mill; ugly women should be light as a linden leaf; and husbands should be made to couch like quails. The problem of exemplary comparison raised in the *Tale* is thus merged into the interpersonal fiction of the frame. This fragmentation of narrative line and voice is familiar to us from the last sections of *Troilus* but the extreme shift towards play, after the exemplary program has been complicated, is not found there. The overtness of the shift suggests that it is more than just a means of individuating the Clerk and thus complicating his clerkliness. Instead it asserts the poet's stylistic freedom over any form of social representation, a wilful play which exploits towards purely poetic ends the dramatic contrasts latent in the combinatorial enterprise of his tale collection.[22] In just the same way one found Chaucer delighting in the literary possibilities of *exempla* even while he was critically analyzing them as a means of understanding. Similarly he exploited the rhetorical possibilities of listing while exposing how inadequate taxonomic classification is for controlling or defining the individual.

6: THE POEM AS *EXEMPLUM*   193

This chapter has been dedicated to showing how Chaucer both promotes and undermines the exemplary possibilities of his poems. Nowhere does he achieve such a paradoxical effect with more success than in the *Wife of Bath's Prologue and Tale* in which comparativism in all its forms is powerfully on display. In this poem he dramatizes comparativism as a political weapon in the relations between the sexes. At a more fundamental level, however, by doing this he is thematizing within the poem the very issues which are involved in reading it. The other *Tales* resist the status of *exemplum* because their tellers cannot be confidently determined as individuals or types—one cannot be sure where the *Clerks' Tale* is the tale of *the* Clerk and where of *a* clerk. But the Clerk does not expose the popular prejudices about clerks which all readers will inevitably employ at some point in trying to understand his *Tale*. In the Wife's case, however, the prejudices which define what is supposedly "known" about woman are exposed by her, and are also invited by her. Her individuality is created through her paradoxical confirmation and subversion of the general "truths" under which women are supposed to lie.[23] At the same time the status of those "truths" forms part of her discourse. It is Chaucer's finest exercise in poetic self-reflexivity: he channels the problems of communication and understanding which have been central to his work into a piece of writing about a woman who is speaking about the way women are written about.

He looks at the use and abuse of example in sexual relations; its susceptibility to attack and to misappropriation. He shows simile, in its creative and conventionally proverbial forms, as a device of degradation and control, sometimes overtly so, sometimes masquerading as illumination, authority, and moral admonition. At a higher fictive level, he creates dramatic tension between what the Wife claims about comparisons, and the value which we give to them as coming from her. Biblical and classical *exempla*, contemporary parallels, supposedly illuminating proverbs, and domestic similes abound as comparison is revealed as a sexual weapon for the Wife and men. When she is not claiming them as her husbands' words, she uses them with bravado herself: she admits that she can bite and whinny like a horse. Elsewhere in the *Prologue* we learn that she is like a cat; he is like a fiend; she is like a scholar learning her craft; a wooden vessel; the patriarch Jacob; he is like a mouse, and claims she is like a spaniel; women's love is like hell, wild fire, worms destroying a tree, and so it goes on.

In exploiting the modes of comparison for her own ends, the Wife reveals their weaknesses as well as her own usurpation of their traditional male authority. She sets one "ensample" against another: Christ and the much married woman of Samaria against Christ's single appearance at a wedding; Jacob's two wives against Lamech's bigamy. She highlights those problems of interpretation, and of missing detail (such as the lack of any specific injunction against marrying more than once), which disable *exempla*. She supplies her own colloquial comparator to interpret St Paul's advice not to touch woman: "For peril is bothe fyr and tow t'assemble; / Ye knowe what this ensample may resemble" (*Wife of Bath's Prologue* 89–90) and thus sinks us imagistically into thoughts of sex. To legitimize a less strenuous Christian life she employs Paul's simile of different domestic vessels having different status, which he used to exhort Christians to strive for perfection (*Wife of Bath's Prologue* 99–101, and 2 Tim. 2:20). With subtle comedy Chaucer shows how *exempla* can themselves be allegorized so as to produce the opposite argument from that originally promised: the Wife cites Christ and the saints as evidence for the perfection of chastity, but she then turns this to allegory: "Lat hem be breed of pured wheteseed, / And lat us wyves hoten barly-breed" (143–44). The terms of this comparison then suggest another story, the Feeding of the Five Thousand, which the Wife can offer implicitly as an *exemplum*, thus making Christ her authority for promiscuity rather than chastity: "And yet with barly-breed, Mark telle kan, / Oure Lord Jhesu refresshed many a man" (145–46). One comparison can be transmuted into another so that dissimilarities which would disable the one can be lost in another, and the resulting meaning changed accordingly.

Individual comparisons serve local needs in the gender war, but one senses a larger battle between men and the Wife for the world of the known. The comparisons are not merely framed to serve the topic but, in the mass, reveal an attempt to appropriate the world of comparators, to reshape its constituent parts round the gender position of the user. Since everything comes from the mouth of the Wife, it is hard to resist the impression that she is engaged in this reconfiguration of the world as much as men are, but she raises it as a specifically male activity in a passage which has larger implication than the allusion it makes to the *Parables* of the misogynistic Solomon (the book of *Proverbs*):

> Been ther none othere maner resemblances
> That ye may likne youre parables to,
> But if a sely wyf be oon of tho?
> (*Wife of Bath's Prologue* 368–70)

It is not simply that she finds men's comparisons for women individually objectionable but that men seem to funnel the known world into providing comparators for the single topic of "woman," when they could illuminate other topics by the same material. Though the effect of the *Prologue* suggests that the Wife wants to grasp men sexually and possess them financially, she bears witness here to the desperation of the male mentally to grasp and possess woman.

Having nothing but the "known" to assist, men substitute the imperfect similarity of comparators for the woman's particularity and inscrutability. Men find it preferable to force through assertions of similarity, against the dissimilarities a particular woman might claim, rather than to acknowledge that they do not understand the woman, and that their knowledge does not constitute the only "known." Unable to possess her, as Chaucer felt himself powerless to represent the sexual consummation of Troilus with Criseyde, men make the woman anew out of "known" wisdom. They reconstitute her through *imago*, simile, and *exemplum*, denying her particularity, and preferring to ignore the dissimilarities latent in the comparisons, or overriding them by tradition, authority, and power. They then present the woman back to herself through their chosen comparators "naming" her as Eve, Dalilah, Dianire, Xantippa, Pasipha, Clytemnestra, etc.

The world of sexual injury is not wholly distinct from the world of poetic creation: Alisoun the Wife is complaining about precisely that assertive, all-inclusive, comparativism which Chaucer, safe within the carapace of fabliau, exploited to create another Alisoun from a multiplicity of similes in the *Miller's Tale*. Similarly, though it is the Wife's garrulousness which is made dramatically explicit by the Friar's "this is a long preamble of a tale!" it is actually male supplementarity which her *Prologue* reveals: one wicked wife is not enough as a comparator to illuminate the nature of women; Jankyn must have a book of them. Individually inadequate, *exempla* are marshalled in crowds, and men show themselves bound to reiterate rather than to understand, to repeat rather than to analyse the failures of their own chosen path of illumination. Just as Chaucer's literary enterprise in creating the Miller's Alisoun appears as an enjoyable version of what the Wife finds offensive in life, so his own long-standing commitment to rhetorical and narratorial multiplication is critically represented in the carefully detailed list of Jankyn's offensive *exempla*. Chaucer reveals, through the Wife's history, the male need to comprehend woman or, failing that, to reconstitute her through comparison, and then to bolster one partial comparison with another. But what he reveals is also intimately linked to what he does himself in fiction, to his own areas of doubt, his own stylistic preferences and narratorial drives. When one considers what the Wife complains of, Chaucer appears as the poetic accomplice, as well as the investigator, of male comparativist perceptions of women. There seems a dangerous complicity between his artistic habits and those attitudes of mind which he uses his art to reveal and criticize. However, one can recognize that complicity without denying his insights into the failures of comparative, and male comparative, thought, and he does manage to rise above it in one respect: he ensures that the Wife herself will be a dangerous *exemplum* for anyone to use.

In some respects, concern for what the Wife represents has overtaken her explicit agenda. She promises to give "ensaumples mo than ten" (*Wife of Bath's Prologue* 179) of the tribulation in marriage. And she reminds the Pardoner of the threatening proverb which underlies all exemplary comparison: "Whoso that nyl be war by othere men, / By hym shul othere men corrected be" (1980–81). Whatever admiration one may feel for her, and whatever interest one may have in her inverting and exposing the traditions of misogyny, her avowed intention is to offer *exempla,* and she does this in her accounts of her marriages.

The subsequent *Prologue* section on her husbands is like the sequence of examples of male betrayal employed in the *House of Fame* Book 1. Like that sequence, this one has its damaging qualification: just as a possible excuse was raised for Aeneas at the end of the list of examples, so at the end of her account of troubled marriages, we get a relationship which does not seem to exemplify tribulation:

> God helpe me so, I was to hym as kynde
> As any wyf from Denmark unto Ynde,
> And also trewe, and so was he to me.
> (*Wife of Bath's Prologue* 823–25)

If this, as much as what she says earlier, is to be believed, the total effect of the exemplary project is not as reliably probative as she threatened to the Pardoner. This shift from sexual antagonism to domestic bliss creates a richness of character for the Wife, but underneath that character portrayal the shift is prompted by Chaucer's much more established formal structure of comparative examples and their qualification. What was textually based, and emerged as a more abstract problem within the philosophical allegories of the *House of Fame,* has become "naturalized" into the psychology of human relations, but the topos of combining exemplary argument with a particular disabling dissimilarity is still sustaining Chaucer's insights.[24]

As we have seen, what is substantially different from earlier instances of this structure is that now, in the dramatized context of the *Tales,* narrators are not merely voices who marshal *exempla* into argument (whether successfully or not). They are the ambiguous conflation of individual features and the "known" wisdom which the reader has about their profession or type. They are sites where the particular and the general uneasily coexist because the reader, Pandarus-like, is supplying the general "truths." Of no one is this more true than the Wife, behind whom lies the heavy traditional use of women as comparators. Typically, although she exposes the practice, she still invites the Pardoner to view her life in an exemplary way. By giving the Wife the power of extended self-description Chaucer challenges the reader to find her own performance exemplary, and to decide what it is an *exemplum* of, for although she offers her life to the Pardoner as exemplary of the misery in marriage (and does not wholly carry that promise through), her autobiographical performance as a whole passes beyond that significance. It is the Wife speaking, rather than any story she tells, which becomes the focus for Chaucer's exploitation of the exemplary.

Much of what she says would seem to qualify her for Jankyn's "Book of Wicked Wives," but equally much is rational, attractive, realistic, illuminating. Although she is a sexual martinet, she resists sexual absolutism: virginity may be most highly praised, but not everyone is bound to be a virgin; even if the private parts were made for sexual purposes, this does not mean that all have to use them in that way. Conversely, some of what she rightly criticizes is actually affirmed by the manner in which she criticizes it: for example, she chides men for saying that women chide men. She exposes the one-sided, repetitive, unthinking male comparators for women, but retransmits them, and partially confirms them, while doing so. She seems to espouse quite contrary ideals of mastery and mutuality, responding in an aggressively masterful way to her own *Tale*, although it has not itself supported such a tone. Although one would expect that, of all people, the Wife would consciously tell an exemplary *Tale*, it is precisely that function which she bypasses in her final comments on it, instead praying to receive the incidentals of the story—young, attractive husbands, and the good fortune of outliving them—rather than asserting the truth of the *Tale* as an important comparator for illuminating relations between men and women.

The power of her autobiography encourages one to read the *Tale* in relation to her *Prologue* life, and to accommodate the two thematically and psychologically, but the *Tale* itself reveals a disturbing difference in voice between that used for content and that used by the narrator when she is commenting. This is obvious if one compares the bald style in which the rape is narrated with the vivid, imagistic, paced, rhetorically structured story of Midas's wife, in which the Wife digresses to prove the standard misogynist claim that women cannot keep a secret. Whatever connections there might be between the Wife in the *Prologue* and the content of the *Tale*, it seems that the Wife who tells the *Tale* is a much simpler creation than the Wife who told the tale of herself. All these paradoxes mean that the Wife escapes being a reliable *exemplum* in the gender war: she is as capable of sustaining the misogynist "wisdom" which some will bring to reading her as she is of defying it with her criticisms and her rich individuality. But she frustrates attempts to make her an *exemplum* not just because she is a very complex creation with qualities which clearly permit contrasting estimation by men and women, and which speak at once to the desires and fears of her hearers of both sexes.

She also escapes exemplary comparativism because she is, in one sense, not a character at all, but a dramatic expression of the univocality which Chaucer has employed throughout his work from the similes shared by narrator and character in *Troilus and Criseyde* to the blurred voices of character, narrator, and author in the *Manciple's Tale*.[25] She is a tangled mass of voices, all rather like each other despite their widely dissimilar opinions, all fighting on the same grounds and using the same arsenal, and all dramatically as well as rhetorically unified by coming from the same mouth.[26] The Wife tells the pilgrims and, through them, the readers, what she said to her husbands, and what she said to her husbands was a quotation of what she claimed they said to, and about, her. Then she acknowledges they said no such thing—it was all a trick—but her hearers know that if these husbands did not say it, other husbands and other men have said and do still say it.

If one focuses upon her apparent motives and feelings one can derive from them a rich character; if one attends to what she says and the complex locutional environment in which it is expressed, the Wife becomes a space filled by contending but similar voices. With either emphasis, she emerges as a creation which all might wish to use as an *exemplum* for their own gender-specific purposes, but none could use securely. She contains too many contrary aspects, too much dissimilarity is built into her, for her to illuminate the unknown as one would wish a comparator to do.

While the *Clerk's Tale* is reminiscent of the earlier exemplary project of *Troilus and Criseyde* with the addition that one can ascribe the problems of comparison to the new social dimension given to the narrator, the *Wife of Bath's Prologue* achieves a greater incorporation of Chaucer's interest in comparative thinking with his dramatizing of the speaker. He manages to construct a female speaker who invites, frustrates, and exposes the exemplary controls put on women by misogynist tradition. In doing this, he leaves a poem poised between rich dramatization and pure speech; between character and the elision of character by voice. The Wife represents his most perfect shorter literary expression of the delights and dangers of comparative thinking.

6: THE POEM AS *EXEMPLUM*

If one wished to comprehend the relations of men and women (and how they read each other), if one wished to understand what women are like, or what they want (as if such generality *could* be more than a temporary delusion), would one then go to the *Wife of Bath's Prologue and Tale*? In a sense one would because Chaucer has created a text of such power and vitality that it cries out for application to the world; it seems a potent *exemplum*. But its application proves fraught with difficulty, as one might expect from a poem which is so explicit about the process of such application. Critics would not still be trying to read the *Prologue and Tale* if the temptation and the frustration were not there in equal measure. This *exemplum* proves to be useful precisely because it exposes the reader's own partiality in configuring the similarities and dissimilarities between *exemplum* and life. Chaucer's art of comparativism reaches its climax here because it draws self-reflexively on his own past literary interests and techniques; it makes comparative thinking into a theme; it encourages the reader to transfer the meanings of the text towards the illumination of life, and it frustrates the attempt, thus leaving the indelible impression that art is *another* life, latently dissimilar to the nontextual one, not a repository of nuggets of wisdom which can be unreflectingly transferred by comparison to the ordinary world outside books.

Conclusion

It will be clear to anyone who has got this far that *Chaucer and Dissimilarity,* unlike much current criticism of Chaucer in various traditions, is not a historicizing account of the poems. However, it is not offered in any sense as a resistance to such readings (or, indeed, to any others). Its intention has been to explore the rhetorical conditions which subsist in Chaucer's works and help to make them writerly texts, encouraging the generation of multiple and contested readings. Specifically, however, it has sought to characterize these rhetorical conditions in a new way. The second half of this century has seen a proliferation of books on metaphor, and a corresponding promotion of metaphor as the metaphor for how language works. There has not been a corresponding degree of interest in simile. No doubt this is because similes (and the other forms of comparison discussed in this book) are not tropes, and western culture has favored tropology because it corresponds to a critical sense that meaning is never stable, always being deferred as other meanings which might fix it are themselves chased after, and meaning is never shared, always somehow twisted (troped) as it passes from language giver to language receiver. We saw in chapter 2 how Chaucer, particularly in the eighties, got drawn into the ambit of this conception of language, though he is not himself a totalizing thinker, and presents the mixing of truth and falsehood as happening only "sometyme." This book argues that the most characteristic features of language as Chaucer uses it in poetic fiction, and as he writes about it, are similaic not tropic. These similaic tendencies are developed most extensively in the middle period of his writing, but continue to inform his later poems where they take on an additional social complexion. For Chaucer, the important condition of language is that it is covered by a mesh of possible likenesses discovered and qualified through the business of comparison. At its most basic, the right words for particular things are arrived at through comparing these things with other things and the words which would be appropriate to them.

Furthermore, Chaucer obviously believes that reality itself, though it may be represented in text, is not itself only textual. For him, a textual representation of reality may be thought to be more or less correct, both in itself by comparison with a prevailing or imagined view of the facts and by comparison with other textual representations. By this acknowledgment of a nontextual reality, Chaucer shifts the emphasis away from language in its essence to language as it is used, and thus away from the tropologically inevitable misprision so prominent in late twentieth-century criticism towards failures in the user: failures of irresponsibility, dishonesty, cowardice, self-interest, ignorance (whether culpable or not), partiality, and so on. He dramatizes some of these failures through his characters' explicit use of comparison, but also exposes them as common to all users of language. The reader or listener is just as capable of malice or goodwill, insight or blindness in receiving language, and it is these motives that exercise Chaucer rather than the unfixable nature of meaning.

Also by this acknowledgment of a nontextual reality, Chaucer commits himself and the reader to the process of comparing the textual world with the nontextual, of trying to establish not just the similarities between the two but also the dissimilarities which are always present and are brought to attention by the tightly wrought contexts of fiction. His work is thus opened up to contrary readings because it acknowledges from the start that disagreements will follow from the comparisons which inflect all language use. At the core of meaning for Chaucer is the comparative process to which language users are committed: comparisons between things and the words which might be applied to them; between genres and particular poems which might or might not rest easily within them; between the literal and the figurative; between the categories of dreams and a particular instance of dream; between the past and the present; between proverb and real life; between real people and text people; between text people and the reader's prejudices or beliefs about their character, sex or profession; between words or images in one context and another; between an *exemplum* and the life it might be thought to illuminate. The list of possible areas for comparison is very great and, because the nontextual world is constantly changing, it should be no surprise if the significant comparisons are constantly being reselected, reordered, reconfigured, revised by speakers and readers, including, most obviously, Chaucer's own readers down the years. Lee Patterson writes, "Chaucer allows Chaucerians to stay in business by handing over his work to a future conceived of as dynamic and appropriative rather than by acquiescing in the reproduction of the past."[1] In my view, that future depends on Chaucer's own dynamic of comparison, and the appropriation which he conceives of is the inevitable, and inevitably contested, practice of comparison in which readers of whatever sophistication engage when they move from the nontextual world to the poem.

Consequently, this book has explored the presence of comparison at different levels in Chaucer's texts from the individual image through its thematics, its structural contribution to poems, and up to the function of a poem as a whole. In doing this it has also shown that the understanding of poems, as Chaucer envisages it, is bound to be plural, partial, disputable, but may be accurate also. The critic understands the shape of the text, its meaning, the problems which it poses, the kinds of cultural or political value which it has by reference to preexisting knowledge, experience, desires, and prejudices. The text is a new thing which has to be understood by reference to the known. Comparison, with its positive and negative forces, will be the condition of this understanding even when the critic is not aware of it. The words which the critic subsequently uses in writing will similarly reflect decisions about similarities and dissimilarities between the unexampled newness of the poem and the nontextual analogues which can be used to illuminate it. In the end this may come down to the choice of a particular word, just like Troilus searching for the right word for what Pandarus did. Personal needs and psychological blindspots may intrude just as Troilus's sexual desire and Phoebus's masculine pride controlled their reception of the meanings offered them. Inevitably, the new will not be wholly subsumed in the known, and readers will differ on what elements of the poem they believe are explicable just as they differ in what knowledge or limitations they bring to a poem. Nevertheless, this reading is far from being a solipsistic activity: Chaucer also acknowledges that readers' frames of reference may overlap so that they share a sense of what alternatives are being selected from, what comparisons are appropriate to draw. After all, Troilus knew that it was the word "bawdrye" that Pandarus was afraid of using, and therefore sought to distinguish his form of soliciting from other less attractive kinds.

Chaucer did not see the problematic of language as defined by the constant deferral of meaning but, more socially, as the constant deferral of *agreement* on whether reality was being represented accurately in a particular communication. The key feature of this problematic, and the centre of all Chaucer's struggles with his own writing as irresponsible, retractable, conducive to sin, or evasive, was that reality might indeed be truly represented, "ryght as hit ys." The truth is indeed out there for Chaucer. Most optimistically, there is nothing in the scheme of language as constructed in the *House of Fame* to prevent a truth emerging unscathed from the House of Rumour and receiving an accurate reputation from Fame before it flies off to the waiting world. So even some of what one is *told* is true may be true in fact: elements of received wisdom in all its forms—tradition, convention, proverbial lore, what our mothers told us, what an author writes, what a literary critic claims—may actually be accurate. The problem is that the receiver of meaning does not know when this is the case, and all subsequent disputations about words and things, poems and lives, and all revisionist poems (like *Troilus and Criseyde*), and all critical rereadings are attempts to negotiate a way to more or less agreement on where the truth can be established. Henryson asked, "Quha wait gif all that Chauceir wrait was trew?" ("The Testament of Cresseid").[2] Nothing could be more Chaucerian in spirit than that question—not just because it is a question or because it acknowledges the importance of truth, but because it acknowledges the possibility that Chaucer wrote the truth and the corollary that we do not know where he did or did not do this.

However, Chaucer does not imply that by critically taking issue with each other readers of poems will eventually come to the truth about them. He refuses this evolutionary notion of progress: the passage from buoyant, though bemused, comparison of different sources to a fragmented or inconclusive ending is figured too prominently in his poems. What he offers instead is the possibility that, even if agreement about the truth is not reached, or to put it more crudely, even if the literary critical industry moves ever onwards in more or less collegial disagreement, an element of the truth or even whole truths may still be present. Such truth may be as present in the first critical intervention as in the latest. Chaucer suggests that it is the need to find that truth that keeps readers reading, engaging them with the world of text as his imprisoned knights, Palamon and Arcite, were committed to the experience of pain by glimpsing through the bars a love from which they were separated. This is not an adumbration of Eden from which one has been for ever expelled: for what is missing is not fully lost; it just cannot be confidently found.

Although comparison may be ubiquitous in language, and prominent in the poems both as a textual feature and as a responsibility expected of both speaker and hearer, it is not simply the general comparative process which drives Chaucer's analysis. Rather what makes that similaic view an important dimension of his poems is that along with it he sees the creative and subversive effect of dissimilarity. As we saw in chapter 1, this was where Chaucer struck away from the path taken by Boethius. This book has therefore been about the "gap" of dissimilarity which opens up whenever comparative writing, speaking, reading, or thinking takes place. This gap frustrates the easy transfer of meaning from one context to another, ensuring that all positive comparisons will have "yes, but" etched into them. Sometimes, as in the case of similes, the presence of dissimilarity is exploited in order to create the desired effect; sometimes, on the other hand, the gap of dissimilarity is an embarrassment to the user or a frustration to the receiver of the comparison. It is the force of dissimilarity which permits Chaucer to question the passage of meaning between past and present, general and particular, proverb and problem, text and life, one context and another. Dissimilarity may give a figurative edge to *similitudo,* but it creates anxiety for the promoter or receiver of *exempla,* and even in its most minimal form, it can unsettle the confidence we would place in an *imago.*

Anxiety is a recognizable feature of the poems, and it issues in the alternating drive to fill up the oeuvre with moral seriousness or scholarship and then with narrative prolixity. It lies behind the moments of disorientation, whether figured as geographical, narratological or poetic, and behind the corresponding moments of assertive direction—stellar ascent with an eagle, recommitment to the narrative line, enthusiastic proliferation of words, new large-scale poetic projects. It lies behind both the confident citation of proverb and the silence which acknowledges the inutility of the proverb in new circumstances. One could figure this anxiety in a number of ways: as sexual or social or to do with the function of writing. This book has figured it as rhetorical, partly because it is expressed in a multitude of ways which can be reasonably described as rhetorical, but also because a rhetorical anxiety is, in a sense, the most prominent anxiety that any writer can disclose to us. The mover of words through the multifarious contexts of life feels an anxiety of transfer: of moving meaning from one place to another, perhaps even from one side of the study door to the other. This is inevitably, therefore, an anxiety about change, and for that reason rhetoric is actually one means by which Chaucer is revealed as an anxious creature of his changing historical circumstances. For him each moment contains in it that shift from the known world of Troy to the new, variegated, unpredictable camp of the Greeks; each moment therefore also contains the drive to compromise, to adjust, to delay by word-spinning, to defer closure by opening up new horizons of subject matter. And all the time commitment to the world and commitment forced on him by the world, like that most worldly Diomede, is urging decisions about meaning, and demanding that comparison between the known and the new be drawn afresh, and its freight of dissimilarity be somehow defined.

Paradoxically, however, the construction of the problem is itself a kind of remedy for it. We saw earlier that at the moment of her greatest distress, faced with the onrush of change and the loss of the securities of the past, Criseyde constructed an *imago* of herself as a grieving lover. In one sense this self-division foreshadowed the betrayal, formally separating her from the problem of losing Troilus. On the other hand, it was a self-division which the narrator supported and strengthened to gain our sympathy. Chaucer also preserves his identity but by reserving it from the medium of his texts in which the problems of transfer in the context of change are given expression. The many Chaucer *personae* are not so much ways of frustrating the reader who might wish to get to the author as they are present to reassure the author and the reader that there is indeed an original existing outside the text for whom these are *imagines*. Similarly, when, as we saw in chapter 3, Chaucer chooses to create figuration not by inventive similes of the kind elaborated in *Pearl* but by employing old similes in new contexts, he is making art out of the very basis of anxiety. He is taking the threat posed to old ideas by new contexts and using that dynamic for local poetic effect. *Similitudo* thus becomes a means of asserting creativity in the face of change. Finally, and most obviously, when Chaucer undermines *exempla* by creating new, complex, changeful, and unstable fictive contexts for them, and undermines the poetic exemplary function by creating poems which cannot easily sustain *exemplum*, he is not simply revealing anxiety but is arrogating to himself the power to recreate the conditions which cause anxiety. He is also offering the poems to his readers as the means by which the successes and failures of comparative thinking can be played out in a constant process of reading and rereading. In that respect, he wants the poems to be recognized as true *exempla*, offering, through the experience of reading them, insight into what life is *like*, and, hopefully, in some places still to be agreed on, telling it "ryght *as* hit ys," but always negatively charged by that latent force of dissimilarity, the strength of which is also open to dispute in the readings of subsequent generations. Chaucer's account of the comparative process thus suggests that readers, of whom literary critics are now the most ubiquitous type for his poems, share in the common paradox by which creativity comes from anxiety. They do not arrive at truth by virtue of their many readings but they continue to live together in the world of words and things by virtue of engaging in the same process of comparison which generated the writer's communication. In the end, it is a commitment to dissimilarity which draws them together.

Notes

Introduction

1. For a discussion, and rejection, of dramatic theories, see C. David Benson, "Beyond the Dramatic Theory," in *Chaucer's Drama of Style: Poetic Variety and Contrast in the "Canterbury Tales"* (Chapel Hill: University of North Carolina Press, 1986), 3–25.

2. Martin Stevens and Kathleen Falvey object to the Pardoner's claim in "Substance, Accident, and Transformations: a Reading of the *Pardoner's Tale*," *Chaucer Review* 17 (1982): 142–58.

3. The case for a "radical separation of words from things" is put interestingly but, I believe, too strongly by Robert R. Edwards in *The Dream of Chaucer: Representation and Reflection in the Early Narratives* (Durham and London: Duke University Press, 1989), 117. The problem which Chaucer sees in such separation is that it is *not* predictably radical.

4. Though fictional, the pilgrimage game of tale-telling can still be "true" in the sense that it represents a social interaction which the reader knows *could* occur, even if this one did not. See Carl Lindahl, "Chaucer and the Shape of Performance," in *Earnest Games: Folkloric Patterns in the "Canterbury Tales"* (Bloomington: Indiana University Press, 1987), 44–61.

5. The tradition of reading the *Manciple's Tale* as metapoetic in significance, and as related to Chaucer's own narrative practice, has been strong over the last twenty to thirty years. See especially James Dean, "The Ending of the *Canterbury Tales*, 1952–1976," *Texas Studies in Literature and Language* 21 (1979): 17–33; F. N. M. Diekstra, "Chaucer's Digressive Mode and the Moral of *The Manciple's Tale*," *Neophilologus* 67 (1983): 131–48; V. J. Scattergood, "The Manciple's Manner of Speaking," *Essays in Criticism* 24 (1974): 124–46; Donald Howard, *The Idea of the Canterbury Tales* (Berkeley: University of California Press, 1976); Helen Cooper, *The Structure of the Canterbury Tales* (London: Duckworth, 1983), and others.

6. For an analysis of the various meanings possible in this Boethian tag, see P. B. Taylor, "Chaucer's *Cousin to the Dede*," *Speculum* 57 (1982): 315–27.

7. Christine may feel that her gender gives her more ready access to the truth in some cases, but she does believe that the same truth is available to all: "And do not believe or let anyone else think, dear Sir, that I have written this defense, out of feminine bias, merely because I am a woman. For, assuredly, my motive is simply to uphold the pure truth." Christine de Pisan's "Letter to Jean de Montreuil" (1401) in Joseph L. Baird and John R. Kane, ed. and trans., *La Querelle de la Rose: Letters and Documents*, North Carolina Studies in the Romance Languages and Literatures, vol. 199 (Chapel Hill: University of North Carolina Press, 1978), 53.

8. Robert Myles, *Chaucerian Realism* (Cambridge: D. S. Brewer, 1994), 22–27.

9. Tropological theories of language particularly underlie deconstructionist criticism. For early formulations of this tradition see, for example, Harold Bloom and others, *Deconstruction and Criticism* (London: Routledge and Kegan Paul, 1979) and Jonathan Culler, "The Turns of Metaphor," in *The Pursuit of Signs: Semiotics, Literature,*

Deconstruction (London: Routledge and Kegan Paul, 1981), 188–209. Culler writes, "today metaphor is no longer one figure among others but the figure of figures," 189. For a broader account of the formative ideas of the tradition see Vincent B. Leitch, *Deconstructive Criticism: an advanced introduction* (London: Hutchinson, 1983). For a recent assertion of the limitations on such a view of reading see Umberto Eco, with others, *Interpretation and overinterpretation*, ed. Stefan Collini (Cambridge: Cambridge University Press, 1992), 23–88. For an analysis of how the status of simile is altered by a metaphorical understanding of language see John J. McGavin, "The Context of Literary Simile," *Cosmos* 3 (1987): 2–20.

10. John J. McGavin, "How Nasty is Phoebus's Crow?" *Chaucer Review* 21 (1987), 455.

11. Philosophers from Aristotle to Cavell, Ricoeur, and Davidson have argued about how, and how far, simile and metaphor are distinct. Tropological theories of meaning, however, depend on promoting the metaphorical.

12. The first recorded use of the word "pander" in the sense which Pandarus feared is in 1530 (*Oxford English Dictionary*, 2d ed.), though it is evidently idiomatic by that time. Giovanni Boccaccio's *Il Filostrato*, which Chaucer used in preparing his poem, is printed in parallel with *Troilus and Criseyde* in Geoffrey Chaucer, *Troilus and Criseyde: A new edition of "The Book of Troilus,"* ed. B. A. Windeatt (Harlow: Longman, 1984).

13. This is the basis of Jill Mann's still seminal study, *Geoffrey Chaucer and Medieval Estates Satire* (Cambridge: Cambridge University Press, 1973). The notions of an estates-based grouping of the pilgrims or of specific estates-based traditions of description may now need qualification. See, for example, H. Marshall Leicester, Jr., "Structure as Deconstruction: 'Chaucer and Estates Satire' in the *General Prologue*, or Reading Chaucer as a Prologue to the History of Disenchantment," *Exemplaria* 2 (Spring 1990): 241–61, and also his critique in *The Disenchanted Self: Representing the Subject in the "Canterbury Tales"* (Berkeley: University of California Press, 1990), 391–406. However, the gap between presumptive and achieved understandings of the pilgrims is still central to appreciating the dynamic of the *General Prologue*.

14. See, for example, Stephen Knight, *Geoffrey Chaucer*, Rereading Literature (Oxford: Blackwell, 1986).

15. Andrew Ortony, "The Role of Similarity in Similes and Metaphors," in *Metaphor and Thought*, ed. Andrew Ortony (Cambridge: Cambridge University Press, 1979), 186–201. Ortony's work is significant not least for having encouraged attention to simile when it was more fashionable to concentrate on metaphor. See also George A. Miller, "Images and Models, Similes and Metaphors," in Ortony, *Metaphor and Thought*, 202–50. For a structuralist continental view of how simile relates to figuration see Michel Le Guern, *Sémantique de la métaphore et de la métonymie* (Paris: Larousse, 1973).

16. Quintilian, *The Institutio Oratoria*, Loeb Classical Library, 4 vols. (1921), 2:281, 285. Quintilian also discusses the nomenclature of comparison in Book 5.11. The Latin text can be found in M. Fabii Quintiliani, *Institutionis Oratoriae*, ed. M. Winterbottom, 2 vols., Scriptorum Classicorum Bibliotheca Oxoniensis (Oxford: Clarendon Press, 1970), 1:279–89.

17. Much has been written about Chaucer's narrator *personae*. For a powerful essay which shifts attention away from them to the nature of the *Tales* told by his pilgrim "Chaucer" see Lee Paterson, "'What Man Artow?': Authorial Self-Definition in *The Tale of Sir Thopas* and *The Tale of Melibee*," *Studies in the Age of Chaucer* 11 (1989): 117–75.

18. Larry Scanlon explores the exemplary tradition which Chaucer uses in *Narrative, Authority, and Power: Medieval Exemplum and the Chaucerian Tradition*, Cambridge Studies in Medieval Literature, vol. 20 (Cambridge: Cambridge University Press, 1994).

19. A. C. Spearing, "The *Canterbury Tales* IV: Exemplum and Fable" in *The Cambridge Chaucer Companion*, ed. Piero Boitani and Jill Mann (Cambridge: Cambridge University Press, 1986), 159–77.

Chapter 1. Traditions of Comparison and Dissimilarity

1. Each of these has attracted monographs. See for instance, V. A. Kolve, *Chaucer and the Imagery of Narrative: The First Five Canterbury Tales* (London: Edward Arnold, 1984); W. J. Aerts and M. Gosman, eds., *Exemplum and Similitudo: Alexander the Great and other heroes as points of reference in medieval literature*, Medievalia Groningiana, vol. 8 (Groningen: Egbert Forsten, 1988); Fritz Kemmler, *"Exempla" in Context: A Historical and Critical Study of Robert Mannyng of Brunne's "Handlyng Synne"* (Tübingen: Gunter Narr, 1984). *Exemplum* has been particularly singled out in recent studies: John D. Lyons, *The Rhetoric of Example in Early Modern France and Italy* (Princeton: Princeton University Press, 1989) and Larry Scanlon, *Narrative, Authority, and Power: Medieval Exemplum and the Chaucerian Tradition*, Cambridge Studies in Medieval Literature, vol. 20 (Cambridge: Cambridge University Press, 1994).

2. James J. Murphy, "A New Look at Chaucer and the Rhetoricians," *Review of English Studies*, n.s., 15 (1964), 15.

3. Murphy, "Chaucer and the Rhetoricians," 15.

4. The *Nun's Priest's Tale* 3347–74 gives a comical version of a set-piece lament by Geoffrey of Vinsauf, and *Troilus and Criseyde* 1.1065–69 translates a passage from Geoffrey's *Poetria Nova*.

5. Murphy, "Chaucer and the Rhetoricians," 11–12.

6. Ibid., 15.

7. For a history of classical comparison see Marsh H. McCall, Jr., *Ancient Rhetorical Theories of Simile and Comparison* (Cambridge, Mass.: Harvard University Press, 1969). For argumentative clarity the present study uses the Latin terms wherever possible, but this does not reflect the variable practice of the writers themselves. The grammarians usually preferred the more stable Greek terms. For a sophisticated working of these terms, including the notion of similarity, into a theory of literature, with an emphasis on the classical and neoclassical sources, see Wesley Trimpi, *Muses of One Mind: The Literary Analysis of Experience and Its Continuity* (Princeton: Princeton University Press, 1983).

8. P. W. Glare, ed., *Oxford Latin Dictionary* (Oxford: Clarendon Press, 1982).

9. There are advantages and disadvantages attaching to any of the words chosen as a working term for comparison of the second kind. *Similitudo* has been chosen to avoid confusion between the superordinate term "comparison" and the Latin term for a specific type of comparison "comparatio." *Similitudo* also keeps in the reader's mind the fact that our "simile" falls within this second type.

10. See, for example, Quintilian, *Institutio Oratoria*, Loeb Classical Library (1921), 2: 285.

11. Contrast, for example, Julius Rufinianus, Victorinus, and the anonymous author of the *Rhetorica ad Herennium* who, respectively, require that the comparator in an *exemplum* be factual, qualitative, or named: Julius Rufinianus, *De Figuris Sententiarum et Elocutionis* in *Rhetores Latini Minores*, ed. Carolus Halm (Leipzig: B. G. Teubner, 1863), 44; Q. Fabius Laurentius Victorinus, *Explanationum in Rhetoricam M. Tullii Ciceronis* in Halm, *Rhetores Latini Minores*, 153–304; ["Cicero"] *Ad C. Herennium, Libri IV, De Ratione Discendi*, Loeb Classical Library (1954), 382.

12. Fritz Kemmler, *"Exempla" in Context: A Historical and Critical Study of Robert Mannyng of Brunne's "Handlyng Synne"* (Tübingen: Gunter Narr, 1984), 60.

13. Martianus Capella, *De Nuptiis Philologiae et Mercurii* ed. J. Willis (Leipzig: BSB B. G. Teubner Verlagsgesellschaft, 1983), 196–97.

14. W. D. Ross, ed., *The Works of Aristotle* (Oxford: Clarendon Press, 1924), 11: 1406b.27–28. The translation is not paginated but follows the divisions of the Greek text, which can be found in Aristotelis, *Ars Rhetorica*, ed. W. D. Ross, Scriptorum Classicorum Bibliotheca Oxoniensis (Oxford: Clarendon Press, 1949), 151.

15. Marcus Cornelius Fronto, *The Correspondence of Marcus Cornelius Fronto*, Loeb Classical Library, 2 vols. (1919), 1: 37. Fronto uses the Greek terms.

16. Fronto, *Correspondence*, 1: 135.

17. ["Cicero"] *Ad C. Herennium, Libri IV; De Ratione Dicendi*, Loeb Classical Library (1954), 385. Except where indicated translations are mine.

18. In general, I believe it is best to leave technical terms like *imago* untranslated. There is a confusing tendency among translators to render *imago* as "simile." This obscures the special nature of *imago* as a depiction of appearance and precludes the word "simile" from translating its proper equivalent, *similitudo*.

19. ["Cicero"] *Ad C. Herennium*, 384 and 385 (Caplan's translation).

20. ["Cicero"] *Ad C. Herennium*, 376.

21. ["Cicero"] *Ad C. Herennium*, 382 and 383 (Caplan's translation).

22. Halm, *Rhetores Latini Minores*, 38–47. Julius uses the Greek terms, *icon* and *parabola*.

23. Halm, *Rhetores Latini Minores*, 44.

24. Quotations and translation from Geoffrey of Vinsauf, *Poetria Nova*, lines 1259–64 in Ernest A. Gallo, *The "Poetria Nova" and its Sources in Early Rhetorical Doctrine* (The Hague: Mouton, 1971), 80 and 82.

25. Gallo, *"Poetria Nova,"* 86. These lines (1361–63) refer to Christ rescuing Adam from the Devil.

26. Compare John of Garland, *Exempla Honestae Vitae* in Edwin Habel, "Die Exempla honestae vitae des Johannes de Garlandia, eine lateinische Poetik des 13. Jahrhunderts," *Romanische Forschungen* 29 (1911): 137–54 (lines 232–33) and John of Garland, *Parisiana Poetria*, ed. and trans. T. Lawler (New Haven and London: Yale University Press, 1974).

27. Aelius Donatus, *Ars Grammatica* in *Grammatici Latini*, ed. H. Keil, 8 vols. (Leipzig: 1853–80; repr., Hildesheim: Georg Olms Verlagsbuchhandlung, 1961), 4: 353–402. Donatus uses the Greek terms for the types of comparison.

28. James J. Murphy, *Rhetoric in the Middle Ages* (Berkeley: University of California Press, 1974), 34.

29. Virgil, *Eclogues, Georgics, Aeneid I–VI*, rev. ed., Loeb Classical Library (1916; reprinted 1974), 160–61 (Fairclough's translation).

30. Diomedis, *Artis Grammaticae*, in Keil, *Grammatici Latini*, 1: 463.

31. Keil, *Grammatici Latini*, 4: 402.

32. Gerardi Joannis Vossii, *Commentariorum Rhetoricorum sive Oratoriarum Institutionum*, (Amsterdami, 1697), 262.

33. Keil, *Grammatici Latini*, 4: col 402. My emphasis.

34. Compare Flavii Sosipatri Charisii, *Artis Grammaticae*, in Keil, *Grammatici Latini*, 1: 277.

35. Isidori Hispalensis Episcopi, *Etymologiarum sive Originum, Libri XX*, ed. W. M. Lindsay (Oxford: Clarendon Press, 1911), 1.37.32–34.

36. Bedae Venerabilis, *Liber De Schematibus et Tropis* in Halm, *Rhetores Latini Minores*, 618.

37. Halm, *Rhetores Latini Minores*, 618.

38. Q. Fabius Laurentius Victorinus, *Explanationum in Rhetoricam M. Tullii Ciceronis* in Halm, *Rhetores Latini Minores*, 153–304.

39. Halm, *Rhetores Latini Minores*, 239.

40. James J. Murphy, *Rhetoric in the Middle Ages*, 184.

41. *Eberhardi Bethuniensis Graecismus*, ed. Joh. Wrobel, Corpus Grammaticorum Medii Aevi, vol. 1 (Bratislava: G. Koebner, 1887), 9–10. Eberhard uses the Greek terms.

42. Wrobel, *Eberhardi Bethuniensis Graecismus*, 75.

43. Alexander of Ville-Dieu, *Doctrinale*, in *Das Doctrinale des Alexander de Villa-Dei*, ed. Dietrich Reichling (Berlin: Hoffman & Comp., 1893), 172–73.

44. See the *Rhetorica ad Herennium* and Geoffrey of Vinsauf's *Poetria Nova*. Geoffrey refers to *effictio* as "a figure allied to this last one [imago], whereby I depict or represent corporeal appearance in so far as is requisite." See *"Poetria Nova" of Geoffrey of Vinsauf,* trans. Margaret F. Nims (Toronto: University of Toronto Press, 1967), 61–62.

45. Isidore used the same example for *characterismus* as for *imago*. Compare Sedulius Scottus, *In Donati Artem Maiorem,* ed. Bengt Löfstedt, Corpus Christianorum, Continuatio Medievalis, vol. 40B (Turnholt: Brepols, 1977), 389.

46. The best place to start investigating this aspect of Christian theology is still provided by Marcia L. Colish's *The Mirror of Language: A Study in the Medieval Theory of Knowledge,* 2d ed. (Lincoln: University of Nebraska Press, 1983). For a wide-ranging study of the cultural reflexivity implicit in this notion of the mirror see Edward Peter Nolan, *Now Through a Glass Darkly: Specular Images of Being and Knowing from Virgil to Chaucer* (Ann Arbor: The University of Michigan Press, 1990).

47. Saint Augustine, *De Trinitate,* ed. W. J. Mountain with Fr. Glorie, Corpus Christianorum, Series Latina, vols. 50 and 50A (Turnholt: Brepols, 1968).

48. See Karlfried Froehlich, "Pseudo-Dionysius and the Reformation of the Sixteenth- Century," in Pseudo-Dionysius, *The Complete Works,* trans. Colm Luibheid, with Paul Rorem, Classics of Western Spirituality (London: SPCK, 1987), 33. Also relevant in this volume is Jean Leclercq, "Influence and noninfluence of Dionysius in the Middle Ages," 25–32. Quotations from Pseudo-Dionysius are from this volume, but the Greek can be consulted in Denys L'Aréopagite, *La Hiérarchie Céleste,* trans. Maurice de Gandillac with introduction by René Roques and Apparatus Criticus by Günter Heil, Sources Chrétiennes, vol. 58 (Paris: Les Éditions du Cerf, 1958).

49. The significance of the Pseudo-Dionysian tradition has been pointed out, together with a valuable introduction and translation of two of its commentaries, in A. J. Minnis and A. B. Scott, with David Wallace, eds., *Medieval Literary Theory and Criticism c.1100–c.1375: The Commentary Tradition,* rev. ed. (Oxford: Clarendon Press, 1991), 165–96.

50. That is "anomoious homoiotētas." Homoeosis is the usual word for comparison in the rhetorical and grammatical manuals. Denys L'Aréopagite, *La Hiérarchie Céleste,* 81.

51. Pseudo-Dionysius, *The Complete Works,* 149.

52. Ibid.

53. The Greek uses the word "dusmorphia" for the nature of the earthly comparators. It is their ugliness, and misshapenness which should prompt us to recognise that they are not literally predicated of God, Denys L'Aréopagite, *La Hiérarchie Céleste,* 80. Compare Thomas Gallus, commenting on Pseudo-Dionysius in the mid-thirteenth century, in Minnis and Scott, *Medieval Literary Theory and Criticism,* 182.

54. Pseudo-Dionysius, *The Complete Works,* 151–52.

55. James Simpson discusses Chaucer's preference for mundane subject matter less susceptible to authoritative pronouncements in "Dante's 'Astripetam Aquilam' and the Theme of Poetic Discretion in the 'House of Fame,'" *Essays and Studies* 39 (1986): 1–18.

56. Robert M. Jordan writes that if Chaucer "was uncertain about his position in the temporal, historical world, he could still place himself, alternatively, in a stable, supranatural reality whose language was unambiguously true." Robert M. Jordan, *Chaucer's Poetics and the Modern Reader* (London: University of California Press, 1987), 173–74.

57. The Latin text of *The Consolation of Philosophy* can be consulted in Anicii Manlii Severini Boethii, *Philosophiae Consolatio,* ed. Ludovicus Bieler, Corpus Christianorum, Series Latina, vol. 94 (Turnholt: Brepols, 1957). Citations here are from Chaucer's *Boece* and indicate Book, Prosa or Metrum number, and then line reference.

58. Chaucer may have been helped to this effectiveness by both his non-Boethian

sources. Minnis notes that Jean de Meun's "nues pleuieuses" and Trevet's "humidans repentinis et impetuosis pluuiis" lie behind the translation of "wete plowngy clowdes." A. J. Minnis, ed., *Chaucer's 'Boece' and the Medieval Tradition of Boethius* (Cambridge: D. S. Brewer, 1993), 97.

59. A. J. Minnis and Tim William Machan, "The *Boece* as Late-Medieval Translation" in Minnis, *Chaucer's 'Boece,'* 183.

60. Chaucer's use of the two main sources, Nicholas Trevet's commentary on the *Consolatio* and Jeun de Meun's *Li Livres de Confort*, is discussed by A. J. Minnis in "Chaucer's Commentator: Nicholas Trevet and the *Boece*" in Minnis, *Chaucer's 'Boece,'* 83–166.

61. He matches Boethius's use of *exemplum* with "ensaumple" in *Boece*, and turns a negative tag into another positive reference (*Boece* 1.Me.3.4; *Phil.Cons* 1.Pr.3.1). He prefers to "English" the Boethian *simulauit* by the close translation "schewede by simylitude" even though "similitude" was not a word to which he naturally turned elsewhere. Sometimes one sees him following the hints of his French source, sometimes Trevet, sometimes neither, in order to present a consistent language of comparison. For his use of clarificatory doublets see 5.Pr.6.16, 85, 131.

62. The Greek term for the second type of comparison, *parabolē*, is used in a restricted context: the *Parables* of Solomon is the title used for the biblical book of *Proverbs* in the *Wife of Bath's Prologue* 679 and in the *Romance of the Rose* 6530. Chaucer also uses the Old English word "forbise" (vb) [to give example] once at *Troilus and Criseyde* 2.1390. Unlike Langland, he never uses the noun "forbisen(e)."

63. See Boethius's use of the term *brevi exemplo* followed by Chaucer at 5.Pr.4.141–43 and elsewhere.

64. We must distinguish between a poem's significance for its author's "poetics," and a self-conscious metapoetic strand in the poem itself. I do not sense the latter in the *Book of the Duchess* whereas it seems very overt in poems like *Troilus and Criseyde*. Here I take a different line from Robert W. Hanning, "Chaucer's First Ovid: Metamorphosis and Poetic Tradition in The Book of the Duchess and The House of Fame" in *Chaucer and the Craft of Fiction*, ed. Leigh A. Arrathoon (Rochester, Mi.: Solaris, 1986), 121–63.

65. Robert W. Hanning notes the alterations made to Ovid to shape this negative exemplum, and further contrasts it with the "positive exemplary use of the same story" by Machaut, Arrathoon, *Chaucer and the Craft of Fiction*, 136.

66. Alfred David indicates that the story of Ceyx and Alcione marks a break from French tradition and the start of Chaucer's concern with "old books." Alfred David, "*Old, New*, and *Yong* in Chaucer," The Presidential Address, *Studies in the Age of Chaucer* 15 (1993), 7.

67. A. C. Spearing, " The *Canterbury Tales* IV: Exemplum and Fable" in *The Cambridge Chaucer Companion*, ed. Piero Boitani and Jill Mann (Cambridge: Cambridge University Press, 1986), 159–77.

68. Boitani and Mann, *Cambridge Chaucer Companion*, 161.

CHAPTER 2. NAMING AND THE *HOUSE OF FAME*

1. See Aelius Donatus, *Ars Grammatica* in *Grammatici Latini*, ed. H. Keil, 8 vols. (Leipzig: 1853–80; repr., Hildesheim: Georg Olms Verlagsbuchhandlung, 1961), 4: 401.

2. The condition of language and its bearing upon literary authority, particularly with respect to Chaucer's own sources, and with a metapoetic slant has been a recurring and productive aspect of criticism of the *House of Fame*. While sharing this gen-

eral topic, the present chapter has different emphases within it, and proposes a different view of language from the prevailing opinion. See especially Robert O. Payne, *The Key of Remembrance: A Study of Chaucer's Poetics* (New Haven: Yale University Press, 1963); Sheila Delany, *Chaucer's "House of Fame": The Poetics of Skeptical Fideism* (Chicago: University of Chicago Press, 1972); A. C. Spearing, *Medieval Dream Poetry* (Cambridge: Cambridge University Press, 1976); Lawrence K. Shook, "*The House of Fame*," in *Companion to Chaucer Studies*, ed. Beryl Rowland, rev. ed. (New York: Oxford University Press, 1979), 414–27; Piero Boitani, *Chaucer and the Imaginary World of Fame* (Cambridge: D. S. Brewer, 1984), a book which extends the linguistic theme into a wide-ranging study of Chaucer's literary affinities; Helen Cooper, "Chaucer and Ovid: A Question of Authority," in *Ovid Renewed: Ovidian Influences on Literature and Art from the Middle Ages to the Twentieth Century*, ed. Charles Martindale (Cambridge: Cambridge University Press, 1988), 71–81. Cooper notes Chaucer's "wholesale rejection" of the traditionally moralized Ovid. Also see Jacqueline T. Miller, *Poetic License: Authority and Authorship in Medieval and Renaissance Contexts* (Oxford: Oxford University Press, 1986); Robert W. Hanning, "Chaucer's First Ovid: Metamorphosis and Poetic Tradition in The Book of the Duchess and The House of Fame," in *Chaucer and the Craft of Fiction,* ed. Leigh A. Arrathoon (Rochester, Mi.: Solaris, 1986), 121–63.

3. Richard Axton rightly affirms Chaucer's sense of responsibility. Writing of the tale of Philomene in the *Legend of Good Women*, Axton says that Chaucer "turns in his anguish from reflection on God's responsibility as author of nature to his own, secondary, authorial responsibility: merely to retell Ovid's story seems to be to pollute the world . . . the sincerity and pain of Chaucer's indignation seem to me to be undeniable and the seriousness of his sense of authorial responsibility is not anything a modern reader can lightly dismiss." Richard Axton, "Gower—Chaucer's heir?" in *Chaucer Traditions: Studies in Honour of Derek Brewer,* ed. Ruth Morse and Barry Windeatt (Cambridge: Cambridge University Press, 1990): 31–32. One might add that even the avowed benign exemplary purpose of the *Legend* is insufficient to allay Chaucer's concern.

4. I do not sense as clear a subversion of Virgil as Cooper, who says that Chaucer "plays off Ovid against Virgil to undermine the master-poet of Western cultural tradition," Cooper, "Chaucer and Ovid," 72.

5. This has long been acknowledged as a characteristic of Chaucer's style. See Charles Muscatine, *Chaucer and the French Tradition: A Study in Style and Meaning* (1957; reprint Berkeley and Los Angeles: University of California Press, 1964). Muscatine writes of "Chaucer's tireless capacity for definition and comparison," 223.

6. Harold Bloom, *A Map of Misreading* (Oxford: Oxford University Press, 1975). For a thoughtful recent discussion of Chaucer and the challenge posed by, and to, modern deconstructionist readings see Andrew Taylor, "Chaucer Our Derridean Contemporary?" *Exemplaria* 5 (fall 1993): 471–86.

7. Hanning, "Chaucer's First Ovid," 145–46.

8. Boitani, *Chaucer and the Imaginary House of Fame,* 210.

9. Friedrich Nietzsche, *On Truth and Falsity in their Ultramoral Sense* in *The Complete Works of Friedrich Nietzsche,* ed. O. Levy, trans. Maximillian A. Mügge (London and Edinburgh: T. N. Foulis, 1911), 2:178.

10. Paul de Man, "The Epistemology of Metaphor," in *On Metaphor,* ed. Sheldon Sacks (London: University of Chicago Press, 1978), 28.

11. Boitani, *Chaucer and the Imaginary House of Fame,* 210.

12. Hanning, "Chaucer's First Ovid," 155.

13. Boitani, *Chaucer and the Imaginary House of Fame,* 211.

14. Robert R. Edwards, *The Dream of Chaucer: Representation and Reflection in the Early Narratives* (Durham and London: Duke University Press, 1989), 117.

15. Mary Carruthers, *The Book of Memory: A Study of Memory in Medieval Cultures,*

Cambridge Studies in Medieval Literature, vol. 10 (1990; reprint Cambridge: Cambridge University Press, 1994): 259.

16. Lee Patterson, "Perpetual Motion: Alchemy and the Technology of the Self," The Biennial Chaucer Lecture, *Studies in the Age of Chaucer* 15 (1993), 39.

17. Patterson, "Perpetual Motion," 38.

18. For the *locus classicus* of discussion on this issue see Stephen A. Barney, "Chaucer's Lists," in *The Wisdom of Poetry: Essays in Early English Literature in honor of Morton W. Bloomfield*, ed. Larry D. Benson and Siegfried Wenzel (Kalamazoo, Mi.: Medieval Institute Publications, 1982): 189–223. In an interesting recent article on the paradox of lists in the *House of Fame* Lara Ruffolo argues that lists "dismember literature" but also "point to a new constitution of literary authority in a way that is more in keeping with the crowded, public, raucous tone" of the poem. Lara Ruffolo, "Literary Authority and the Lists of Chaucer's *House of Fame:* Destruction and Definition through Proliferation," *Chaucer Review* 27 (1993), 338.

19. James Simpson, "Dante's 'Astripetam Aquilam' and the Theme of Poetic Discretion in the 'House of Fame'," *Essays and Studies* 39 (1986): 1–18. Compare also David Wallace, "Chaucer's Continental Inheritance: The Early Poems and *Troilus and Criseyde*," in *The Cambridge Chaucer Companion*, ed. Piero Boitani and Jill Mann (Cambridge: Cambridge University Press, 1986), 19–37; Lisa Kiser, "Eschatological Poetics in Chaucer's *House of Fame*," *Modern Language Quarterly* 49 (1990 for 1989): 99–119 on Chaucer's refusal of Dantean judgment of souls, and Karla Taylor, who writes, "Chaucer uses the eagle, his chief Dantean borrowing, to steer clear of poetry in the Dantean vein," in *Chaucer Reads "The Divine Comedy"* (Stanford: Stanford University Press, 1989), 36.

20. For a discussion of the iconographic sources of Aeolus, but without comment on Chaucer's striking contemporary simile of bearbaiting, see J. A. W. Bennett, *Chaucer's Book of Fame: An Exposition of the "House of Fame"* (Oxford: Clarendon, 1968), 150–64.

21. J. A. W. Bennett holds back from positively endorsing the division into books, though he appreciates why a division was made here. "The interruption of the action at this point by a proem to what Caxton calls the *liber secundus* prepares us for a change of scene and atmosphere. The pause is deliberate, and the position as well as the content of the proem counts against the view that the poem as a whole is casual or extemporized." Bennett, *Chaucer's Book of Fame*, 52.

22. This can be productive of interesting, though I would argue, overschematic, readings. See Elizabeth Buckmaster, "Meditation and Memory in Chaucer's *House of Fame*," *Modern Language Studies* 16 (1986): 279–87, and John Finlayson, "Seeing, Hearing and Knowing in *The House of Fame*," *Studia Neophilologica* 58 (1986): 47–57.

23. John M. Ganim discusses Chaucer's representation of the destructive language of the people in "Chaucer and the Noise of the People," *Exemplaria* 2 (spring 1990): 71–88, and in *Chaucerian Theatricality* (Princeton: Princeton University Press, 1990).

24. Bennett discusses the eagle, *Chaucer's Book of Fame*, 56–57. Other interpretations can be found in John M. Steadman, "Chaucer's Eagle: A Contemplative Symbol," *PMLA* 75 (1960): 153–59, and John Leyerle, "Chaucer's Windy Eagle," *University of Texas Quarterly* 40 (1971): 247–65. An extended analysis of the eagle, which, significantly for the present discussion, traces its line of association ultimately to the eagle formed out of words in Dante's *Paradiso* 18 is Karla Taylor's "First Readings: 'The House of Fame'," in Taylor, *Chaucer Reads 'The Divine Comedy,'* 22–23.

25. David Wallace, *Chaucerian Polity: Absolutist Lineages and Associational Forms in England and Italy, Figurae:* Reading Medieval Culture (Stanford: Stanford University Press, 1997), 249.

26. The *Riverside Chaucer* mentions earlier interpretations and notes, "The pre-

sumed joke here is hard to decipher," 979. Previous explanations have suggested allusion to an unhappy marriage, or to St Leonard as the patron saint of prisoners.

27. Each of these multiple narratives has generated strikingly different judgments about the function of the narrative project. For example, Jill Mann attempts to accommodate the iterative monotony of the *Legend of Good Women* with the cultural value of its project, when she writes that it "can only be understood *as* a riposte to misogyny— as adopting a single-mindedness and refusal of compromise which mirrors its own intransigence." Jill Mann, *Geoffrey Chaucer,* Feminist Readings (London: Harvester Wheatsheaf, 1991), 32. See also Sheila Delany, *The Naked Text: Chaucer's "Legend of Good Women"* (Berkeley and Los Angeles: University of California Press, 1994), who argues that variety at many levels clothes the "minimalism of topos (the woman faithful in love)," 2. Michaela Paasche Grudin discusses contrary modern views of the *Monk's Tale,* and its significance for Chaucer's interest in the capacities of the listener, in "The *Monk's Tale* and Chaucer's Idea of the Listener," in *Chaucer and the Politics of Discourse* (Columbia: University of South Carolina Press, 1996): 135–48. Judgment on Dorigen's list of exemplary suicides has recently stressed deliberate failure in the exemplary project. See, for example, Susan Crane, *Gender and Romance in Chaucer's "Canterbury Tales"* (Princeton: Princeton University Press, 1994), 111. But contrast Gerald Morgan's unfairly neglected "A Defence of Dorigen's Complaint," *Medium Ævum* 46 (1977): 77–97. As the present study indicates, it is not necessary to subvert the rhetorical list itself in order to claim that its dramatic or psychological functions are complex.

28. See also Robert R. Edwards's description of the work, as coming to a "poetic dead end" despite its sophistication, scholarliness, and elaboration in Edwards, *The Dream of Chaucer,* 94.

29. John Burrow discusses the incompleteness of several of Chaucer's poems, reviews past attempts to find significance in their lack of endings, and cautions against "undiscriminating overinterpretation" in "Poems Without Endings," *Studies in the Age of Chaucer* 13 (1991): 17–37, 37.

30. For the sharing of simile see the chapter on "Patterns of Comparison" in this book.

31. See above "Introduction," footnote 5. More recently, David Wallace has stated that "the Manciple and Chaucer share a line and have a lot in common" but he understands the similarity as fundamentally social and professional in character. Wallace, *Chaucerian Polity,* 249. Compare Louise Fradenburg who also sees the metapoetics of the Tale as lying in anxieties about Chaucer's role at court: Louise Fradenburg, "The Manciple's Servant Tongue: Politics and Poetry in *The Canterbury Tales,*" *ELH* 52 (1985): 85–118.

32. On the "movement of characters among the normally mutually exclusive levels of reality represented in the *Canterbury Tales,*" though as part of a rather over-elaborate theory, see Jeff Henderson, "Chaucer's Experiment in Narrative Metadrama: The General Prologue as *Dramatis Personae,*" *Publications of the Arkansas Philological Association* 14: 1 (1988), 23.

Chapter 3. Similes

1. Though the immediate context of a literary simile is much larger than for a casual simile in conversation, and the reflection needed to understand it may be much greater, the demand of relevance, which governs the processing of the information and the interpreting of the simile, is not essentially different. I would agree with the claim of Dan Sperber and Deirdre Wilson "that the lengthy and highly self-conscious processes of textual interpretation that religious or literary scholars engage in are

governed just as much by the principle of relevance as is spontaneous utterance comprehension." Dan Sperber and Deirdre Wilson, *Relevance: Communication and Cognition* (Oxford: Basil Blackwell, 1986), 75.

2. The point is generally made in theoretical discussion of figurativeness, but see for example, Michel Le Guern, *Sémantique de la métaphore et de la métonymie* (Paris: Larousse, 1973), 53. Le Guern writes that such comparison "au sens restreint n'est pas une image, parce qu'elle reste dans l'isotopie du contexte: on ne compare quantitativement que des réalités comparables." What structuralists call the semantic isotopy of the context, that is the equable condition in which language supposedly exists prior to figuration, is not disrupted by the quantitative comparison. That kind of comparison says nothing strange and does not prevent us from grasping the immediate meaning of the statement, as figuration does. One can reject the notion of semantic isotopy, and Le Guern himself finds it difficult as a measure of similaic figuration, and still agree that quantitative comparison does not normally create a figurative effect. See Paul Ricoeur, *The Rule of Metaphor: Multi-disciplinary studies of the creation of meaning in language*, trans. Robert Czerny, Kathleen McLaughlin and John Costello, S. J. (London: Routledge and Kegan Paul), 138–43, and John J. McGavin, "The Context of Literary Simile," *Cosmos* 3 (1989 for 1987) 14–16.

3. W. Aldis Wright, ed., *Generydes*, Early English Text Society, o.s., 55, 70 (London: N. Trübner & Co., 1878).

4. Donald B. Sands, ed., *Middle English Verse Romances* (London: Holt, Rinehart and Winston, 1966): 130–53.

5. Julius Zupitza, ed., *The Romance of Guy of Warwick*, Early English Text Society, e.s., 42, (London: N. Trübner & Co., 1883), 1: 208 [Auchinleck MS].

6. George A. Panton and David Donaldson, eds., *The "Gest Hystoriale" of the Destruction of Troy*, Early English Text Society, o.s., 39, 56 (London: N. Trübner & Co., 1869 and 1874).

7. J. Ernst Wülfing, ed., *The Laud Troy Book*, Early English Text Society, o.s., 121, 122 (London: Kegan Paul, Trench, Trübner, 1902–3).

8. Walter Hoyt French and Charles Brockway Hale, eds., *Middle English Verse Romances*, (New York: Russell and Russell, 1964), 1: 381–419.

9. Spenser uses the same trick when he says that Archimago, dressed as a hermit, knocked his breast "as one that did repent" (*Faerie Queene* 1.1.29). What Archimago presented as *imago* was only a deceitful *similitudo*. I do not believe that this is part of Spenser's conscious medievalising of his romance. The deceit which reformers claimed was intrinsic to the religious *imago* would be enough to suggest the device. Edmund Spenser, *The Faerie Qveene*, ed. A. C. Hamilton, Longman Annotated English Poets (New York: Longman, 1977), 37.

10. French and Hale, eds., *Middle English Metrical Verse Romances*, 1: 287–320.

11. Richard Beadle, ed., *The York Plays*, York Medieval Texts, second series (London: Edward Arnold, 1982).

12. All references to the work of this author are to Malcolm Andrew and Ronald Waldron, eds., *The Poems of the Pearl Manuscript: Pearl, Cleanness, Patience, Sir Gawain and the Green Knight*, rev. ed., Exeter Medieval Texts and Studies (Exeter: University of Exeter Press, 1987).

13. Malcolm Andrew, "The Realizing Imagination in Late Medieval English Literature," *English Studies* 76 (1995): 113–28.

14. The local effects which I have been describing are to be distinguished from the general "assimilation of the iconographic to the mimetic," the uniting of "symbolic image and mimetic verisimilar action" which V. A. Kolve describes as the common condition and aim of Chaucer's employment of traditional imagery in his fiction. They do not contradict Kolve's claim but have a different value in the present different pro-

ject. V. A. Kolve, *Chaucer and the Imagery of Narrative: The First Five Canterbury Tales* (London: Edward Arnold, 1984), 68, 359.

15. Ernest A. Gallo, *The "Poetria Nova" and its Sources in Early Rhetorical Doctrine* (The Hague: Mouton, 1971), 44–47 (lines 567–626).

16. Kolve, *Chaucer and the Imagery of Narrative*, 73.

17. I understand "irony" in the medieval sense, that is, a figure in which one meaning is *replaced* by another. See the important article by Joseph A. Dane, "The Myth of Chaucerian Irony," *Papers on Language and Literature* 24 (1988): 115–33. Modern critical use of the term "irony" leaves two meanings in play, one of which (usually that which the critic wishes to prioritize) is considered more authoritative.

18. For a more detailed investigation of the incongruity at the heart of this *comparatio* see Robert Boenig, "January's Trumpets," *English Language Notes* 32, no. 1 (1994): 19–23.

19. See Derek Pearsall, *The Canterbury Tales* (Boston: G. Allen & Unwin, 1985), 192–93. Pearsall senses an overenthusiasm at the start of this curtailed poem.

20. The author of *Sir Gawain and the Green Knight* predictably factualises this idea rather than making it figurative (459 and 671).

21. As one would expect, the source, Guido delle Colonne, does not have a reference to turnips. Milk is his chosen comparator. Guido de Columnis, *Historia Destructionis Troiae*, ed. Nathaniel Edward Griffin, Medieval Academy of America Publications, vol. 26 (Cambridge, Ma.: Medieval Academy of America, 1936), 73.

22. In Gallo, *"Poetria Nova,"* 44 (lines 570–71).

23. Donald B. Sands, ed., *Middle English Verse Romances*, 313–22.

24. This is how the editors of the Selected Plays interpret it. Richard Beadle and Pamela King, eds., *York Mystery Plays: A Selection in Modern Spelling* (Oxford: Clarendon, 1984), 215.

25. L. F. Casson, ed., *Sir Degrevant*, Early English Text Society, o.s., 221 (London: Oxford University Press, 1949 for 1944). [Lincoln Manuscript]

26. Alice Miskimin, ed., *Susannah: An Alliterative Poem of the Fourteenth Century* (New Haven: Yale University Press, 1969).

27. O. S. Pickering, ed., *The South English Nativity of Mary and Christ*, Middle English Texts, vol. 1 (Heidelberg: Carl Winter, 1975).

28. Sidney J. Herrtage, ed., *Sir Ferumbras*, Early English Text Society, e.s., 34 (London: Kegan Paul, Trench, Trübner & Co., 1879).

29. In French and Hale, eds., *Middle English Metrical Romances*, 1: 421–55.

30. Derek Pearsall and Elizabeth Salter, *Landscapes and Seasons of the Medieval World* (London: Paul Elek, 1973), 105. Much *Pearl* criticism has drawn attention to the revision of earthly values which the dreamer has to undergo and the way in which the poem structures itself on this revision. See for example, Louis Blenkner, "The Pattern of Traditional Images in *Pearl*," *Studies in Philology* 68 (1971): 26–49 and "The Theological Structure of *Pearl*," in John Conley, ed., *The Middle English "Pearl": Critical Essays* (Notre Dame and London: University of Notre Dame Press, 1970): 220–71; Theodore Bogdanos, *Pearl: Image of the Ineffable: A Study in Medieval Poetic Symbolism* (Univ. Park.: Pennsylvania State University Press, 1983); Marie Borroff, "Pearl's 'Maynful Mone': Crux, Simile, and Structure," in *Acts of Interpretation: The Text in its Contexts, 700–1600. Essays on Medieval and Renaissance Literature in Honor of E. Talbot Donaldson*, ed. Mary J. Carruthers and Elizabeth D. Kirk (Norman, Okla.: Pilgrim, 1982), 159–72; Paul Reichardt, "Animal Similes in *Pearl*," in *Text and Matter: New Perspectives of the Pearl-Poet*, ed. Robert J. Blanch, M. M. Youngerman, and Julian N. Wasserman (Troy, N.Y.: Whitson, 1991), 17–30.

31. For discussion of this simile see Malcolm Andrew, "*Patience:* the 'Munster Dore'," *English Language Notes* 14 (1976–77): 164–67.

32. Pearsall and Salter, *Landscapes and Seasons*, 103–4.

33. W. A. Davenport, *The Art of the Gawain Poet* (London: The Athlone Press, 1978), 12.

34. Andrew and Waldron, *Poems of the Pearl Manuscript*, 60, note. See this note also for references to parallels and sources for the image.

35. Analysis of this simile supports the recent discussion of the poem's Ockhamism by Lawrence Clopper who, writing of the poem's "system of analogies" describes the river's significance thus: "the river flowing from the throne of God remains between— and the only face of God that man can know is that which, through his *ordinata*, God chooses to turn towards mankind, and that anthropomorphic one that man constructs in his own image in the face of God's *potentia absoluta*." Lawrence M. Clopper, "The God of the *Gawain*-Poet," *Modern Philology* 94 (1996–97), 18. I would modify this judgment only to cite the optimistic exuberance of the art which constructs the analogy.

36. J. A. Burrow and Thorlac Turville-Petre, eds., *A Book of Middle English* (Oxford: Blackwell, 1992): 110–29.

37. See *impen* (v), in Hans Kurath and Sherman M. Kuhn, *Middle English Dictionary* (Ann Arbor, Mi.: University of Michigan Press, 1956–).

Chapter 4. Patterns of Comparison in *Troilus and Criseyde*

1. So extensive has been the work on this poem that the reader in search of bibliographical guidance on any points not specifically noted here is directed to Barry Windeatt, *Troilus and Criseyde*, Oxford Guides to Chaucer (Oxford: Clarendon, 1992), where past criticism is gathered and scrutinized at length.

2. David Burnley argues that the word "lyne" has mathematical significance for Chaucer and retains its technical resonance elsewhere. "On more than one occasion, a *lyne* is regarded as the epitome of straightness or directness. The fact that a simile is used . . . is a good indication of the technicality of the word." The idiomatic use of this simile outside Chaucer rather tells against the second part of Burnley's claim for how *Troilus and Criseyde* 2.1460–62 should be read, though not, of course, against its being a technical term for him in technical contexts. David Burnley, *A Guide to Chaucer's Language* (Frome: Macmillan, 1983), 160. See also Linda Tarte Holley, *Chaucer's Measuring Eye* (Houston, Tex.: Rice University Press, 1990).

3. Critics have previously noted the pairing of scenes. See, for example, Ian Bishop, *"Troilus and Criseyde": A Critical Study* (Bristol: University of Bristol Press, 1981), 25–29, 61–64, and Brenner's remarks on "parallels of action": Gerry Brenner, "Narrative Structure in Chaucer's 'Troilus and Criseyde'," in *Chaucer's "Troilus": Essays in Criticism*, ed. Stephen A. Barney, (London: Scolar Press, 1980), 137.

4. With an emphasis on the dialectic of the poem, Barry Windeatt points out that this is part of a larger pattern which "progressively educates its reader into accepting that there can be no single fixed point of view in this world," Windeatt, *Troilus and Criseyde*, Oxford Guides to Chaucer, 299.

5. For a study of this motif as thematically significant see Elizabeth A. Dobbs, "Seeing Through Windows in Chaucer's *Troilus*," *Chaucer Review* 32 (1998): 400–22.

6. Critics have seen this in terms of the feminization of Troilus. See Jill Mann, *Geoffrey Chaucer*, Feminist Readings Series (London: Harvester Wheatsheaf, 1991), 166, and Gayle Margherita, *The Romance of Origins: Language and Sexual Difference in Middle English Literature* (Philadelphia: University of Pennsylvania Press, 1994), 117–18.

7. For studies of the importance of "looking" in the poem see B. A. Windeatt, "Gesture in Chaucer," *Medievalia et Humanistica* 9 (1979): 143–61 and, more recently, Sarah Stanbury, "The Voyeur and the Private Life in *Troilus and Criseyde*," *Studies in the Age*

of Chaucer 13 (1991): 141–58. Stanbury's essay includes substantial reference to other writings on this topic.

8. This image, and the surrounding passage on the ennobling effect of love, is closely modeled on Boccaccio's "come falcon ch' uocisse di capello," but its significance is determined by the imagistic pattern of Chaucer's poem into which it is brought. For other alterations made by Chaucer in adopting the simile, see B. A. Windeatt, ed., *Troilus and Criseyde: "The Book of Troilus" by Geoffrey Chaucer*, Longman Annotated Texts (Harlow: Longman, 1990), 343.

9. Stanbury, "The Voyeur and the Private Life," 144.

10. Boccaccio repeats the sentiment, but it is Chaucer who makes the link by repeating the key words; Boccaccio uses the phrases "il nero manto" and "la bruna vesta." See Windeatt, *Troilus and Criseyde: "The Book of Troilus" by Geoffrey Chaucer*, 106, 178.

11. This is a widely noted aspect of Chaucer's style, but for a specific study of Chaucer's false "authority" for *Troilus,* see Bella Millett, "Chaucer, Lollius, and the Medieval Theory of Authorship," in *Studies in the Age of Chaucer Proceedings 1. 1984: Reconstructing Chaucer,* ed. Paul Strohm and Thomas J. Heffernan (Knoxville, Tenn.: The New Chaucer Society, 1985): 93–108.

12. H. Marshall Leicester Jr. stresses Chaucer's art in the Canterbury Tales as one of "learning—and practicing—to speak in the voices of others" but conversely as the generating of a textual voice in its own right. H. Marshall Leicester Jr., *The Disenchanted Self: Representing the Subject in the "Canterbury Tales"* (Berkeley: University of California Press, 1990), 414.

13. See Windeatt, *Troilus and Criseyde,* Oxford Guides to Chaucer, 319–20.

14. Karla Taylor discusses this group of images, and others related to it, with an emphasis on the functions of conventional language. Karla Taylor, "Proverbs and the Authentication of Convention in 'Troilus and Criseyde'," in *Chaucer's "Troilus": Essays in Criticism,* ed. Stephen A. Barney (London: Scolar Press, 1980), 281–86.

15. John M. Ganim discusses this passage with an eye on Chaucer's politics in *Chaucerian Theatricality* (Princeton: Princeton University Press, 1990), 110–13.

16. The analogy has long been seen to include the poem's narrator also. See John M. Fyler, "The Narrator and His Double," in *Chaucer and Ovid* (New Haven and London: Yale University Press, 1979), 124–47, and A. C. Spearing, *The Medieval Poet as Voyeur: Looking and Listening in Medieval Love-Narratives* (Cambridge: Cambridge University Press, 1993.)

17. See Jane Chance, "The Medieval 'Apology for Poetry': Fabulous Narrative and Stories of the Gods," in *The Mythographic Art: Classical Fable and the Rise of the Vernacular in Early France and England,* ed. Jane Chance (Gainesville: University of Florida Press, 1990), 3–44.

18. For discussion of the substance and source of these borrowings see Barry Windeatt, "Sources" in Windeatt, *Troilus and Crisyede,* Oxford Guides to Chaucer, 37–137.

19. Robert M. Jordan, *Chaucer's Poetics and the Modern Reader* (London: University of California Press, 1987).

20. The most extensive analysis of Chaucer's use of earlier writers is Winthrop Wetherbee's *Chaucer and the Poets: An Essay on "Troilus and Criseyde"* (Ithaca: Cornell University Press, 1984). For a critique of critical readings based on allusions see A. C. Spearing, *"Troilus and Criseyde:* the Illusion of Allusion," *Exemplaria* 2 (Spring 1990): 263–77.

21. See Jill Mann, "Parents and Children in the *Canterbury Tales,"* in *Literature in Fourteenth-Century England,* ed. Piero Boitani and Anna Torti (Tübingen: Narr, 1983), 165–83, and A. C. Spearing, "Father Chaucer," in *Writing after Chaucer: Essential Readings in Chaucer and the Fifteenth Century,* ed. Daniel J. Pinti (New York: Garland Publishing Inc., 1998), 145–66.

22. See Norman Blake, "The Wife of Bath and her *Tale*," *Leeds Studies in English*, n.s, 13 (1982): 42–55.

23. Spearing questions the extent to which readers or hearers would know the details of the story being alluded to, though Chaucer might take an independent pleasure in creating the link. Spearing, "Illusion of Allusion," 271.

Chapter 5. Persuasive Comparisons in *Troilus and Criseyde*

1. Barry Windeatt, *Troilus and Criseyde*, Oxford Guides to Chaucer (Oxford: Clarendon, 1992), 321.

2. Also in this section is his cynical shift of bird imagery to the functionalism of heron and falcon, discussed in the previous chapter.

3. Umberto Eco, with others, *Interpretation and overinterpretation*, ed. Stefan Collini (Cambridge: Cambridge University Press, 1992), 65.

4. See Jill Mann, *Chaucer and Medieval Estates Satire: The Literature of Social Classes and the General Prologue to the Canterbury Tales* (Cambridge: Cambridge University Press, 1973), 195–96.

5. For a recent study of Criseyde which explores Chaucer's problem with her as a resistant object of fictional sympathy, see Laura D. Kellogg, *Boccaccio's and Chaucer's Cressida*, Studies in the Humanities, vol. 16 (Frankfurt am Main and Berne: Peter D. Lang, 1995).

6. Susan Yager points out that this is increasingly a problem in the later books of the poem. Susan Yager, "'As she that': Syntactical Ambiguity in Chaucer's *Troilus and Criseyde*," *Philological Quarterly* 73 (1994): 151–66.

7. Judith Ferster, *Chaucer on Interpretation* (Cambridge: Cambridge University Press, 1985). Ferster was taking issue with a line of thought represented by H. Marshall Leicester Jr., "The Art of Interpretation: A General Prologue to the *Canterbury Tales*," *PMLA* 95 (1980): 213–24.

8. See, for example, Evan Carson, "Complicity and Responsibility in Pandarus' Bed and Chaucer's Art," *PMLA* 94 (1979): 47–61, and John M. Fyler, "The Fabrications of Pandarus," *Modern Language Quarterly* 41 (1980): 115–30.

9. This borrowing from Geoffrey may be indirect. See Larry D. Benson, ed., *The Riverside Chaucer*, 3d ed. (Boston: Houghton Mifflin, 1989), 1030.

10. Ruth Morse argues for the characterizing function of the comparisons: "In Chaucer's *Troilus and Criseyde*, Pandarus's fondness for proverbs which support his view of events helps to characterize him as an almost pedagogic type, aware of and not overmuch moved by the changeableness of life, yet that he uses so many proverbs also suggests a certain literary as well as social vulgarity about him. Overuse is an ironizing mechanism." Ruth Morse, *Truth and Convention in the Middle Ages: Rhetoric, Representation, and Reality* (Cambridge: Cambridge University Press, 1991), 67–68.

11. However, as I pointed out in an earlier chapter, it is not always easy to judge precisely what constitutes indecorum in a figure which exploits dissimilarities between topic and comparator.

12. See Stephen A. Barney, "Chaucer's Lists," in *The Wisdom of Poetry: Essays in Early English Literature in honor of Morton W. Bloomfield*, ed. Larry D. Benson and Siegfried Wenzel (Kalamazoo, Mi.: Medieval Institute Publications, 1982): 189–223.

13. Stephen A. Barney, "Chaucer's Lists," 198.

14. Helen Cooper, *The Structure of the Canterbury Tales* (London: Duckworth, 1983), 198–200. Cooper argues that the *Tale* "questions the activity of storytelling within a fiction," 199. For a contrasting view of the positive values and implications of the *Man-*

ciple's Tale see David Raybin, "The Death of a Silent Woman: Voice and Power in Chaucer's Manciple's Tale," *Journal of English and Germanic Philology* 95 (1996): 19–37.

15. David Wallace sees silence in the *Manciple's Tale* less in a metapoetic dimension as in a social one: Chaucer the court poet has to learn when to speak and when to be silent. David Wallace, *Chaucerian Polity: Absolutist Lineages and Associational Forms in England and Italy, Figurae:* Reading Medieval Culture (Stanford: Stanford University Press, 1997), 259–60. Pandarus, however, seems to be prompted by less political motives. Though perhaps his need to remain included in Troilus's society plays a part in his restraint, his apparent motive is more moral in its metapoetic significance.

16. Carolyn Dinshaw, *Chaucer's Sexual Poetics* (Madison, Wi.: University of Wisconsin Press, 1989), 29.

CHAPTER 6. THE POEM AS *EXEMPLUM*

1. A. C. Spearing, "The *Canterbury Tales* IV: Exemplum and Fable" in *The Cambridge Chaucer Companion*, ed. Piero Boitani and Jill Mann (Cambridge: Cambridge University Press, 1986): 159–77. The *Canterbury Tales* also formed a substantial part of Larry Scanlon's major study of exemplary authority. Larry Scanlon, *Narrative, Authority, and Power: The medieval exemplum and the Chaucerian tradition*, Cambridge Studies in Medieval Literature, vol. 20 (Cambridge: Cambridge University Press, 1994).

2. For the importance of female authorship of the lyric at this key point, see Clare Regan Kinney, "'Who made this song?': The Engendering of Lyric Counterplots in *Troilus and Criseyde*," *Studies in Philology* 89 (1992): 272–92.

3. David Wallace writes, "Troilus and Criseyde manages to suggest something of the experience of a medieval walled city, and in 1381 London, often termed 'New Troy,' bore a resemblance to its ancient namesake in being walled, besieged, and finally overrun. But . . . the Troy of Troilus plainly differs from Chaucer's London." David Wallace, *Chaucerian Polity: Absolutist Lineages and Associational Forms in England and Italy, Figurae:* Reading Medieval Culture (Stanford: Stanford University Press, 1997).

4. Troilus means "Little Troy." See Jacqueline de Weever, *Chaucer Name Dictionary: A Guide to Astrological, Biblical, Historical, Literary, and Mythological Names in the Works of Geoffrey Chaucer* (London: Garland, 1988), 355–56.

5. Related to this difference in function is the long-lived strand in criticism which has pointed up the narrator's contrary claims to both historical objectivity and distance and also personal sympathy and insight. See Morton W. Bloomfield, "Distance and Predestination in *Troilus and Criseyde*," *PMLA* 72 (1957): 14–26, and more recently Karla Taylor, who writes that Chaucer's "subjective and objective authenticating devices work against each other." Karla Taylor, *Chaucer Reads "The Divine Comedy"* (Stanford: Stanford University Press, 1989), 109. Also in this tradition, though feminist criticism has moved beyond it in major respects, is E. T. Donaldson, "Criseyde and Her Narrator," in *Speaking of Chaucer* (London: Athlone Press, 1970): 65–83.

6. This is a device which Chaucer uses again in the *Pardoner's Tale* where the Pardoner's moralizings only develop once the narrative has started, and thus cut across the structural integrity of the *exemplum* he is is promoting.

7. For a similar view, see Barry Windeatt, *Troilus and Criseyde*, Oxford Guides to Chaucer (Oxford: Clarendon, 1992), 314. The ambivalent proximity of the poem to its audience extends to its proverbial bases, as is shown by Nancy Mason Bradbury, who argues that "familiar folkloric traditions" (324) are drawn into the learned ambit of the poem. Nancy Mason Bradbury, "Gentrification and the *Troilus*," *Chaucer Review* 28 (1993–94): 305–29.

8. Attempts to fashion a distinctive character for Arcite seem to me to cut against

Chaucer's evident desire to make the lovers similar in all respects except their ultimate fates. See for example the claim of sexual vengefulness made by Lorraine Kochanske Stock, "The Two Mayings in Chaucer's *Knight's Tale*," *Journal of English and Germanic Philology* 85 (1986): 206–21. Like many modern readings, this bears out Chaucer's own expectations about subsequent reading of his poems in that it fashions a creative similarity between the ethos of the *Tale* and that of the critic's own world.

9. Alfred David, "*Old, New,* and *Yong* in Chaucer," The Presidential Address, *Studies in the Age of Chaucer* 15 (1993), 20.

10. They certainly did for Christine de Pisan who objects to the violence and triumphalism of partisan male imagery for love: "Learn . . . how to make traps, capture the forts, deceive them, condemn them, attack this castle, take care that no woman escape from you men, and let everything be given over to shame!" Christine de Pisan, "Reply to Pierre Col" (2 October 1402) in Joseph L. Baird and John R. Kane, ed. and trans., *La Querelle de la Rose: Letters and Documents,* North Carolina Studies in the Romance Languages and Literatures, vol. 199 (Chapel Hill: University of North Carolina Press, 1978), 136.

11. Spearing remarks with memorable understatement, "The attitude conveyed by the end of the poem is not single or simple." A. C. Spearing, *Readings in Medieval Poetry* (Cambridge: Cambridge University Press, 1987), 132.

12. "Where does Chaucer's *Troilus* begin to end?" asks Barry Windeatt in his extended discussion of whether the poem achieves closure. Windeatt, *Troilus and Criseyde,* Oxford Guides to Chaucer, 304. This volume also contains an account (310–13) of the different readings which critics have given of the ending. The fragmentation of the poem's structure at the end has long attracted discussion.

13. In a recent investigation of whether Chaucer's language bears out claims that he is a literary theorist, David Burnley concludes that Chaucer's and Gower's "attitude to their composition is strikingly one of personal responsibility." David Burnley, "Chaucer's Literary Terms," *Anglia* 114 (1996), 228.

14. Christine de Pisan, "Reply to Pierre Col" (2 October 1402) in Baird and Kane, *La Querelle de la Rose: Letters and Documents,* 136.

15. Here, as in other places in this book, I would wish to distinguish Chaucer's problematics from those of deconstructionist reading. I agree with Murray J. Evans, when he writes that "Chaucer 'defamiliarizes,' holds in tension *without apparently rejecting,* the traditional medieval rhetorical relationship of author, poem, audience and moral" (my emphasis). Murray J. Evans, "'Making Strange': The Narrator (?), the Ending (?), and Chaucer's 'Troilus,'" *Neuphilologische Mitteilungen* 87 (1986), 228. A recent article argues that Chaucer stresses the textuality of the poem at the end, expects the readers' interpretative struggles, and celebrates inconclusiveness. Claudia Rattazzi Papka, "Transgression, the End of Troilus, and the Ending of Chaucer's *Troilus and Criseyde,*" *Chaucer Review* 32 (1998): 267–81.

16. Saul N. Brody explores the moral inconclusiveness which extends between middle and late-period works in "*Troilus and Criseyde* and *The Nun's Priest's Tale:* The Drawing and Undrawing of Morals," in *Religion in the Poetry and Drama of the Late Middle Ages in England,* The J. A. W. Bennett Memorial Lectures, ed. Piero Boitani and Anna Torti (Cambridge: D. S. Brewer, 1990): 133–48.

17. See Lesley Johnson, "Reincarnations of Griselda: contexts for the *Clerk's Tale?*" in *Feminist Readings in Middle English Literature: The Wife of Bath and all her sect,* ed. Ruth Evans and Lesley Johnson (London and New York: Routledge, 1994): 195–220. Johnson rejects recurring attempts to present the meaning of the *Tale* as unified. An account of the various sources for and interpretations of the *Tale,* can be found in Judith Bronfman, *Chaucer's "Clerk's Tale": The Griselda Story Received, Rewritten, Illustrated,* Garland Studies in Medieval Literature, vol. 11 (New York: Garland: 1994).

18. David Weisberg similarly contrasts the two dimensions of this poem, setting

"stanzas of ethereal, abstruse, prefigural writing" against this "representative of an alternative narrative realism." David Weisberg, "Telling Stories about Constance: Framing and Narrative Strategy in the *Canterbury Tales*," *Chaucer Review* 27 (1992–93), 60.

19. There has been much recent criticism of the *Tale* because of its significance for a feminist reading of Chaucer. A challenging interpretation of Griselda's apparent complaisance is that she is actually mimicking conventional male ideals of female behavior, and thus "the *Clerk's Tale* is inherently fissured in a manner that goes beyond Chaucer's deliberate opening up and multiplication of perspective." Gail Ashton, "Patient Mimesis: Griselda and the *Clerk's Tale*," *Chaucer Review* 32 (1998), 232.

20. David Wallace sees the Tale's "terminating contradictions and incoherencies" as the product of a similarly fractured narrative. David Wallace, *Chaucerian Polity*, 293.

21. Wallace, *Chaucerian Polity*, 65.

22. For a review of critical problems with the Clerk's *Envoy*, with an accompanying hermeneutic reading, see John M. Ganim, "Carnival Voices in the Clerk's *Envoy*," in *Chaucerian Theatricality* (Princeton: Princeton University Press, 1990), 79–91. More recently, Howell Chickering argues that the *Envoy*, "stabilizes the double ironies and undecidables of interpretation *as* undecidables." Howell Chickering, "Form and Interpretation in the *Envoy* to the *Clerk's Tale*," *Chaucer Review* 29 (1994–95), 352.

23. Carolyn Dinshaw writes, "The Wife of Bath's Prologue . . . renovates the patriarchal hermeneutic to accommodate the feminine." Carolyn Dinshaw, *Chaucer's Sexual Poetics* (Madison: University of Wisconsin Press, 1989), 126. Compare H. Marshall Leicester Jr., who stresses the "unresolvable tensions" which constitute the Wife as a textual presence. H. Marshall Leicester Jr., *The Disenchanted Self: Representing the Subject in the "Canterbury Tales"* (Berkeley: University of California Press, 1990), 138.

24. For discussion of the Wife's loving relationship with Jankyn see H. Marshall Leicester Jr., *The Disenchanted Self*, 114–39. For an article locating the Wife's preaching in the context of tradition and late medieval sermon argument see Andrew Galloway, "Marriage Sermons, Polemical Sermons, and *The Wife of Bath's Prologue:* A Generic Excursus," *Studies in the Age of Chaucer* 14 (1992): 3–30. For an important feminist account of the Wife see Carolyn Dinshaw, *Chaucer's Sexual Poetics*, 113–31.

25. In rejecting various monologic readings of the Wife, Arthur Lindley argues that "We create the Alisoun we see, Chaucer's Alysoun is an absence." Arthur Lindley, "'Vanysshed Was This Daunce, He Nyste Where': Alysoun's Absence in the *Wife of Bath's Prologue and Tale*," *ELH* 59 (1992), 18. This is a different kind of absence from that caused by the silences which a male author may impose on his female speaker. See Sheila Delany, "Strategies of Silence in the Wife of Bath's Recital," *Exemplaria* 2 (Spring 1990): 49–69.

26. A valuable recent essay in this area is Lynne Dickson's, "Deflection in the Mirror: Feminine Discourse in *The Wife of Bath's Prologue* and *Tale*," *Studies in the Age of Chaucer* 15 (1993): 61–90. Its value lies not least in its assertion of the textual level rather than the character as the place where Chaucer "dramatizes the irresolvable antagonism between such [patriarchal] constructions of the feminine and the female subject," 72. See also Catherine Cox, "Holy Erotica and the Virgin Word: Promiscuous Glossing in the *Wife of Bath's Prologue*," *Exemplaria* 5 (1993): 207–37, where neither feminist nor misogynist readings are found adequate to explain the Wife's text.

Conclusion

1. Lee Patterson, "Perpetual Motion: Alchemy and the Technology of the Self," The Biennial Chaucer Lecture, *Studies in the Age of Chaucer* 15 (1993), 57.

2. Robert Henryson, *The Poems*, ed. Denton Fox (Oxford: Clarendon, 1987), 113.

Bibliography

GEOFFREY CHAUCER: PRIMARY TEXTS

Benson, Larry, et al., eds. *The Riverside Chaucer*. 3d ed. Boston: Houghton Mifflin Company, 1987.

Chaucer, Geoffrey. *Troilus and Criseyde: A new edition of "The Book of Troilus."* Edited by B. A. Windeatt. Longman Annotated Texts. Harlow: Longman, 1984.

OTHER AUTHORS: PRIMARY TEXTS

Alexander of Ville-Dieu. *Doctrinale*. In *Das Doctrinale des Alexander de Villa-Dei*, edited by Dietrich Reichling. Berlin: Hoffman & Comp., 1893.

Andrew, Malcolm and Ronald Waldron, eds. *The Poems of the Pearl Manuscript: Pearl, Cleanness, Patience, Sir Gawain and the Green Knight*. Rev. ed. Exeter Medieval Texts and Studies. Exeter: University of Exeter Press, 1987.

Aristotle. *Ars Rhetorica*. Edited by W. D. Ross. Scriptorum Classicorum Bibliotheca Oxoniensis. Oxford: Clarendon Press, 1949.

Aristotle. *The Works of Aristotle*. Edited in translation by W. D. Ross. 12 vols. Oxford: Clarendon Press, 1928–52.

Augustine, Saint. *De Trinitate*. Edited by W. J. Mountain with Fr. Glorie. Corpus Christianorum, Series Latina, vols. 50 and 50A. Turnholt: Brepols, 1968.

Beadle, Richard, ed. *The York Plays*. York Medieval Texts, second series. London: Edward Arnold, 1982.

Beadle, Richard and Pamela King, eds. *York Mystery Plays: A Selection in Modern Spelling*. Oxford: Clarendon, 1984.

[Bede] Bedae Venerabilis. *Liber De Schematibus et Tropis*. In *Rhetores Latini Minores*, edited by Carolus Halm, 607–18. Leipzig: B. G. Teubner, 1863.

Boethius, Anicius Manlius Severinus. *Philosophiae Consolatio*. Edited by Ludovicus Bieler. Corpus Christianorum, Series Latina, vol. 94. Turnholt: Brepols, 1957.

Casson, L. F., ed. *Sir Degrevant*. Early English Text Society, o.s., 221. London: Oxford University Press, 1949 for 1944.

Charisius, Flavius Sosipater. *Artis Grammaticae*. In *Grammatici Latini*, edited by H. Keil, 1: 1–296. 8 vols. 1853–80. Reprint, Hildesheim: Georg Olms Verlagsbuchhandlung, 1961.

[Christine de Pisan] *La Querelle de la Rose: Letters and Documents*. North Carolina Studies in the Romance Languages and Literatures, edited and translated by Joseph L. Baird and John R. Kane, vol. 199. Chapel Hill: University of North Carolina Press, 1978.

["Cicero"] *Ad C. Herennium, Libri IV, De Ratione Discendi.* Edited, with translation, by Harry Caplan. Loeb Classical Library. London: Heinemann, 1954.

Diomedes. *Artis Grammaticae.* In *Grammatici Latini,* edited by H. Keil, 1: 297–529. 8 vols. 1853–80. Reprint, Hildesheim: Georg Olms Verlagsbuchhandlung, 1961.

Donatus, Aelius. *Ars Grammatica.* In *Grammatici Latini,* edited by H. Keil, 4: 353–402. 8 vols. 1853–80. Reprint, Hildesheim: Georg Olms Verlagsbuchhandlung, 1961.

Eberhard of Béthune. *Eberhardi Bethuniensis Graecismus.* Edited by Joh. Wrobel. Corpus Grammaticorum Medii Aevi, vol. 1. Bratislava: G. Koebner, 1887.

French, Walter Hoyt and Charles Brockway Hale, eds. *Middle English Verse Romances.* New York: Russell and Russell, 1964.

Fronto, Marcus Cornelius. *The Correspondence of Marcus Cornelius Fronto.* Edited, with translation, by C. R. Haines. 2 vols. Loeb Classical Library. London: Heinemann, 1919.

Geoffrey of Vinsauf. *Poetria Nova.* In Ernest A. Gallo, *The "Poetria Nova" and its Sources in Early Rhetorical Doctrine.* The Hague: Mouton, 1971.

Geoffrey of Vinsauf. *"Poetria Nova" of Geoffrey of Vinsauf.* Translated by Margaret F. Nims. Toronto: University of Toronto Press, 1967.

Guido de Columnis. *Historia Destructionis Troiae.* Edited by Nathaniel Edward Griffin. Medieval Academy of America Publications, vol. 26. Cambridge, Ma.: Medieval Academy of America, 1936.

Herrtage, Sidney J., ed. *Sir Ferumbras.* Early English Text Society, e.s., 34. London: Kegan Paul, Trench, Trübner & Co., 1879.

[Isidore of Seville] Isidori Hispalensis Episcopi. *Etymologiarum sive Originum, Libri XX.* Edited by W. M. Lindsay. Oxford: Clarendon Press, 1911.

John of Garland. *Exempla Honestae Vitae.* In Edwin Habel, "Die Exempla honestae vitae des Johannes de Garlandia, eine lateinische Poetik des 13. Jahrhunderts." *Romanische Forschungen* 29 (1911): 137–54.

John of Garland. *Parisiana Poetria.* Edited and translated by T. Lawler. New Haven and London: Yale University Press, 1974.

Martianus Capella. *De Nuptiis Philologiae et Mercurii.* Edited by J. Willis. Leipzig: BSB B. G. Teubner Verlagsgesellschaft, 1983.

Miskimin, Alice, ed. *Susannah: An Alliterative Poem of the Fourteenth Century.* New Haven: Yale University Press, 1969.

Nietzsche, Friedrich. "On Truth and Falsity in their Ultramoral Sense." Vol. 2, *The Complete Works of Friedrich Nietzsche,* edited by O. Levy, translated by Maximillian A. Mügge. London and Edinburgh: T. N. Foulis, 1911.

Panton, George A. and David Donaldson, eds. *The "Gest Hystoriale" of the Destruction of Troy.* Early English Text Society, o.s., 39, 56. London: N. Trübner & Co., 1869 and 1874.

Pickering, O. S. ed. *The South English Nativity of Mary and Christ.* Middle English Texts, vol.1. Heidelberg: Carl Winter, 1975.

Pseudo-Dionysius. *The Complete Works.* Translated by Colm Luibheid, with Paul Rorem. Classics of Western Spirituality. London: SPCK, 1987.

[Pseudo-Dionysius] Denys L'Aréopagite. *La Hiérarchie Céleste.* Translated by Maurice de Gandillac with introduction by René Roques and Apparatus Criticus by Günter Heil. Sources Chrétiennes, vol. 58. Paris: Les Éditions du Cerf, 1958. [This contains the Greek text.]

Quintiliani, M. Fabii. *Institutionis Oratoriae*. Edited by M. Winterbottom. 2 vols. Scriptorum Classicorum Bibliotheca Oxoniensis. Oxford: Clarendon Press, 1970.

Quintilian. *The Institutio Oratoria*. Edited, with translation, by H. E. Butler. 4 vols. Loeb Classical Library. London: Heinemann Ltd., 1921–22.

Rufinianus, Julius. *De Figuris Sententiarum et Elocutionis*. In *Rhetores Latini Minores*, edited by Carolus Halm, 38–47. Leipzig: B. G. Teubner, 1863.

Sands, Donald B., ed. *Middle English Verse Romances*. London: Holt, Rinehart and Winston, 1966.

Sedulius Scottus. *In Donati Artem Maiorem*. Edited by Bengt Löfstedt. Corpus Christianorum, Continuatio Medievalis, vol. 40B. Turnholt: Brepols, 1977.

Spenser, Edmund. *The Faerie Qveene*. Edited by A. C. Hamilton. Longman Annotated English Poets. New York: Longman, 1977.

Victorinus, Q. Fabius Laurentius. *Explanationum in Rhetoricam M. Tullii Ciceronis*. In *Rhetores Latini Minores*, edited by Carolus Halm, 153–304. Leipzig: B. G. Teubner, 1863.

Virgil. *Eclogues, Georgics, Aeneid I—VI*. Edited, with translation, by H. Rushton Fairclough. Rev. ed. Loeb Classical Library. Cambridge, Ma.: Harvard University Press, 1916; reprinted 1974.

Vossius, Gerardus Johannes. *Commentariorum Rhetoricorum sive Oratoriarum Institutionum*. Amsterdam, 1697.

Wright, W. Aldis, ed. *Generydes*. Early English Text Society, o.s., 55, 70. London: N. Trübner & Co., 1878.

Wülfing, J. Ernst, ed. *The Laud Troy Book*. Early English Text Society, o.s., 121, 122. London: Kegan Paul, Trench, Trübner, 1902–3.

Zupitza Julius, ed. *The Romance of Guy of Warwick*. Early English Text Society, 3 parts, e.s., 42, 49, 59. London: N. Trübner & Co., 1883–91.

Secondary Works

Aerts, W. J., and M. Gosman, eds. *Exemplum and Similitudo: Alexander the Great and other heroes as points of reference in medieval literature*. Medievalia Groningiana, vol. 8. Groningen: Egbert Forsten, 1988.

Andrew, Malcolm. "*Patience:* the 'Munster Dore'." *English Language Notes* 14 (1976–77): 164–67.

Andrew, Malcolm. "The Realizing Imagination in Late Medieval English Literature." *English Studies* 76 (1995): 113–28.

Arrathoon, Leigh A, ed. *Chaucer and the Craft of Fiction*. Rochester, Mi.: Solaris, 1986.

Ashton, Gail. "Patient Mimesis: Griselda and the *Clerk's Tale*." *Chaucer Review* 32 (1998): 232–38.

Axton, Richard. "Gower—Chaucer's heir?" In *Chaucer Traditions: Studies in Honour of Derek Brewer*, edited by Ruth Morse and Barry Windeatt, 21–38. Cambridge: Cambridge University Press, 1990.

Bennett, J. A. W. *Chaucer's Book of Fame: An Exposition of the "House of Fame."* Oxford: Clarendon, 1968.

Benson, C. David. *Chaucer's Drama of Style: Poetic Variety and Contrast in the "Canterbury Tales."* Chapel Hill: University of North Carolina Press, 1986.

Bishop, Ian. *"Troilus and Criseyde": A Critical Study.* Bristol: University of Bristol Press, 1981.

Blake, Norman. "The Wife of Bath and her *Tale.*" *Leeds Studies in English,* n.s, 13 (1982): 42–55.

Blanch, Robert J., M. M. Youngerman, and Julian N. Wasserman, eds. *Text and Matter: New Perspectives of the Pearl-Poet.* Troy, N.Y.: Whitson, 1991.

Blenkner, Louis. "The Pattern of Traditional Images in *Pearl.*" *Studies in Philology* 68 (1971): 26–49.

Blenkner, Louis. "The Theological Structure of *Pearl.*" In *The Middle English "Pearl": Critical Essays,* edited by John Conley, 220–71. Notre Dame and London: University of Notre Dame Press, 1970.

Bloom, Harold. *A Map of Misreading.* Oxford: Oxford University Press, 1975.

Bloom, Harold, and others. *Deconstruction and Criticism.* London: Routledge and Kegan Paul, 1979.

Bloomfield, Morton W. "Distance and Predestination in *Troilus and Criseyde.*" *PMLA* 72 (1957): 14–26.

Boenig, Robert. "January's Trumpets." *English Language Notes* 32, no. 1 (1994): 19–23.

Bogdanos, Theodore. *Pearl: Image of the Ineffable: A Study in Medieval Poetic Symbolism.* Univ. Park: Pennsylvania State University Press, 1983.

Boitani, Piero. *Chaucer and the Imaginary World of Fame.* Cambridge: D. S. Brewer, 1984.

Boitani, Piero, and Jill Mann, eds. *The Cambridge Chaucer Companion.* Cambridge: Cambridge University Press, 1986.

Boitani, Piero, and Anna Torti, eds. *Literature in Fourteenth-Century England.* The J. A. W. Bennett Memorial Archives, Perugia, 1981–82. Tübingen: Narr; Cambridge: D. S. Brewer, 1983.

Borroff, Marie. "Pearl's 'Maynful Mone': Crux, Simile, and Structure." In *Acts of Interpretation: The Text in its Contexts, 700–1600. Essays on Medieval and Renaissance Literature in Honor of E. Talbot Donaldson,* edited by Mary J. Carruthers and Elizabeth D. Kirk, 159–72. Norman, Okla.: Pilgrim, 1982.

Bradbury, Nancy Mason. "Gentrification and the *Troilus.*" *Chaucer Review* 28 (1993–94): 305–29.

Brenner, Gerry. "Narrative Structure in Chaucer's 'Troilus and Criseyde'." In *Chaucer's "Troilus": Essays in Criticism,* edited by Stephen A. Barney, 131–44. London: Scolar Press, 1980.

Brody, Saul N. "*Troilus and Criseyde* and *The Nun's Priest's Tale:* The Drawing and Undrawing of Morals." In *Religion in the Poetry and Drama of the Late Middle Ages in England,* The J. A. W. Bennett Memorial Lectures, 1988, edited by Piero Boitani and Anna Torti, 133–48. Cambridge: D. S. Brewer, 1990.

Bronfman, Judith. *Chaucer's "Clerk's Tale": The Griselda Story Received, Rewritten, Illustrated.* Garland Studies in Medieval Literature, vol. 11. New York: Garland: 1994.

Buckmaster, Elizabeth. "Meditation and Memory in Chaucer's *House of Fame.*" *Modern Language Studies* 16 (1986): 279–87.

Burnley, David. "Chaucer's Literary Terms." *Anglia* 114 (1996): 202–35.

Burnley, David. *A Guide to Chaucer's Language.* Frome: Macmillan, 1983.

Burrow, John. "Poems Without Endings." *Studies in the Age of Chaucer* 13 (1991): 17–37.

Burrow, J. A. and Thorlac Turville-Petre, eds. *A Book of Middle English.* Oxford: Blackwell, 1992.

Carruthers, Mary. *The Book of Memory: A Study of Memory in Medieval Cultures.* Cambridge Studies in Medieval Literature, vol. 10. 1990. Reprint, Cambridge: Cambridge University Press, 1994.

Chance, Jane, ed. *The Mythographic Art: Classical Fable and the Rise of the Vernacular in Early France and England.* Gainesville: University of Florida Press, 1990.

Chickering, Howell. "Form and Interpretation in the *Envoy* to the *Clerk's Tale*." *Chaucer Review* 29 (1994–95): 352–72.

Clopper, Lawrence M. "The God of the *Gawain*-Poet." *Modern Philology* 94 (1996–97): 1–18.

Colish, Marcia L. *The Mirror of Language: A Study in the Medieval Theory of Knowledge.* 2d ed. Lincoln, Nebr.: University of Nebraska Press, 1983.

Cooper, Helen. "Chaucer and Ovid: A Question of Authority." In *Ovid Renewed: Ovidian Influences on Literature and Art from the Middle Ages to the Twentieth Century,* edited by Charles Martindale, 71–81. Cambridge: Cambridge University Press, 1988.

Cooper, Helen. *The Structure of the Canterbury Tales.* London: Duckworth, 1983.

Cox, Catherine. "Holy Erotica and the Virgin Word: Promiscuous Glossing in the *Wife of Bath's Prologue*." *Exemplaria* 5 (1993): 207–37

Crane, Susan. *Gender and Romance in Chaucer's "Canterbury Tales."* Princeton: Princeton University Press, 1994.

Culler, Jonathan. *The Pursuit of Signs: Semiotics, Literature, Deconstruction.* London: Routledge and Kegan Paul, 1981.

Dane, Joseph A. "The Myth of Chaucerian Irony." *Papers on Language and Literature* 24 (1988): 115–33.

Davenport, W. A. *The Art of the Gawain Poet.* London: The Athlone Press, 1978.

David, Alfred. "*Old, New,* and *Yong* in Chaucer." The Presidential Address. *Studies in the Age of Chaucer* 15 (1993): 5–21.

Dean, James. "The Ending of the *Canterbury Tales,* 1952–1976." *Texas Studies in Literature and Language* 21 (1979): 17–33.

Delany, Sheila. *Chaucer's "House of Fame": The Poetics of Skeptical Fideism.* Chicago: University of Chicago Press, 1972.

Delany, Sheila. *The Naked Text: Chaucer's "Legend of Good Women."* Berkeley: University of California Press, 1994.

Delany, Sheila. "Strategies of Silence in the Wife of Bath's Recital." *Exemplaria* 2 (Spring 1990): 49–69.

Dickson, Lynne. "Deflection in the Mirror: Feminine Discourse in *The Wife of Bath's Prologue* and *Tale*." *Studies in the Age of Chaucer* 15 (1993): 61–90.

Diekstra, F. N. M. "Chaucer's Digressive Mode and the Moral of *The Manciple's Tale*." *Neophilologus* 67 (1983): 131–48.

Dinshaw, Carolyn. *Chaucer's Sexual Poetics.* Madison, Wi.: University of Wisconsin Press, 1989.

Dobbs, Elizabeth A. "Seeing Through Windows in Chaucer's *Troilus*." *Chaucer Review* 32 (1998): 400–422.

Donaldson, E. T. *Speaking of Chaucer.* London: Athlone Press, 1970.

Eco, Umberto, with others. *Interpretation and overinterpretation.* Edited by Stefan Collini. Cambridge: Cambridge University Press, 1992.

Edwards, Robert R. *The Dream of Chaucer: Representation and Reflection in the Early Narratives.* Durham and London: Duke University Press, 1989.

Evans, Murray J. "'Making Strange': The Narrator (?), the Ending (?), and Chaucer's 'Troilus.'" *Neuphilologische Mitteilungen* 87 (1986): 218–28.
Finlayson, John. "Seeing, Hearing and Knowing in *The House of Fame*." *Studia Neophilologica* 58 (1986): 47–57.
Fradenburg, Louise. "The Manciple's Servant Tongue: Politics and Poetry in *The Canterbury Tales*." *ELH* 52 (1985): 85–118.
Froehlich, Karlfried. "Pseudo-Dionysius and the Reformation of the Sixteenth-Century." In Pseudo-Dionysius, *The Complete Works*, translated by Colm Luibheid, with Paul Rorem, 33–46. Classics of Western Spirituality. London: SPCK, 1987.
Fyler, John M. *Chaucer and Ovid*. New Haven and London: Yale University Press, 1979.
Galloway, Andrew. "Marriage Sermons, Polemical Sermons, and *The Wife of Bath's Prologue*: A Generic Excursus." *Studies in the Age of Chaucer* 14 (1992): 3–30.
Ganim, John M. "Chaucer and the Noise of the People." *Exemplaria* 2 (spring 1990): 71–88.
Ganim, John M. *Chaucerian Theatricality*. Princeton: Princeton University Press, 1990.
Glare, P. W., ed. *Oxford Latin Dictionary*. Oxford: Clarendon Press, 1982.
Grudin, Michaela Paasche. *Chaucer and the Politics of Discourse*. Columbia: University of South Carolina Press, 1996.
Hanning, Robert W. "Chaucer's First Ovid: Metamorphosis and Poetic Tradition in The Book of the Duchess and The House of Fame." In *Chaucer and the Craft of Fiction*, edited by Leigh A. Arrathoon, 121–63. Rochester, Mi.: Solaris, 1986.
Henderson, Jeff. "Chaucer's Experiment in Narrative Metadrama: The General Prologue as *Dramatis Personae*." *Publications of the Arkansas Philological Association*, 14: 1 (1988): 13–24.
Holley, Linda Tarte. *Chaucer's Measuring Eye*. Houston, Tex.: Rice University Press, 1990.
Howard, Donald. *The Idea of the Canterbury Tales*. Berkeley: University of California Press, 1976.
Johnson, Lesley. "Reincarnations of Griselda: Contexts for the *Clerk's Tale?*" In *Feminist Readings in Middle English Literature: The Wife of Bath and All Her Sect*, edited by Ruth Evans and Lesley Johnson, 195–220. London: Routledge, 1994.
Jordan, Robert M. *Chaucer's Poetics and the Modern Reader*. London: University of California Press, 1987.
Kemmler, Fritz. *"Exempla" in Context: A Historical and Critical Study of Robert Mannyng of Brunne's "Handlyng Synne."* Tübingen: Gunter Narr, 1984.
Kinney, Clare Regan. "'Who made this song?': The Engendering of Lyric Counterplots in *Troilus and Criseyde*." *Studies in Philology* 89 (1992): 272–92.
Kiser, Lisa. "Eschatological Poetics in Chaucer's *House of Fame*." *Modern Language Quarterly* 49 (1990 for 1989): 99–119.
Knight, Stephen. *Geoffrey Chaucer*. Rereading Literature. Oxford: Blackwell, 1986.
Kolve, V. A. *Chaucer and the Imagery of Narrative: The First Five Canterbury Tales*. London: Edward Arnold, 1984.
Kurath, Hans and Sherman M. Kuhn. *Middle English Dictionary*. Ann Arbor, Mi.: University of Michigan Press, 1956–
Leclercq, Jean. "Influence and noninfluence of Dionysius in the Middle Ages." In Pseudo-Dionysius, *The Complete Works*, translated by Colm Luibheid, with Paul Rorem, 25–32. Classics of Western Spirituality. London: SPCK, 1987.

Le Guern, Michel. *Sémantique de la métaphore et de la métonymie.* Paris: Larousse, 1973.

Leicester, H. Marshall, Jr. *The Disenchanted Self: Representing the Subject in the "Canterbury Tales."* Berkeley: University of California Press, 1990.

Leicester, H. Marshall, Jr. "Structure as Deconstruction: 'Chaucer and Estates Satire' in the *General Prologue*, or Reading Chaucer as a Prologue to the History of Disenchantment." *Exemplaria* 2 (1990): 241–61.

Leitch, Vincent B. *Deconstructive Criticism: an advanced introduction.* London: Hutchinson, 1983.

Leyerle, John. "Chaucer's Windy Eagle." *University of Texas Quarterly* 40 (1971): 247–65.

Lindahl, Carl. *Earnest Games: Folkloric Patterns in the "Canterbury Tales."* Bloomington: Indiana University Press, 1987.

Lindley, Arthur. "'Vanysshed Was This Daunce, He Nyste Where': Alysoun's Absence in the *Wife of Bath's Prologue and Tale.*" *ELH* 59 (1992): 1–21.

Lyons, John D. *The Rhetoric of Example in Early Modern France and Italy.* Princeton: Princeton University Press, 1989.

McCall, Marsh H., Jr. *Ancient Rhetorical Theories of Simile and Comparison.* Cambridge, Ma.: Harvard University Press, 1969.

McGavin, John J. "The Context of Literary Simile." *Cosmos* 3 (1987): 2–20.

McGavin, John J. "How Nasty is Phoebus's Crow?" *Chaucer Review* 21 (1987): 444–58.

Man, Paul de. "The Epistemology of Metaphor." In *On Metaphor,* edited by Sheldon Sacks, 11–28. London: University of Chicago Press, 1978.

Mann, Jill. *Geoffrey Chaucer.* Feminist Readings. London: Harvester Wheatsheaf, 1991.

Mann, Jill. *Geoffrey Chaucer and Medieval Estates Satire.* Cambridge: Cambridge University Press, 1973.

Mann, Jill. "Parents and Children in the *Canterbury Tales.*" In *Literature in Fourteenth-Century England,* edited by Piero Boitani and Anna Torti (Tübingen: Narr, 1983), 165–83.

Margherita, Gayle. *The Romance of Origins: Language and Sexual Difference in Middle English Literature.* Philadelphia: University of Pennsylvania Press, 1994.

Martindale, Charles, ed. *Ovid Renewed: Ovidian Influences on Literature and Art from the Middle Ages to the Twentieth Century.* Cambridge: Cambridge University Press, 1988.

Miller, George A. "Images and Models, Similes and Metaphors." In *Metaphor and Thought,* edited by Andrew Ortony, 202–50. Cambridge: Cambridge University Press, 1979.

Miller, Jacqueline T. *Poetic License: Authority and Authorship in Medieval and Renaissance Contexts.* Oxford: Oxford University Press, 1986.

Millett, Bella. "Chaucer, Lollius, and the Medieval Theory of Authorship." In *Studies in the Age of Chaucer Proceedings 1. 1984: Reconstructing Chaucer,* ed. Paul Strohm and Thomas J. Heffernan, 93–108. Knoxville, Tenn.: The New Chaucer Society, 1985.

Minnis, A. J., ed. *Chaucer's 'Boece' and the Medieval Tradition of Boethius.* Cambridge: D. S. Brewer, 1993.

Minnis, A. J., and Tim William Machan. "The *Boece* as Late-Medieval Translation." In *Chaucer's 'Boece' and the Medieval Tradition of Boethius,* edited by A. J. Minnis, 167–88. Cambridge: D. S. Brewer, 1993.

Minnis, A. J., and A. B. Scott, with David Wallace, eds. *Medieval Literary Theory and Criticism c.1100–c.1375: The Commentary Tradition.* Rev. ed. Oxford: Clarendon Press, 1991.

Morgan, Gerald. "A Defence of Dorigen's Complaint." *Medium Ævum* 46 (1977): 77–97.

Morse, Ruth and Barry Windeatt, eds. *Chaucer Traditions: Studies in Honour of Derek Brewer.* Cambridge: Cambridge University Press, 1990.

Muscatine, Charles. *Chaucer and the French Tradition: A Study in Style and Meaning.* 1957. Reprint, Berkeley and Los Angeles: University of California Press, 1964.

Murphy, James J. "A New Look at Chaucer and the Rhetoricians." *Review of English Studies*, n.s., 15 (1964):1–20.

Murphy, James J. *Rhetoric in the Middle Ages.* Berkeley and Los Angeles: University of California Press, 1974.

Myles, Robert. *Chaucerian Realism.* Cambridge: D. S. Brewer, 1994.

Nolan, Edward Peter. *Now Through a Glass Darkly: Specular Images of Being and Knowing from Virgil to Chaucer.* Ann Arbor: The University of Michigan Press, 1990.

Ortony, Andrew, ed. *Metaphor and Thought.* Cambridge: Cambridge University Press, 1979.

Papka, Claudia Rattazzi. "Transgression, the End of Troilus, and the Ending of Chaucer's *Troilus and Criseyde.*" *Chaucer Review* 32 (1998): 267–81.

Patterson, Lee. "Perpetual Motion: Alchemy and the Technology of the Self." The Biennial Chaucer Lecture. *Studies in the Age of Chaucer* 15 (1993): 25–57.

Patterson, Lee. "'What Man Artow?': Authorial Self-Definition in *The Tale of Sir Thopas* and *The Tale of Melibee.*" *Studies in the Age of Chaucer* 11 (1989): 117–75.

Payne, Robert O. *The Key of Remembrance: A Study of Chaucer's Poetics.* New Haven: Yale University Press, 1963.

Pearsall, Derek. *The Canterbury Tales.* Boston: G. Allen & Unwin, 1985.

Pearsall, Derek and Elizabeth Salter. *Landscapes and Seasons of the Medieval World.* London: Paul Elek, 1973.

Reichardt, Paul. "Animal Similes in *Pearl.*" In *Text and Matter: New Perspectives of the Pearl-Poet*, edited by Robert J. Blanch, M. M. Youngerman, and Julian N. Wasserman, 17–30. Troy, N.Y.: Whitson, 1991

Ricoeur, Paul. *The Rule of Metaphor: Multi-disciplinary studies of the creation of meaning in language.* Trans. Robert Czerny, Kathleen McLaughlin and John Costello, S. J. London: Routledge and Kegan Paul, 1986.

Rowland, Beryl, ed. *Companion to Chaucer Studies.* Rev. ed. New York: Oxford University Press, 1979.

Ruffolo, Lara. "Literary Authority and the Lists of Chaucer's *House of Fame:* Destruction and Definition through Proliferation." *Chaucer Review* 27 (1993): 325–41.

Sacks, Sheldon, ed. *On Metaphor.* London: University of Chicago Press, 1978.

Scanlon, Larry. *Narrative, Authority, and Power: Medieval Exemplum and the Chaucerian Tradition.* Cambridge Studies in Medieval Literature, vol. 20. Cambridge: Cambridge University Press, 1994.

Scattergood, V. J. "The Manciple's Manner of Speaking." *Essays in Criticism* 24 (1974): 124–46.

Shook, Lawrence K. "*The House of Fame.*" In *Companion to Chaucer Studies*, ed. Beryl Rowland, 414–27. Rev. ed. New York: Oxford University Press, 1979.

Simpson, James. "Dante's 'Astripetam Aquilam' and the Theme of Poetic Discretion in the 'House of Fame'." *Essays and Studies* 39 (1986): 1–18.

Spearing, A. C. "The *Canterbury Tales* IV: Exemplum and Fable." In *The Cambridge Chaucer Companion*, edited by Piero Boitani and Jill Mann, 159–77. Cambridge: Cambridge University Press, 1986.

Spearing, A. C. "Father Chaucer." In *Writing after Chaucer: Essential Readings in Chaucer and the Fifteenth Century*, edited by Daniel J. Pinti, 145–66. New York: Garland Publishing, Inc., 1998. First published in A. C. Spearing, *Medieval to Renaissance in English Poetry* (Cambridge: Cambridge University Press, 1985), 88–110.

Spearing, A. C. *Medieval Dream Poetry*. Cambridge: Cambridge University Press, 1976.

Spearing, A. C. *The Medieval Poet as Voyeur: Looking and Listening in Medieval Love-Narratives*. Cambridge: Cambridge University Press, 1993.

Spearing, A. C. *Readings in Medieval Poetry*. Cambridge: Cambridge University Press, 1987.

Spearing, A. C. "*Troilus and Criseyde:* the Illusion of Allusion." *Exemplaria* 2 (Spring 1990): 263–77.

Sperber, Dan and Deirdre Wilson. *Relevance: Communication and Cognition*. Oxford: Basil Blackwell, 1986.

Steadman, John M. "Chaucer's Eagle: A Contemplative Symbol." *PMLA* 75 (1960): 153–59.

Stanbury, Sarah. "The Voyeur and the Private Life in *Troilus and Criseyde*." *Studies in the Age of Chaucer* 13 (1991): 141–58.

Stevens, Martin and Kathleen Falvey. "Substance, Accident, and Transformations: a Reading of the *Pardoner's Tale*." *Chaucer Review* 17 (1982): 142–58.

Stock, Lorraine Kochanske. "The Two Mayings in Chaucer's *Knight's Tale*." *Journal of English and Germanic Philology* 85 (1986): 206–21.

Taylor, Andrew. "Chaucer Our Derridean Contemporary?" *Exemplaria* 5 (fall 1993): 471–86.

Taylor, Karla. *Chaucer Reads "The Divine Comedy."* Stanford: Stanford University Press, 1989.

Taylor, Karla. "Proverbs and the Authentication of Convention in 'Troilus and Criseyde'." In *Chaucer's "Troilus": Essays in Criticism*, edited by Stephen A. Barney, 277–96. London: Scolar Press, 1980.

Taylor, P. B. "Chaucer's *Cousin to the Dede*." *Speculum* 57 (1982): 315–27.

Wallace, David. "Chaucer's Continental Inheritance: The Early Poems and *Troilus and Criseyde*." In *The Cambridge Chaucer Companion*, edited by Piero Boitani and Jill Mann, 19–37. Cambridge: Cambridge University Press, 1986.

Wallace, David. *Chaucerian Polity: Absolutist Lineages and Associational Forms in England and Italy. Figurae:* Reading Medieval Culture. Stanford: Stanford University Press, 1997.

Weisberg, David. "Telling Stories about Constance: Framing and Narrative Strategy in the *Canterbury Tales*." *Chaucer Review* 27 (1992–93):45–64.

Wetherbee, Winthrop. *Chaucer and the Poets: An Essay on "Troilus and Criseyde."* Ithaca: Cornell University Press, 1984.

Weever, Jacqueline de. *Chaucer Name Dictionary: A Guide to Astrological, Biblical, Historical, Literary, and Mythological Names in the Works of Geoffrey Chaucer*. London: Garland, 1988.

Windeatt, B. A. "Gesture in Chaucer." *Medievalia et Humanistica* 9 (1979): 143–61.

Windeatt, Barry. *Troilus and Criseyde*. Oxford Guides to Chaucer. Oxford: Clarendon, 1992.

Index

adnominatio, 176
Alexander of Ville-Dieu: *Doctrinale*, 41–42
allegoria, 41
allusion: intertextual, 104, 123–24, 138–39, 141, 144, 152; dissimilarity in, 144; and patterns of comparison, 78, 120, 138–44; problematic, 146
analogy, 113, 115, 124, 143, 154, 162–63, 164; ambivalent, 150; as persuasion, 43
Anelida & Arcite, 54–55
anxiety, 204–5
appearance: similarity of, 34, 36. See also *imago*
apposition, 86–90, 91; ambiguity, 89; proximity to similaic comparison, 87
Aristotle, 33; *Rhetoric*, 36
Athelston, 87
Augustine, 43; *De Trinitate*, 43–44
author: responsibility of, 186, 202

"Barbarismus," 33
Barney, Stephen A., 167
Blanche of Castille, 54
blurring of literal and figurative. *See* figurative and literal
Bede, 40–41, 43
Bible, 43, 44, 194
Bloom, Harold, 65
Boccaccio, 20, 123, 125–26, 127, 128, 130, 131, 143, 168, 171
Boece, 16, 32, 47, 48, 49, 50, 51
Boethius, 31, 33, 35, 43, 50, 51, 55, 74, 138, 147, 203, 212; *De Consolatione Philosophiae*, 27, 32, 44, 47–50, 51, 52–53, 56, 77, 78
Boitani, Piero, 65, 66

Book of the Duchess, The, 24, 53–54, 98, 99, 100; *exempla* in, 53, 54

Canon's Yeoman's Tale, The, 69, 94
Canterbury Tales, The, 15, 51, 53, 55, 56, 59, 69, 82, 138, 191, 192; dramatic theories of, 15
Carruthers, Mary, 67
Caxton, William, 72
characterismus, 42
Cecily de Champagne, 107
children. *See* familial relationships
Christine de Pisan, 18, 186, 207 n
Cicero: *De Inventione*, 41
circularity (hermeneutic), 22–23, 45–46, 180
Cleanness, 102–3, 113. See also *Pearl*-Poet
Clerk's Tale, The, 103 (Prologue), 140, 187–93, 198; as *exemplum*, 187–88, 190–92, 198
cliché(s), 84, 87, 92, 97, 101, 104-5, 108, 109, 110
collatio, 34, 50
collation, 50
comparatio, 34, 72, 143
comparison: ambiguity, 90, 91, 157–60, 161; ambivalence in, 127, 132; Chaucer inviting, 24; as Chaucerian term, 50, 52; circularity of, 22–23, 45–46; clusters of, 49, 151, 158–59; consoling, 47; contest, as site of, 23, 46; in context, 11, 93, 99, 119–20, 121, 140, 144, 159; danger of, 45, 47, 152; disrupting patterns of, 132–34; dissimilarity inherent in, 22, 26, 31, 38, 51, 63; doubleness of, 89, 112, 118, 159–61; educating function of, 46, 47, 147, 184; empowering, 80; failures of, 12, 22, 79, 96, 153–57, 196;

235

INDEX

comparison (*continued*)
  good and bad, employed for, 145, 147, 168, 169; as intellectual device 161; and intensification 88, 97; and limits of persuasion, 149–50, 153–54, 155; mixed, 90; and morality, 145, 188; multiplicity of, 151–52, 164, 165; as narrative strategy, 90; negotiation of, 11, 161; and otherness, 84, 112–18; paired scenes of, 124–25; paradox, 45, 46; and past knowledge, 21, 22, 23; patterns of 27, 78, 119–44; persuasion by, 23, 34, 51, 145–69; poetic process, assisting, 96; pleasure, 88; problematic, 11; proof, serving as, 23; qualified by language, 68; quantitative, 148–50; reader's role in, 16, 23, 24, 25, 26, 27, 45, 100, 105, 120, 122, 132, 141, 145, 157, 169, 173, 187, 201; reading(s) of, 11, 122, 123, 124, 131, 134, 140, 142, 144, 169, 187, 199; reflective nature of, 161; repetition, 119; responsibility for, 16, 18; self-defeating, 52; self-serving, 69, 146, 154; source of Chaucer's interest in, 31–36, 47, 57; as theme, 51, 187; underlying language, 11, 12, 15, 16, 22, 23, 201; and understanding, 19–20, 69; unreliability of, 73; variety of, 164; vocabulary of, 35–36, 50
comparison: traditions of; academic, 22–23, 32–35; Chaucer closer to grammatical than rhetorical, 33, 36, 41; Christian, 32, 43–46, 56; common usage, 33; grammatical, 23–24, 38–41, 56; versus rhetorical, 33, 35–36, 38–39, 40, 41; rhetorical, 35–38, 56;
comparative thinking, 12, 22, 23, 28, 34, 56, 137, 184, 198, 205; discredited, 158; failure of, 22; and judgement, 147, 149, 161; limits of, 153, 154–57; natural, 146; as theme, 199
comparativism, 44, 49, 56, 137, 191, 192, 193, 195, 198, 199
contextuality, 99
conventionality, 24, 25, 26, 28, 87, 88, 93–94, 99, 100, 105, 108, 111, 126, 151, 183

Cook's Tale, The, 101
Culler, Jonathan, 207–8 n

Dante, 31, 73, 74, 78, 138–39, 141, 142–43; *Inferno*, 139; *Purgatorio*, 77
Davenport, W. A., 115
David, Alfred, 181
decorum, 16, 17, 25, 85, 94, 176; failure of 101, 165. *See also* indecorum
descriptio, 101–2
Destruction of Troy, The, 88, 102
difference. *See* comparison, dissimilarity
Diomedes (the Grammarian), 39
Dinshaw, Carolyn, 169
dissimilarity, 31, 33; ambivalence towards, 44; awareness of, 11; co-present with similarity, 21, 32, 82; consolation of acknowledging, 47; context of, 16–17; and cultural perceptions, 15; and doubt, 47, 104; educative function of, 162, 175; failure of, 54; and figuration, 84, 86, 89–96; "gap" created by, 203; quantitative, 86; reader's role in, 144, 146, 199; removal of, 92; in similes, 203–4; in *similitudo*, 35–42, 56, 94, 112–18, 179; subversive nature of, 25; taxonomy and, 33, 43; tension created by, 51, 150. *See also* comparison
domestic imagery, 102
Donatus, 33, 38, 39–40, 41, 50; *Ars Grammatica*, 33, 38, 212
drama, religious: comparison in, 90–91; "Massacre of the Innocents" plays, 104; York Cycle, 91–92, 109–10, 121

Earl of Toulouse, The, 90
Eberhard of Béthune: *Graecismus*, 41, 42
Eco, Umberto, 146
Edwards, Robert R., 66
effictio, 42
eikon, 34. See also *icon*
Émaré, 111, 117
emotionalism, 189, 191
entrelacement, 127
example (as Chaucerian term), 50–51, 132, 185, 186, 187, 193
exemplum, 23, 31, 34–35, 43, 50, 55, 61, 64, 66, 69, 70, 74, 83, 96, 107, 120, 144, 147–48, 156, 165, 167–69, 175,

182, 204; ambivalence towards, 62, 63, 68; avoidance of, 169; Chaucer's works as, 26, 28, 181 (see also *Clerk's Tale, Troilus and Criseyde, Wife of Bath's Tale*); derogatory, 52; dramatic potential, 42; educative function of, 42, 78, 170; failure of, 111, 137, 191; fragile foundation of, 63, 192; and gender, 52, 187, 195; in grammatical tradition of comparison, 41; limits of, 147, 178, 179, 192; and narrative, 81, 163; patterns of, 195; people as, 60–61, 63–64; as persuasion, 162; poem as, 132, 170–99, 205; as proof, 34, 49; reading(s) of, 73, 199; in Renaissance, 73, 74; and reputation, 90; subversion, 25, 54; and thematic focus, 51; as threat to fiction, 188–89; and truth, 94; undermining of, 56, 62, 191, 192, 205; unreliable, 67, 83, 158–59; from women, 53, 60;
experience, 74, 190; comparisons explaining, 67, 74; and listing, 70; relationship to books, 54; and taxonomy, 68; and truth, 189

fabliau, 95, 101, 103, 104; Chaucer's, 18, 100, 195
falsification, 141–43, 144
familial relationships, 139, 140–41
Ferster, Judith, 161
figurae, 31, 32, 38, 41, 42
figurative and literal, blurring of, 84, 88, 93, 94, 96, 127, 131, 151; play of, 53, 89, 135
Franklin's Tale, The, 81, 165
Friar's Tale, The, 55, 171
Fronto, M. Cornelius, 36, 37

"Geffrey," 12, 19, 25, 46, 53, 69, 74, 75–76, 78, 80, 105, 136, 140, 161, 163, 178
gender, 52, 103, 169, 187, 188; and comparison, 194–95; war, 26, 192, 193, 194, 198
General Prologue, The, 14, 16–17, 21–22, 25, 56, 97, 103, 104, 149–50, 191; portrayal of monk, 95; prioress, 100
Generydes, 87

Geoffrey of Vinsauf, 32, 38, 94–95; *Poetria Nova*, 102, 163, 211
generic expectations, 98, 100
genre, 28, 92, 98, 101, 102, 103, 111; and *exempla*, 35; dream, 79–80; fairy tale, 116–17; and simile, 104, 117. See also drama, romance
Guy of Warwick, 87, 89, 94, 160

Hanning, Robert W., 65–66
Harry Bailley, 60
Henryson, Robert: *Testament of Cresseid*, 203
hermeneutic circularity, 22–23, 45–46, 180
historicism, 200
House of Fame, The, 12, 18–19, 24, 25, 27, 46, 50, 51, 53, 55, 58–83, 105, 106, 107, 111, 112, 119, 135–36, 140, 163, 178, 191, 196, 200, 202, 205; ambivalence of, 73; *exempla*, 64; expansion and constraint, 70–73; incompleteness, 81; internal divisions, 72; lack of names, 76; narrative dynamic, 72; tropological language, 65

icon, 39, 42. See also *eikon*
Iliad, The, 102
illumination: comparison as, 21, 22, 31, 58, 67, 74, 148, 162, 182; and dissimilarity, 25, 47, 56; and doubt, 79; *exemplum*, 34, 83; failure of, 79; limits of, 147; past as, 21, 23, 173; and persuasion, 35; problematic, 26; untruth disguised as, 65
image, 50
imago, 23–25, 34–35, 43, 50, 51, 56, 86, 88, 89, 90, 91, 92, 95, 96, 112, 120, 124, 137, 150, 159–62, 163, 172, 183, 191, 195, 204, 205; in academic tradition of comparison, 42; as Chaucerian term, 42; in Christian thought, 44; conflated with *similitudo*, 41–42; dissimilarity in, 36, 39–40, 84, 87, 94; emotional force, 42; in grammatical tradition of comparison, 39, 40; in rhetorical tradition of comparison, 36–37, 38, 40
indecorum, 104, 112. See also decorum
intertextuality, 59, 77, 104, 108, 120, 138–39. See also allusion, intertextual

Isidore of Seville, 40, 211

Janus, 11–12
John of Gaunt, 54
Julius Rufinianus: *De Figuris Sententiarum et Elocutionis*, 37, 39
juxtaposition, 63; to disrupt pattern of comparison, 132–34

Kemmler, Fritz, 35
Knight's Tale, The, 17, 50, 51, 52, 67, 70, 93, 98, 100–101, 105, 165, 180–81, 203
knowledge, 46, 58–59, 61, 67, 68, 118, 195; gap in, 81; sacred, 45; transfer of, 21, 22, 26, 58, 64, 70, 83, 95, 124, 199
Kolve, V. A., 98

Laud Troy Book, The, 89, 102, 108, 110, 112
language: appropriateness of, 18, 19; association of violence with, 75–76, 78, 106–8, 135–36; authenticated by reader, 14, 149; Chaucer's attitude to, 66, 105, 135; contest, as site of, 13, 19; dangerous, 21; deferring reality, 166; and difference, 11; and experience, 14, 105–7; failure of, 17, 106–7; falsehood in, 65–66; inability to vocalise, 12, 105–6, 137; irresistibility of, 105; misunderstanding of, 19; negotiation of meaning, 19; particular versus general, 19; and pleasure, 13, 57, 88, 94; problematic, 202; proliferation of words, 13, 19, 69, 166–68; sound of, 74, 97; threat of, 12, 79, 105, 136; as topic, 75; and truth, 14, 16–19, 66–67, 79, 83, 202–203; uncontrollable, 75; unreliable, 17, 18, 66–67, 74, 78, 79, 81, 137; user, failures of, 201
Legend of Good Women, The, 51, 53, 60, 61, 81, 96, 103, 105, 107
likeness: as Chaucerian term, 50; degrees of, 42
listing, 53, 62–63, 69, 79, 82, 88, 103, 165-67, 171, 192; foregrounding language, 166; revealing particularity, 69

literal and figurative: blurring of, 53, 84, 88, 93–96, 135
Lucan: *Pharsalia*, 40

Machaut, Guillaume de: *Jugement du Roi de Nevarre*, 77
Man, Paul de, 66
Man of Law's Tale, The, 97, 98, 100, 140, 188–90; *exemplum* in, 189–90
Manciple's Tale, The, 16–17, 19, 50, 51, 52, 55, 61, 82, 97, 98, 129, 165, 167–68, 171, 187, 198
Martianus Capella, 36
meaning: transfer of, 146, 170, 181, 191, 199, 203, 204
Melibee, 60, 167
Merchant's Tale, The, 99–100, 103–4, 129, 165
metafiction, 70
metaphor, 19, 20, 45, 119, 182, 200; functioning as simile, 137
metapoetics, 27, 52, 72, 81, 106, 108, 136–38, 147, 157–165, 166–67, 168, 169, 195–96; and comparison, 136–37, 146; and silence, 167
Miller's Tale, The, 94–95, 101, 104, 151, 195–96
Monk's Tale, The, 51, 81, 167
Murphy, James J., 31, 32, 33, 38, 41

name(s): bad reputation and, 61; contest, as site of, 21; context, and, 20; diachronic meanings of, 20; as *exempla*, 60–61; and expectations, 21; and judgement, 12–13; and reputation, 20–22, 25, 58–62, 76, 90, 191; shaping understanding, 61, 64; and taxonomy, 67, 69; and truth, 15, 63, 70, 76
naming, 12–14, 58–83, 89, 90, 172; comparison's role in, 13, 15; credibility, 14; and interpretation, 173; negotiation of, 15; problematic, 17, 20; reliability of judgement, 13; social prejudice, 16; and truth, 14
narrative, 81, 191; dissimilarity in, 25, 179; in drama, 92; exemplum as generator of, 49, 56, 81; and pleasure, 82; proliferation of, 81; structure as context for comparison, 121; voice, mixed, 82, 96, 109, 129, 198

narrator *personae*, 23–24, 46, 136, 161, 163, 191, 205; as *imago* of Chaucer, 24; as preserving an external original author, 205. *See also* "Geffrey"
Nietzsche, 65–66
Nun's Priest's Tale, The, 51, 55, 100, 101, 165, 171; Prologue to, 82

occupatio, 68
oral communication, 59, 66
Ortony, Andrew, 208 n
Ovid, 62, 138–39, 142–43, 212; *Epistles*, 63; *Metamorphosis*, 139

paganism, 132, 139, 144, 147, 175, 180, 185
Pandarus as artist, 136, 163, 165, 166–67, 173–74
parable, 144
parabole, 34, 41, 42
paradeigma, 34
paradox, 82
Pardoner's Tale, The, 55, 97, 136, 167, 171
parent-child relationship. *See* familial relationships
Parliament of Fowls, The, 24, 53, 93, 165–66
parody, 84, 101–2, 111
paronomasia, 97
particularity, 19, 181, 182–83, 191, 192; and representations of women, 195–96; revealed by lists, 69; tension with *exemplum*, 182
Patience, 114
Patterson, Lee, 69, 201, 208
Paul, Saint, 43
Pearl-Poet, 41, 99, 112–16, 123; *Pearl*, 112–18, 205
Pearsall, Derek, 113; and Elizabeth Salter, 115
persuasion, 145–69; poetry as, 147. *See also* comparison, exemplum
playfulness, 16, 18, 19, 51, 62, 95, 100, 104, 192
positive comparison, 46, 47, 115
Prioress's Tale, The, 140
proverb, 31, 35, 174, 204
Pseudo-Dionysius, 44–46, 85; *Celestial Hierarchy*, 44; *Mystical Theology*, 44

Quintilian, 23, 209 n

reader, 100, 111, 157, 163; authorial power over, 182; constrained by context, 107; expectations of, 21–22, 24; fashions meaning, 99, 149, 184
readings, 169, 179, 200; variety of, acknowledged by Chaucer, 17, 108
realism, 51
reality, nontextual, 200–201
Reeve's Tale, The, 94, 100, 101
religious drama. *See* drama
reputation: acquisition of, 64; untrustworthiness of, 63
reputational names. *See* names
Rhetorica ad Herennium, 36–37, 38, 40, 211
rhetoric, 145, 204; French literary models, 31; limits of, 157
rhetoricians, 23, 32, 34, 35, 36, 147. *See also* comparison, traditions of
romance, 86–90, 92, 95, 98, 100–101, 126, 160
Romance of the Rose, The, 186

Salter, Elizabeth, 113, 115
satire, 84
Saussure, 65
self-reflexivity, 193
sexual misdemeanour, 139, 143, 144, 156
Shipman's Tale, The, 17, 98, 105
silence, 17, 106, 167–68
simile(s), 27, 34, 45, 49, 74–6, 84–118, 127, 182, 184, 193, 200, 203; and character, 108, 110, 123; clustering of, 56, 84, 87, 92, 95, 101, 104; in context, 53, 85, 96–112, 118, 128; conventional, 84, 93–94, 97, 98–99, 100, 104–5, 108–9, 110–11, 117, 118, 121, 122, 126, 131; from dissimilarity, 38; double, 113–14; doubleness, 115, 116, 118; extended between speakers, 128–32, 133; for intensification, 102, 121; and knowledge, 22; limits of, 74; and literal, 53, 89; as microcosm of reading, 84–85; original, 96, 87–98; paired, 98, 110; pattern(ing), 75, 78, 84, 88, 122; and phrasal patterning, 88; and pleasure, 94; quantitative, 114;

simile(s) (*continued*)
  reading(s) of, 85, 86, 88, 99, 100, 103–4, 108, 119–20, 123, 127, 133; and reflection, 76; repetition, 97, 98, 99, 119, 123; shared simile, 128–32; for sound of language, 74–75, 77, 97; subversive, 110; tension inherent in, 22; for threat of language, 75–76; used by character, 109–10; variety, 96, 97–98
similitude, 50, 82
similitudo, 23, 34–35, 36, 39, 40, 41, 42, 43, 50, 56, 84–118, 124, 127, 150, 160, 163, 179, 204, 205; conflated with imago, 41–42; conventional, 170; dissimilarity elided by Chaucer, 94, 96; empowered by context, 98; in grammatical tradition of comparison, 39–41; in rhetorical tradition of comparison, 37, 38
Simpson, James, 73
simulare, 50
Sir Dégaré, 90
Sir Degrevant, 109
Sir Ferumbras, 110
Sir Gawain and the Green Knight, 92–93, 110, 113–14
Sir Orfeo, 116–18
Sir Thopas, 24, 60, 101–3, 110, 167
South English Nativity, The, 109–10
Spearing, A. C., 55–56, 69, 171
Squire's Tale, The, 94
Summoner's Tale, The, 166
supplementarity, 81, 82, 165, 195
Susannah, 109–10

taxonomy, 13, 28, 67, 67–68, 69, 73, 79, 80–81, 192; and dissimilarity, 27, 33, 35, 37, 43; and meaning, 20; and multiplicity, 79; qualified by language, 68

Tournament of Tottenham, The, 108
traductio, 176
Troilus and Criseyde, 12–18, 20, 35, 50, 51, 53, 54, 55, 56, 81, 82, 96, 97, 98, 105–7, 108, 111, 119–88, 198, 202–5; comparison in, 27, 85, 177; as *exemplum*, 51, 170–88; *imago* and, 24–25; 143, 168, 171–79, 185–86, 187, 191; name in, 60; and paradigm of reading process, 175; and reader, 180, 185
tropology, 19, 38, 41, 65–66, 161, 200, 207, 208
truth, 18, 64, 170, 193, 203; and experience, 189; and failure of comparison, 96; and falsehood, 65, 67, 70; independent of source, 14, 15; negotiation of, 203; possibility of, 66–67; reader and, 25, 197; replaced by narrative, 147. *See also* language

univocality, 53, 82, 96, 128, 129, 198

Victorinus: *Explanationum in Rhetoricam M. Tullii Ciceronis*, 41
Virgil, 39; *Aeneid*, 39, 40, 62, 63, 68
Vossius, 39

Wallace, David, 79, 191
Wife of Bath, 26, 28, 50–51, 140, 191, 193–99; and *exempla*, 61, 193–94; as unreliable *exemplum*, 196, 197, 198, 199; *Prologue*, 51, 98, 99, 100, 186, 193–99; *Tale*, 59, 61, 193–99
Windeatt, Barry, 145
word(s): and deed, relationship of, 17, 18; process of choosing correct, 12, 17, 20–21, 200, 202; tension with silence, 167. *See also* language